PRELIMINARY EXCAVATION REPORTS AND OTHER ARCHAEOLOGICAL INVESTIGATIONS

Tell Qarqur,
Iron I Sites in the North-Central Highlands of Palestine

THE ANNUAL OF
THE AMERICAN SCHOOLS OF ORIENTAL RESEARCH

Volume 56 (1999)

Series Editor
Nancy Lapp

Billie Jean Collins
ASOR Director of Publications

PRELIMINARY EXCAVATION REPORTS AND OTHER ARCHAEOLOGICAL INVESTIGATIONS

Tell Qarqur,
Iron I Sites in the North-Central Highlands of Palestine

Edited by

Nancy Lapp

American Schools of Oriental Research • Boston, MA

ANNUAL OF THE AMERICAN SCHOOLS OF ORIENTAL RESEARCH
VOLUME 56

© 2003
American Schools of Oriental Research

ISBN: 0-89757-026-X

Library of Congress Cataloging-in-Publication Data

Preliminary excavation reports and other archaeological investigations :
Tell Qarqur, Iron I sites in the North-Central highlands of Palestine /
edited by Nancy Lapp.
        p. cm. -- (Annual of the American Schools of Oriental Research ;
v. 56)
Includes bibliographical references.
  ISBN 089757026X
 1. Qarqur, Tall (Syria) 2. Excavations (Archaeology)--Syria--Qarqur,
Tall. 3. Excavations (Archaeology)--Palestine. 4.
Palestine--Antiquities. 5. Iron age--Syria--Qarqur, Tall. 6. Iron
age--Palestine. I. Lapp, Nancy L., 1930- II. Series.

DS99.Q228P74 2002
939'.44--dc21
                                2002156214

Printed in the United States of America on acid-free paper

CONTENTS

SEVEN SEASONS OF AMERICAN SCHOOLS OF ORIENTAL RESEARCH EXCAVATIONS AT TELL QARQUR, SYRIA, 1993–1999

RUDOLPH H. DORNEMANN

INTRODUCTION

American Schools of Oriental Research excavations were conducted at Tell Qarqur in 1983 and 1984 under the direction of Dr. John Lundquist and resumed under my direction in 1993 after a break of nine years. I would like to thank Dr. Lundquist for his cooperation in getting the renewed excavations started and for sharing significant information with me. I would like to acknowledge the encouragement and support of Dr. Sultan Muhesen, Director General of the Directorate General of Antiquities and Museums of Syria; Dr. Adnan Bounni, the Directorate's past Director of Excavations; Dr. Michel al Maqdassi, the current Director of Excavations; Bassam Jamous, the current Director of the Museums of Syria; Abdurazaq Zaqzuq the Director of the Directorate's Hama District, as well as many staff members of the Directorate who have worked with and assisted me over the past seven years.[1] I would like to thank the ASOR Board of Trustees for its continued support of the project and for affiliation and advice offered by ASOR's Committee on Archaeological Policy. We greatly appreciate the continued major financial support from the Catholic Biblical Association and its Executive Director, the Rev. Joseph Jensen, OSJ, support from private donors,

in particular P.E. MacAllister, V. Rebecca MacAllister and Charles and Janet Harris, and the Concordia Archaeological Society.[2] LeMoyne College, Concordia Theological Seminary, Emory University, Marquette University, Seton Hall University and Brigham Young University all provided support for staff members affiliated with their institutions that participated in the excavations in the past seven years.[3] Each excavation season varied in the number of staff members participating and in the length of the season.[4]

The seven seasons of excavation at Tell Qarqur, from 1993 to 1999, have provided valuable information on the importance of the ancient site and its long history of occupation. One of the reasons for the choice of Tell Qarqur for archaeological investigation was its possible identification with the ancient Karkara/Qarqar mentioned in Assyrian historical records. These records mention a number of battles that were fought near Karkara/Qarqar by Assyrian armies, first under the Assyrian king Shalmaneser III and later under Sargon II, against coalitions of states in Syria and Palestine. The coalitions covered areas from as far south as Israel and Amman in the Transjordan, east to Arabs from the desert, west to the Mediterranean coast and north to the kingdom of Hama. Karkara/Qarqar apparently represented a significant city on the northern boarder of this area. If Tell Qarqur were to be equated with Karkara/ Qarqar, then the excavation of this site will help us to better understand the history and archaeology of the area.

It has become clear that Tell Qarqur has an important Iron Age settlement that is contemporary with the Assyrian records just mentioned. The excavations have also made it clear that Tell Qarqur has a very long history and must have played an equally important role in the northern Orontes area in many other periods. Particularly well attested so far in addition to Iron II, are the Ayyubid, Early Bronze Age and Iron I periods. Evidence of important Middle Bronze, Persian, Hellenistic and Roman period occupations are also represented from the excavations but so far very little is known about the nature and extent of the settlement on the site in these periods.

This report is not intended as a final report, since much of the excavated levels and structures have been disturbed by continuous rebuilding projects. Recent seasons and continuing excavations were and are focused on building solid, well-stratified, architecturally defined sequences for future reports. Since the excavations are ongoing, it is difficult to draw a line between seasons for a summary report. We have tried to limit our discussion of the information obtained from seasons after 1999 and to block out the finds of these seven seasons of excavation so that a reliable record of the important materials and their excavated contexts are available for comparison at this point. We have included references from individual seasons to indicate how our understanding of the site has changed over the years, as the excavations progressed.

The preliminary analysis of our materials has provided many clear parallels and connections, but has also raised a series of important problems that need to be dealt with in the future. It is not appropriate here to go into long discussions on many points, since much of our evidence is still suggestive and more evidence is needed to make it conclusive. It is important at this point to highlight the problems that exist and the evidence that raises important questions.

I have continued to use a modified Albright/ Wright periodization, though others are available. None, however, seems so far to fit comfortably all of the available information. More work needs to be done to establish a periodization for northwestern Syria that can stand on its own, based solely on locally significant criteria and not shaped by the archaeological sequences from other areas and the literature supporting the associated periodizations.

In the Iron Age, we have considered using the Tarsus periodization of Early–Middle–Late Iron (Goldman 1963), the recently suggested periodization of S. Mazzoni (Mazzoni 2000) and other possibilities. Mazzoni provides a thorough reassessment of the currently available information. She basically maintains the Iron I divisions that were used by Wright (Wright 1961: 94–101) but thoroughly reworks the remainder of the Iron Age with different characterizations of Iron IIB (roughly the eighth century B.C.) and Iron III (seventh century B.C.). Some of the unresolved questions that remain are, for example, where is the break between Late Bronze Age and Iron I?–1200 B.C., 1187 B.C., 1150 B.C.? And what are the artifactual indicators and cultural configurations that support the designations? How late do Iron I and Iron IIA last, and how is Iron IIB to be characterized? Is Iron III a valid designation? What features define the dividing line between the end of the Iron Age and the Persian period, and the Persian and Hellenistic periods?

Until the study of the ceramic materials from Tell Qarqur is farther along, we will continue to use Iron I for the period from just after 1200 B.C. to just before 900 B.C. We will use the Iron IIA designation for the period from the end of the tenth century B.C. down to the middle of the eighth century B.C. and Iron IIB for the remainder of the Iron Age. Serious consideration is being given to shortening Iron I and starting Iron II around 1000 B.C. but this is premature on the basis of the information in hand. It has been very difficult, on the basis of the Tell Qarqur ceramics available so far, to see a shift in the Iron IIA tradition that would define a break point to Iron IIB. On the other hand, the length of Iron IIA seems excessive. Hopefully continued excavations will provide a better ceramic corpus for the latest Iron Age occupation at Tell Qarqur.

What roughly is the end date for the Early Bronze Age? Is it 2000 B.C., 1900 B.C. or 1800 B.C.? Should Early Bronze Age IVB be considered contemporary with the Akkad period in Mesopotamia or should it last longer? Where is the dividing line between Early Bronze IVB and IVA? And the dividing line between Early Bronze IVA and III? The information from Tell Qarqur bears directly on all of these questions and suggests important adjustments in current interpretations.

The renewed excavations at Tell Qarqur have as major objectives the development of basic documentation with which to understand the site's settlement sequence, the size and nature of the settlement in different periods, to obtain a good sample of the cultural materials Qarqur has to offer in its major periods of occupation and gather as complete a record as possible of paleozoological, paleobotanical and other remains. As this report indicates, a good start has been made towards realizing these objectives. Also, as the expedition continues its work, investigations will move out from the tell to the neighboring countryside to work to understand how the site functioned within the local ecosystem.

Since the historical references to Tell Qarqur provide a possible link between archaeological sequences and artifacts, and historical records and established chronologies, I begin with a brief, selective overview of the historical records pertaining to northwestern Syria. This is followed by a brief discussion of the available archaeological information in the same region. I conclude with an overview of the architecture and levels encountered in the seven seasons of excavation and a basic discussion of some of the artifactual and sample materials derived from the excavations. The discussion is basically in chronological units starting with Iron II, since it is the first extensive phase exposed so far. The upper layers, which are unevenly preserved or nearly eliminated, are discussed next. The Bronze Age and earlier remains are discussed last. The discussion throughout is keyed closely to the photographs illustrating the

text and some references to materials from the later levels are intended to provide orientation for the illustrated features under discussion, particularly where later walls of structures are still in place.

GENERAL DISCUSSION AND HISTORICAL REFERENCES CONCERNING EXCAVATED ARCHAEOLOGICAL SITES IN THE REGION AROUND TELL QARQUR

Iron Age

Tell Qarqur has been equated with the Karkara/Qarqar mentioned in Neo-Assyrian texts of the ninth and eighth centuries B.C. (Pritchard 1955: 278, 279, 285 and 287). Many questions have been raised by these references concerning the location and nature of the ancient city, its apparent strategic location and the indication that it clearly played an important role in history. The excavations at Tell Qarqur in the Orontes Valley (fig. 1) are providing an increasing body of evidence to support identification with the Qarqar/Karkara of the texts, but have not yet provided definitive proof. It is important to try to settle this question as quickly as possible to be able to evaluate the historical records properly and to understand better the historical situation that existed at the time.

Early Iron Age records of the Assyrian ruler Tiglath Pileser I (1114–1076 B.C.) mention campaigns in which his armies moved through the Khabur area of Syria, continued along the Euphrates and reached the Mediterranean coast (Pritchard 1955: 275). The records mention that cedar trees were cut down in Lebanon, that tribute was received from Sidon, Byblos, and Arvad on the coast, and that the country of Amurru was conquered. On his return, tribute was imposed on the country called Hatti. From this time on Arameans groups are mentioned as a military concern from Syria in the west to Assyria and Babylonia in the east. It is impossible to tell to what degree political power in Syria was decentralized and fragmented or to what extent some of the city and state structures of the Late Bronze Age retained a degree of effectiveness in the twelvth century B.C.

Fig. 1. View of Tell Qarqur in the Orontes Valley, from the east.

Elements of the Bronze Age cultural and political structures clearly remained, as the evidence of excavations at Carchemish and Ain Dara (Hawkins 1974; Bunnens 2000a, 2000b; Mazzoni 2000) particularly indicate, but many small "Aramean" states developed as well. By the tenth century, many small states existed throughout northern Syria and southeastern Anatolia and in Palestine. Assyrian power was consolidated along the Khabur and a relentless push began against the states that existed over a broad area from Bit Halupe and Laqe in the east to Bit Adini and Aram in the west.

Much work remains to be done to understand the relationships between "Neo-Hittite" and "Aramean" states and their relationships through time with the Assyrian State. The Kingdoms of Hamath and Aram-Damascus became primary entities in the resistance to Assyrian encroachment, and Assyrian records, particularly those of Shalmaneser III (858–824) and Sargon II (721–705), indicate that the focus of Assyrian attack against the Kingdom of Hamath was apparently at its northern border, at the city of Karkara/Qarqara.

Karkara is called a "royal city" in Shalmaneser's inscriptions and said to have been destroyed at this time. Accounts of Assyrian campaigns by Shalmaneser III in subsequent years mention repeated battles taking place near Karkara. A later record of the Assyrian king Sargon II (721–705 B.C.) mentions a battle against the army of Ilubi'di of Hamath at Qarqar and also the siege and destruction of the city which is called "his favorite city" (Pritchard 1955: 285).

An inscription from Tell Afis (50 km northeast of present-day Qarqur) is a dedication stele of Zakir, King of Hamath and Lu'ath. The site is possibly mentioned in the text as Apish (Pritchard 1955: 501), but Mazzoni now argues for its identification with Hazrek (Mazzoni 2000). Additional written records have been found at Qalat Sheisar and Tell 'Acharneh (roughly half way between Qarqur and Hama; Thureau-Dangin 1933) and the ancient citadel of Hama (Riis and Buhl 1987); all provide local records to supplement to the Assyrian accounts (Pritchard 1955: 276–80).

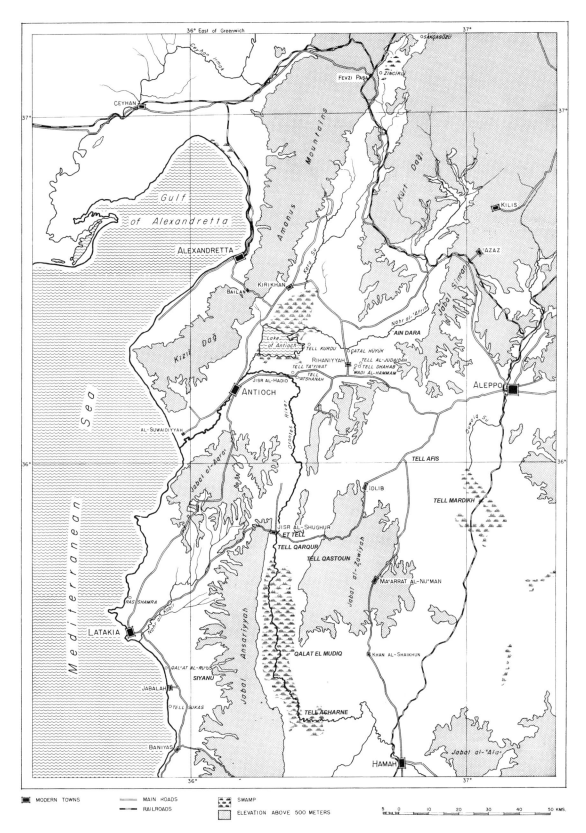

Fig. 2. Map of Northeastern Syria. Adapted from Haines, Excavations in the Plain of Antioch, II, pl. 1.

Fig. 3. View of the present-day village of Qarqur, looking west from the high tell.

Bronze Age

To my knowledge, no references to Qarqur exist in Late Bronze Age records. One possible Middle Bronze Age reference to Qarqur occurs in an Egyptian Middle Kingdom execration text where there is a reference to q–r–q–r–m (Helck 1962: 61). Again, no reference to Qarqur is available in Early Bronze Age cuneiform texts. It has been only recently, in the 1950s, that the marshy areas south of the modern village and tell at Qarqur have been drained as part of the extensive irrigation system in this part of the Orontes Valley (figs. 2, 3). Such marshy areas are known to have existed in antiquity. Egyptian New Kingdom records mention pharaohs hunting elephants in marshes near the Orontes (Klengel 1992: 87–94). Establishing a good record for the ancient ecology of the Qarqur area is as much an objective of the ongoing excavations as the documentation of the cultural sequence. The study of the botanical, osteological and other remains will allow us to provide comparative materials for the surrounding areas

and help to define the distinctive characteristics that influenced its cultural and historical development.

THE ARCHAEOLOGICAL SETTING FOR THE REGION AROUND TELL QARQUR

Iron Age

Archaeologically, the picture is similar to the one sketched out by the historical texts. The basic outline exists but reconstruction of the detailed picture still requires extensive work. Hama was excavated between 1929 and 1939, but many questions remain concerning its Iron Age ceramic sequence, architecture and the date of specific buildings and levels. A tantalizing sample of inscriptional and artistic remains was found but almost nothing in the way of osteological, botanical or other non-artifactual material remains are published. At roughly an equal distance to the north of Qarqur (fig. 2) excavations in the Amuq plain have yielded an excellent Iron Age sequence at the sites of Çatal Hüyük, Judeideh and Tayinat. These excavations, conducted between 1932 and 1938, provide distinct assemblages for the beginning of the Iron Age, Phase N, and the remainder of the Iron Age in Phase O (Swift 1958). The body of ceramics and small finds are yet to be published. The ceramics of the earliest phases of the Hilani area at Tell Tayinat parallel the materials from the gateway area at Tell Qarqur in considerable detail.

In contrast, the materials published so far from the excavations at Tell Afis, nearer to Qarqur, where an Italian expedition has been digging for more than 25 years, illustrate several phases of Iron I occupation (Mazzoni 1990a, 1990c, 1995a; Mazzoni and Cecchini 1995, 1998). These seem to show a distinctive character and require careful work to evaluate the geographical and chronological variations between the two adjacent regional cultures. Our Areas B and D excavations are moving down into earlier Iron Age levels but, though there seem to be changes in the ceramic inventory, the overall trends are not yet clear. At Afis, several phases of Iron I and Iron II occupation have been excavated, but ceramics similar to the ninth–early eighth centuries B.C. materials at Qarqur are not well represented in the materials published so far. Some parts of this sequence may not be represented at Afis and later Iron II wares are poorly represented so far at Qarqur. We are hopeful that the Area B sequence will carry down through these levels and come down to the Late Bronze Age.

The materials excavated by the Japanese expedition at Tell Mastuma, about 7 km south of Idlib and 20 kilometers west of Afis, are valuable in defining the features of a regional assemblage (Egami, et al. 1984; Egami, 1988; Wakita, et al. 1994 and Wakita, et al. 1995) and provide additional information to link the Idlib plateau and the northern Orontes Valley. Materials from contemporary levels at Abou Danné, between Aleppo and the Euphrates, Ain Dara and Tell Jindaris, both on the Afrin River, and renewed salvage excavations at the rich site of Til Barsib (University of Melbourne excavations) should provide a critical mass of evidence that, over the next decade, may well revolutionize our understanding of the material culture of this period. For Iron I, it seems that

the "dark age" may be more the result of a lack of evidence available for consideration in years past and that an actual "dark age" never occured.

Bronze Age

In the region around Tell Qarqur good Bronze Age sequences have been excavated at many important sites. Particularly to be noted are Tell Tayinat, Tell Judeidah, Çatal Hüyük, and Alalakh to the north in the Amuq plain; Hama, Tell Afis, Tell Mardikh/Ebla, and Tell Umm el-Marra to the south and east; and numerous sites in the "big bend" area of the Euphrates River Valley that were investigated as salvage projects in connection with the flooding caused by the Assad and Tishrin dams. The growing corpus of Early Bronze pottery and other artifacts from Tell Qarqur will be instrumental in refining the periodization developed for this region and in giving us a better understanding of the social and political interaction of the area (see pp. 103–16 below).

RENEWED AMERICAN SCHOOLS OF ORIENTAL RESEARCH EXCAVATIONS

The renewed excavations at Tell Qarqur, starting in 1993, continued the excavation in three of the four areas excavated earlier and opened one new area. The locations of all squares that have been excavated are shown on the topographic map of the site (fig. 4),[5] and the grid of excavated squares is shown in fig. 5. The elevations, numbering of the north–south and east–west grid lines and the pattern of square identification was continued from the 1983–1984 excavators with the zero-point of the grid located on the northwest edge of the high southern tell. Elevations on the tell are measured from an arbitrary level of 1000 m on a marker on the highest point of the tell, just southeast of Area B. A long sequence of occupation is now clear and we are tentatively blocking out the strata represented on the site. In the list below, only sherds represent some strata at this point but architectural remains are clearly to be expected; those strata, which are also represented by architecture, are indicated with an asterisk.

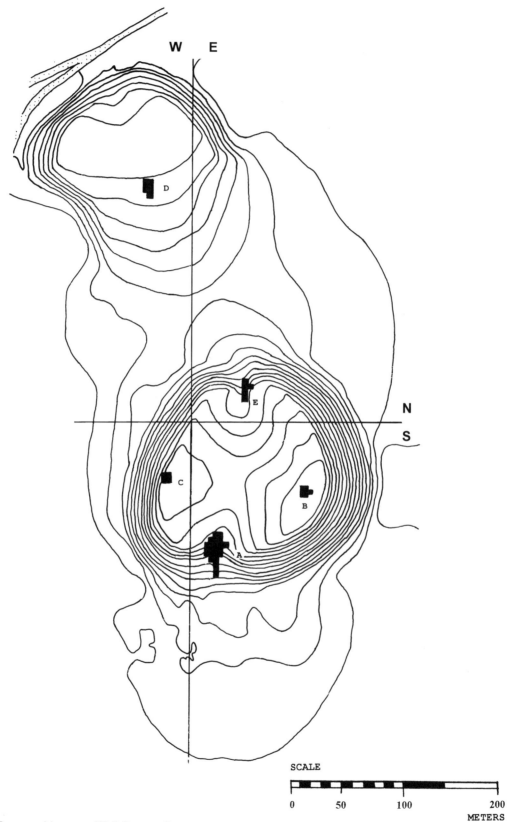

Fig. 4. Topographic map of Tell Qarqur. Contours are in 2 m intervals.

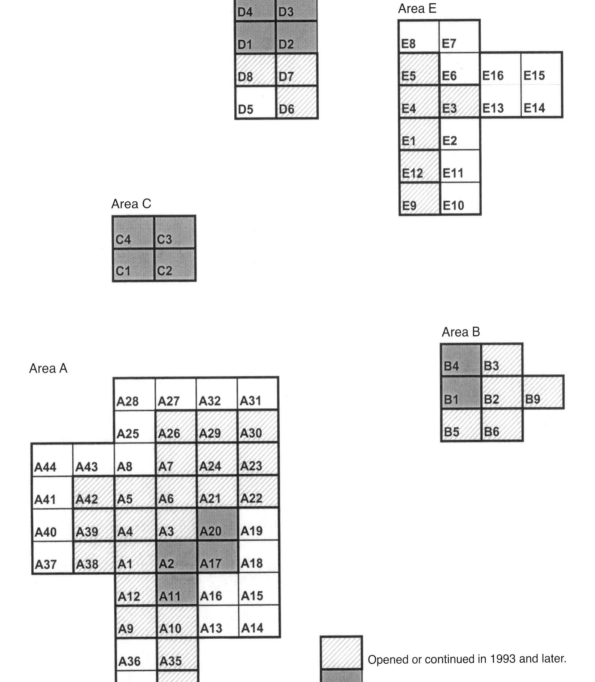

Fig. 5. Graphic illustration of layout of squares in excavation areas.

Stratum 1.   Mamluk
Stratum 2.   Ayyubid*
Stratum 3.   Early Islamic*
Stratum 4.   Byzantine
Stratum 5.   Roman*
Stratum 6.   Hellenistic*
Stratum 7.   Persian*
Stratum 8.   Iron II*
Stratum 9.   Iron I*
Stratum 10.   Late Bronze
Stratum 11.   Middle Bronze II*
Stratum 12.   Latest Early Bronze IV*
Stratum 13.   Early Bronze IVB*
Stratum 14.   Early Bronze IVA*
Stratum 15.   Early Bronze III
Stratum 16.   Early Bronze II
Stratum 17.   Early Bronze I
Stratum 18.   Uruk
Stratum 19.   Chalcolithic
Stratum 20   Neolithic

IRON AGE REMAINS IN AREA A

Excavations in 1983–84 exposed a portion of an Iron Age gateway on the southern slope of the high southern tell (figs. 6, 7). The greatest part of the excavation effort in 1993 through 1999 continued to focus on this area as well (fig. 10). The area has proved to be quite difficult and many details about the sequence of occupation are still unclear despite the effort. There has been extensive pitting and erosion of the area's architectural features so the sequence that has emerged has required much patience to develop as the excavations broaden. It has been essential to create a composite picture by adding more and more pieces as the excavation proceeds. Also, modern intrusion by large and small animals, root disturbance from a variety of plants and major disturbance from later building has left very few intact or continuous surfaces over extended areas.

Though the greater portion of the gateway plan is preserved (fig. 8) very little that is contemporary with the gateway other than the contemporary street and approaching stairway have been found (fig. 39). Kite photographs of the gateway area were taken at the end of the 1995 season (fig. 9). As sections have been removed and walls

traced, the sequence has been reconstructed. Some critical features came to light only in the 1997–1999 seasons (figs. 10, 25). Critical information on the sequence of Iron Age gateways came to light in the 1999 season.

At this point, the major phases of occupation are represented by very deep layers stratified with a later, Ayyubid tower AF42 set over an Iron Age street, AF78/300 (fig. 11). Though there was a major component of earlier pottery in the associated layers, twelvth and thirteenth centuries A.D. pottery was present consistently. Only in the 1997 season did it become clear that a circular structure AF 329, preliminarily assigned to the Roman period (a dating confirmed in 1999) stood east of this tower. It was not connected with any other remains in the area (figs. 8, 11–14, 152, 158, 159 and 161). The northern half of this structure was not as well preserved when it was exposed in 1995 (fig. 13). Walls of a room built against the north wall of the Iron Age gateway, AF149/306, had only one good associated floor but represented a Hellenistic occupation (fig. 15 and on the left in figs. 16–18). In several places, evidence for reuse of the gateway in the Persian Period was found but was poorly preserved. One of these rebuildings is associated with the remains of a circular, 0.90 m–diameter oven, AF312, built against the northern wall of the gateway (figs. 16, 17). This oven was covered with fallen stones and was stratified in a layer beneath wall AF303 and a rebuilding of wall AF306. A thin layer of earth separated the bottom of oven AF312 and the underlying Iron II stone feature AF305. Though we had no solid dating evidence for this feature through 1998, it became apparent in the 1999 excavations that it was actually the remains of an earlier Iron II A gateway. The rebuilt gateway, defined primarily by AF30, 44, 46, 57, 126, 310–312 and 315, had been shifted to the south and east (figs. 14, 16–18, 23–25, 152, 153 and 159). The stones that defined wall AF305, were not uniform in size and orientation, indicating several phases of use (figs. 8, 16, 152 and 158).

The basic plan of the central portion of the last phase of the Iron Age II gateway is clear but only a portion of the entire gateway has been cleared. The objective of exposing other buildings related to the gateway just inside the city, have

Fig. 6. View of Tell Qarqur from the south, taken at the end of the 1998 season.

Fig. 7. View of the Iron Age II gateway area, from the south.

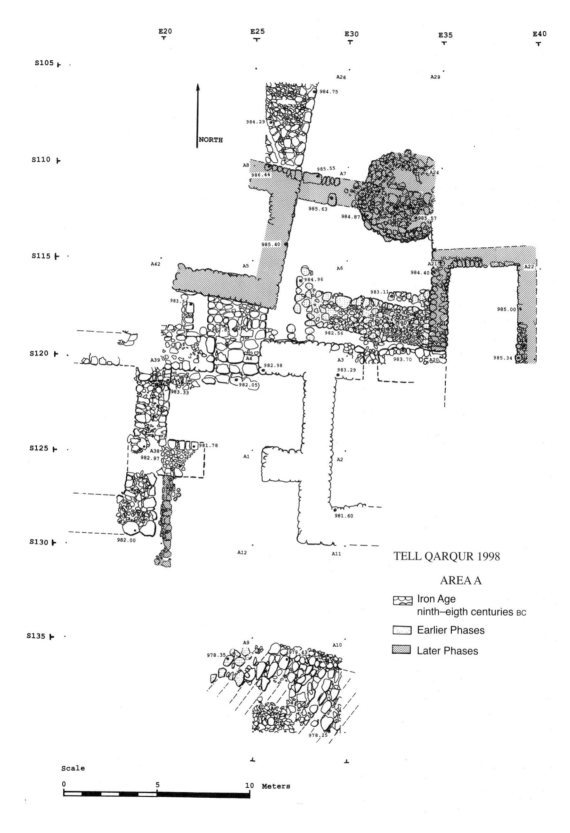

Fig. 8. Plan of the gateway area, through the 1998 excavation season.

Fig. 9. Aerial view of Area A, taken in the 1995 season.

Fig. 10. Panoramic view of Area A taken from the east in 1998.

Fig. 11. Ayyubid tower AF42 covering a portion of the Iron Age II stone paved street, AF78/300.

Fig. 12. View of Roman tower AF329 in A24, from the south. Portions of two of the Iron Age II gravel layers are exposed beneath and to the south of the Roman Tower.

Fig. 13. View of Roman tower AF329 in A24, from the north.

Fig. 14. View of Roman tower AF329 on the left, from the northwest, near the end of the 1999 sea-son as the sections between the Roman and Islamic towers were removed.

Fig. 15. View of Hellenistic room with oven in corner of walls AF308 and 309, from the southwest.

Fig. 16. View of west wall AF303 of room in A22 on the left, and oven AF312 and collapse with Persian remains over AF305 and against gateway wall F306, from the north.

Fig. 17. View of west wall AF303 of room in A22 on the left, and oven AF312 and collapse with Persian remains over AF305 and against gateway wall F306, from the northwest.

Fig. 18. Foundation wall AF305 from the north at the end of the 1998 season, show-ing Early Bronze IV architecture beneath AF305 and in the foreground.

Fig. 19. Wine storage jar found in place in the northwest corner of the main gate chamber.

Fig. 20. West corner of gateway entrance porch, intersection of walls AF310 and AF311, from the northwest.

Fig. 21. Wall AF319 in front of wall AF310 the west wall of the gateway entrance porch, from the east.

met with little success. The plan of the gateway is simple (fig. 8). It consists of a single gate chamber measuring 7.30 m east to west and 3.80 m north to south. It is entered through an open entrance room or porch 7.30 m east to west and 3.20 m north to south. Erosion in the gateway was such that no good floors were preserved in either room. In the northwest corner of the gate chamber, a stone plat-

form was preserved with a wine jar still in place (fig. 19). A stone-lined drain came down to the gateway from the north, ran through the northern wall on the east side and through that portion of the gate chamber. Several pits destroyed portions of the short wall AF312 separating the gate chamber from the porch. The corner at the west side of the entrance porch, the intersection of AF310 and

Fig. 22. Stairway through the northern gateway wall, from the southwest.

Fig. 23. General view of Area A in the 1995 season, with the section over wall AF310, from the east.

AF311 were well preserved (figs. 8, 20 and 21). North of wall AF312, the east and west faces of wall AF310 shift slightly to the east, indicating a rebuilding of the wall. Only a portion of the western room and portions of two associated walls have been excavated so far. A stone foundation, AF319, was later built against the west wall of the entrance room (figs. 8 and 21). No pottery could reliably be associated with this wall, so its association with other features in the gateway area can not be determined.

The gateway was built on a slope so that in its final Iron II phase, a stairway of five steps was needed for the rise of about 1.00 m from the gateway chamber to the street inside the gateway (figs. 22–26). The north wall of the gateway was preserved to a maximum height of six courses of stone, to 0.75 m below the level of the street. At the south end of the gateway, the base of the southeast corner was 2.45 m below the level of the street inside the gateway and 1.60 m below the base of the northern wall, AF30/315. The area east of the gate-

Fig. 24. View of stairway, beginning of street, and north wall of gateway in 1998. General view of features exposed north of the gateway in A42 and extension of wall AF315 to the west, from the east.

Fig. 25. General view of Area A from southeast, showing main north–south section at end of the 1999 season.

Fig. 26. Section over wall AF310 in 1995 season showing Persian period rebuilding in the northeast corner of A39, from the southwest.

Fig. 27. Primary floor excavated in the storeroom west of the main gate chamber of the gateway, from the north.

way has not yet been opened but the exterior corner of the gateway on the northeast has been cleared. No evidence has been found for a fortification wall connected with the gateway, so additional excavation is needed to determine the full plan of the gateway and determine a possible point of connection with a fortification wall. In Area C, a portion of an Iron Age casemate wall was excavated in the 1983–1984 excavations, so a wall connected to the gateway can be expected.

Even less of the Iron Age occupation was encountered in square A22 on the east, shown in the distance in fig. 152. Early Bronze Age IVB walls of A22 are visible in the foreground in fig. 153, while later levels are still exposed in the background in the 1996 view to the west. The gravel layers in A21, and further north, were apparently disrupted when stone walls F303, 308, 309, were constructed (figs. 8, 11 and 12). The north and west sections of A22 (figs. 154–157) show that the clearance for this complex of Persian/Hellenistic walls sloped about 40 cm toward the southwest. As a result, little remained of the Iron Age occupation in the area. Few loci could be ascribed to this period and it was represented primarily by a small percentage of Iron Age sherds in the building fills and where later construction had cut into early destruction debris. West of wall AF303 an oven and a tumble of stones contained Persian Period pottery (figs. 16, 17).

Fig. 28. Storage jars preserved in patches of sherds up to 0.50 m above the main floor of the storeroom west of the main gate chamber of the gateway, from the south.

Two small stone circles with depressions in the middle were found beneath and to the west of wall AF309 in the southeastern corner of A22. They were apparently the remains of stone foundations for storage jars. This seems to be one of the few Iron II loci preserved in this square. Beneath the floor associated with the Hellenistic phase doorsill in AF309, the remains were fragmentary for more than 0.50 m and contained many fragments of fallen clay plaster and major concentrations of Early Bronze Age pottery. In some places substantial sections of vessels were preserved, and in others there were heavy concentrations of Early Bronze Age sherds but occasional Iron Age sherds continued to be found for most of this depth.

Only patches of fallen stones, and destruction debris in the way of ash, broken sun-dried brick, plaster fragments, were found throughout the area at roughly contemporary levels with the Iron Age street surface. Beneath this debris very compact gravel surfaces which included pebbles as large as 2–3 cm were found in 10–15 cm layers and alternated with ash and destruction debris. At least seven of those gravel layers were encountered and were found extending from A26–29 in the north and A6 and A21 in the south. It is difficult to interpret anything other than a courtyard expanse that was reused for a considerable period of time in the Iron Age. In 1999, we removed sections that

had been left standing in previous seasons (fig. 158–161). In the process we confirmed the series of Iron Age gravel layers (figs. 11–14, 152, 153, 158 and 159). The lowest of these layers ran over several phases of Early Bronze Age construction (fig. 158). The gravels sloped steeply to the southwest so that to the northeast we encountered Early Bronze Age IVB architecture while in the southwest that phase had been destroyed and Early Bronze Age IVA was encountered immediately beneath the gravel layer. Re-examination of the major north–south sections (fig. 25), indicated that the highest gravel surface was only poorly preserved and came to a level about 0.20 m below the upper surface of the Iron Age street. Two primary gravel surfaces were found at levels lower than the street. The highest of these gravels ran up against stone feature AF305 and is associated with an earlier rebuilding of the gateway. The lower gravel surface, also dated by associated pottery to Iron Age IIA, ran up against a patch of stones that resemble the pavement of the Iron Age street.

Unfortunately we have had to work in a restricted area because we do not want to undermine the highest phase of that street and it is difficult to see how we can get to additional confirming evidence easily. It will be essential to remove the Ayyubid tower to expose all of this section of the Iron Age street and excavation west of the street may provide the evidence we are looking for, in-

Fig. 29. Base of west wall of entrance room to gate chamber, AF310, with fill and possible single course of an earlier phase of the gateway shown over Early Bronze IV remains, from the west.

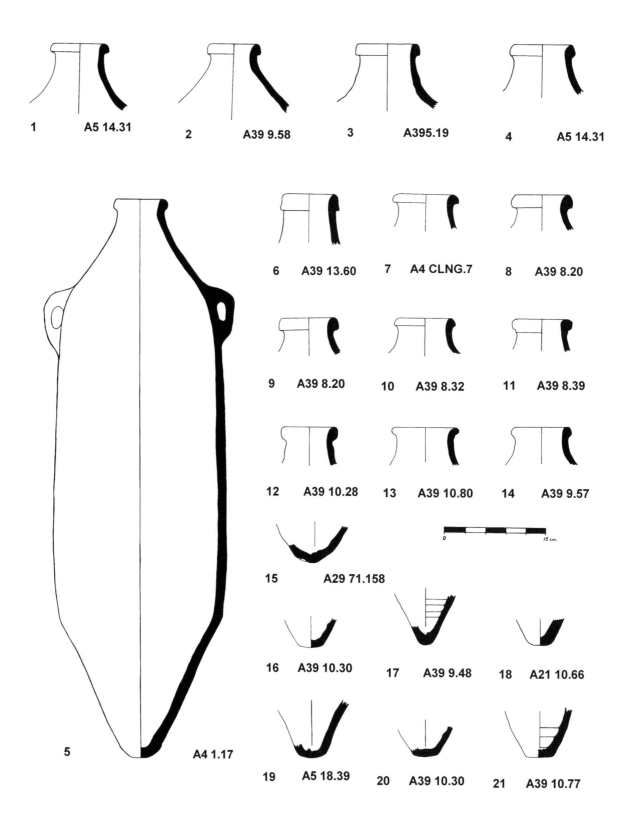

Fig. 30. Profile drawings of Iron Age II storage jars from the main chamber of the gateway and similar sherds from the western room of the gateway and elsewhere.

Drawing Figure	Sherd Number	Area	Plot	Locus	Basket	Form	Exterior	Color	Interior	Color	Ware	Color	Inclusions	Surface Treatment	Height in mm.	Dia. in mm.	Thick ness
30 : 01	TQ95-0201	A	5	14	31	J-023									95	88	10
30 : 02	TQ95-0200	A	39	9	58	J-023									100	70	10
30 : 03	TQ95-0039	A	39	5	19	J-023	7.5YR7/6	RED.YELLOW	7.5YR7/6	RED.YELLOW	10YR7/2	LT. GRAY	SOME FINE BLACK SOME MED GRAY		92	95	11
30 : 04	TQ95-0071	A	5	14	31	J-071	10YR7/4	V. PALE BR.	10YR7/4 10YR7/2	V. PALE BR. LT.GRAY	10YR7/2	LT.GRAY	FEW COR. RED FEW COR. GRAY MANY FINE BLACK		70	85	9
30 : 05	TQ95-0019	A	4	1	17	J-115 BB-19									800	68	14
30 : 06	TQ95-0077	A	39	13	60	J-074	7.5YR7/4 7.5YR5/0	PINK GRAY	7.5YR7/4 7.5YR5/0	PINK GRAY	7.5YR4/0	DK GRAY	FEW MED WHITE MANY FINE BLACK		72	90	10
30 : 07	TQ95-0070	A	4	CLNG	7	J-023	10YR8/2	WHITE	10YR8/2	WHITE	10YR8/2	WHITE	FEW MED RED FEW MED WHITE		50	100	6
30 : 08	TQ95-0042	A	39	8	20	J-023	7.5YR8/4 7.5YR8/0	PINK LT. GRAY	7.5YR8/4 7.5YR8/0	PINK LT. GRAY	7.5YR8/4	PINK	MANY MED BLACK	PLAIN	51	70	7
30 : 09	TQ95-0202	A	39	8	20	J-023									54	80	8
30 : 10	TQ95-0038	A	39	8	32	J-015	10YR4/1 10YR7/3	DK.GRAY V.PALE BR.	7.5YR7/3 10YR4/2	PINK DK.GRAY.BR	7.5YR7/3	PINK	MANY FINE BLACK SOME FINE RED SOME FINE WHITE SOME FINE GRAY		50	90	8
30 : 11	TQ95-0076	A	39	8	39	J-070	7.5YR7/6	RED.YELLOW	7.5YR7/6	RED.YELLOW	10YR7/2	LT.GRAY	MANY FINE BLACK SOME MED GRAY		47	88	8
30 : 12	TQ95-0040	A	39	10	28	J-072	10YR6/2	LT. BR. GRAY	10YR6/2	LT. BR. GRAY	10YR6/2	LT. BR. GRAY	SOME MED WHITE MANY FINE BLACK		55	85	8
30 : 13	TQ96-0043	A	39	10	80	J-069	10YR6/3	PALE BROWN	10YR6/3	PALE BROWN	10YR6/2	LT.BR.GRAY	MANY FINE BLACK SOME FINE WHITE		54	90	8
30 : 14	TQ95-0041	A	39	9	57	J-015	10YR7/3	V.PALE BR	10YR5/2 7.5YR7/4	GRAY.BROWN PINK	7.5YR7/4	PINK	MANY FINE BLACK MANY FINE WHITE		54	90	8
30 : 15	TQ95-0021	A	29	71	158	BB-18	7.5YR7/4	PINK	10YR8/4	V.PALE BR.	7.5YR7/4	PINK	MANY FINE BLACK SOME COR. WHITE		58	22	10
30 : 16	TQ95-0023	A	39	10	30	BB-21	10YR8/4	V.PALE BR.	10YR8/4	V.PALE BR.	5YR3/1 10YR8/4	V.DK. GRAY V.PALE BR.	MANY FINE BLACK		45	36	10
30 : 17	TQ95-0020	A	39	9	48	BB-20	7.5YR7/4	PINK	10YR6/2	LT.BR.GRAY	10YR6/2	LT.BR.GRAY	MANY FINE BLACK		75	24	10
30 : 18	TQ93-0163	A	33	10	66	BB-07	7.5YR8/4 7.5YR7/6	PINK RED.YELLOW	10YR7/2	LT. GRAY	10YR7/2	LT. GRAY	MANY FINE BLACK MANY COR.WHITE FEW COR.RED	PLAIN	40	35	14
30 : 19	TQ95-0022	A	5	18	39	BB-19	10YR8/4	V.PALE BR.	10YR8/4	V.PALE BR.	10YR8/4 10YR7/4	V.PALE BR. PINK	MANY FINE BLACK		80	45	10
30 : 20	TQ95-0023	A	39	10	30	BB-07	10YR8/4	V.PALE BR.	10YR8/4	V.PALE BR.	5YR3/1 10YR8/4	V.DK. GRAY V.PALE BR.	MANY FINE BLACK		42	40	10
30 : 21	TQ96	A	39	10	77	BB-22	10YR6/1 10YR6/2	GRAY LT.BR.GRAY	10YR8/2 10YR5/1	WHITE GRAY	10YR8/2 10YR5/1	WHITE GRAY	MANY FINE BLACK		72	40	11

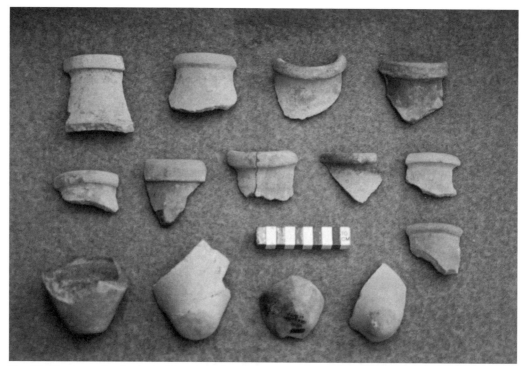

Fig. 31. Photograph of selected Iron Age II storage jar rim and base sherds.

Fig. 33. Bent nails of iron and bronze from the destruction on locus 45 floor in western room of the gateway.

Fig. 32. Iron spear point from destruction on locus 45 floor in western room of the gateway.

Fig. 34. Cylinder seal found in the destruction debris inside the western room of the gateway, with modern impression.

Fig. 35. Stratification of the Islamic tower over the Iron Age stone paved street was clarified during the removal of the south section of A26, from the north.

Fig. 36. Iron Age stone-paved street as exposed in 1995, after removal of the south section of A26.

cluding the line of an intermediate street. In order to obtain additional details of the various phases and plans of the gateway, considerable additional excavation will be required, if indeed enough is preserved after the later rebuildings. There are many critical, unanswered questions. If the gateway was shifted in the upper phase, did it also shift in the intermediate phase from an initial location close to that of the final phase? Since, if we are correct, the lower street is built in the same location as the upper phase but about 0.50 m lower. There are large stones on the level of this lower street but it is impossible to interpret their original function at this time. At this point the evidence and possibilities need to be made clear and the correlation of three possible gateway phases with the stairway to the south cannot yet be attempted. We should emphasize, however, that several phases of the Iron Age II gateway construction probably indicate a fairly long period of continuous use for the gateway within the ninth and the eighth centuries B.C.

Two rooms flanked the gate chamber on the east and the west. The outline of the western part of the eastern room was established in the 1983–1984 seasons and the narrow, 0.70 m wide doorway providing access to the room from the north was excavated in 1995. A portion of the western

Fig. 37. Iron Age stone paved street as first exposed in the 1993 season, from the east.

room was excavated between 1995–1998. Only one good earth floor was encountered in this room (fig. 27). It was covered with materials, which demonstrated extensive burning and stone collapse from the surrounding walls, and was filled with broken wine jars (figs. 30 and 31; similar to the one found in 1995 when the north section was re-cut to reveal a jar in the northwest corner of the gateway chamber [fig. 19]) and other store jars.

Scatters of similar storage jar sherds were present at higher levels, fig. 28, but only small patches of floors were preserved. When the eastern balk and part of the southern balk were removed its eastern wall, F310, was clarified (figs. 8, 25 and 26). Wall F 310 was partially destroyed by a large pit but the foundation stones of the wall at this point continued down for over a meter. A little over a meter to the north and on the west side of this wall the

Fig. 38. Iron Age stone paved street photographed at the end of the 1993 season, from the southeast.

foundation was not set down to a similar depth but was set on fill and large fallen stones from earlier construction in the area (fig. 29). When excavation proceeded beneath the floor of the room, no other good Iron Age floors were encountered, but Iron Age fill extended down for 1.80 m at which point a destruction layer of Early Bronze Age IV was found. The line of stones beneath the foundation of the final phase of the gateway, as well as lines of stones below gateway floor levels in the main chamber of the gateway, is probably to be connected with the earlier phases of the gateway. Additional excavation will be required in this area to clarify the phasing of the gateway.

Among the objects found in this room were a number of iron spear points (fig. 32), several bent bronze and iron nails (fig. 33). The most interesting object was found fairly high in the destruction debris. It was a small cylinder seal with the impression of two quadrupeds in front of a small chariot (fig. 34). A double arc is the most prominent filling feature, situated above the back of the lead animal. The contents of the chariot are indistinct, possibly representing a human figure holding a spear and sitting behind a shield or the chariot front. Though I know of no exact parallels, chariot scenes are not unusual in Neo-Assyrian glyptic and the simple rendering is in keeping with the Neo-

Fig. 39. General view of gateway area from approaching stairway, taken from the southeast.

Fig. 40. View of stairway leading to the gate after clearance in the 1995 season, from the southwest.

Assyrian linear style of the ninth–seventh centuries B.C. (Buchanan 1966: 106–13).

In the northeast corner of the western room, the gateway wall showed signs of rebuilding, on the left side of figs. 22 and 26, but no higher floors were in association with it. A buttress seems to be built into wall AF315, but it is unclear how it relates to north–south running wall AF310. A well-preserved wall surface on the south face of the buttress indicates a possible doorway, or it is possible that wall AF310 did not continue south in this period, and the single chambered gateway was replaced by buttresses flanking a gateway door. The evidence is scanty, so it is difficult to be sure of the architectural configuration of the gateway in this phase. Little more can be said other than that the date of this rebuilding is possibly indicated by the presence of Persian period pottery. The gateway had been constructed with large, unshaped stones at the faces and with smaller stones filled in at the core, as shown in figs. 19–22, 24, 25 and other photographs. Fragments of the plaster that once covered the clay surface of the walls were found in patches on the walls and fallen in the destruction debris.

The street running north from the gateway is still partially covered by the Islamic tower (figs. 8–12, 23–25, 35 and 36). It measured 3.20 m wide

Fig. 41. View of stairway and trench in square A9, taken from the east. West section at rear of photograph shows ash layer covering Middle Bronze Age remains.

Fig. 42. View of earlier stairway AF321 in foreground beneath later Iron II stairway AF320, from the west.

at the gateway and was constructed with a single layer of stones. Larger, roughly shaped stones were used to line its edges (figs. 36–38). Patches of a white clay plastered surface were preserved on top of the stones near the gateway. The street was traced to a distance of 14.00 m to the north and rose 1.9 m over that stretch, rising at an angle of 8 degrees. A drain was constructed at an angle across the street in square A26. The size of the stones varied in different sections of the street, indicating areas of rebuilding or change in function of different segments of the street.

East of the street and beneath the level of the Roman Tower, AF329, only patches of fallen stones and destruction debris in the way of ash, broken sun-dried brick and plaster fragments, were found throughout the area at roughly contemporary levels with the street surface. This debris was found in 10–15 cm layers and alternated with gravel surfaces, as mentioned earler. The top of these layers has been reached farther south in A24 at the center of the area, where they sloped steeply toward the center of the gateway. As indicated above, it is difficult to interpret anything other than a courtyard expanse that was reused in this area for a considerable period of time in the Iron Age.

Below the gateway, 5 m to the south, a stairway approached the gateway at an angle (figs. 8, 39–41). Ten steps were cleared to a maximum width of 3.60 m; the height of the steps averaged 0.15 m and their depth 0.50 m. The stairs abutted a retaining wall, AF313, on its north side but the south side was destroyed. The stairs descended to the southeast but also sloped in a southerly direction, away from wall AF313. A small portion of the stairway was excavated in 1984 and the remainder came to light when we tried to extend a test trench south from the gateway area to explore early occupations on the tell. Pits had robbed sections of the stairs and a heavy scree of fallen stones that contained a concentration of Ayyubid pottery covered most of it. Additional pitting was encountered south of the stairway and domestic architecture of the Umayyad period was encountered close to the surface in the lowest plot of the test trench (fig. 92). Our attempt to connect the gateway and the stairway was unsuccessful. West of square A10 nothing remained of the stairway, but three steps

of an earlier stairway AF321 were encountered immediately beneath it (fig. 42). At the northwest corner of square A9, additional stones indicated another stone feature, possibly a still earlier stairway, but the stones were so badly disrupted by later pitting that no pattern could be discerned. Ash layers and destruction debris covered the lower levels of stairs AF321 and the stone feature AF322 in the southwest corner. The pottery associated with these ash layers was Middle Bronze II. The excavations were extended to the north of A9 but again contemporary features were not obvious there. Many wall lines are evident in the heavy concentration of stones between the stairway and the gateway, and may be the remains of wall foundations of the Middle Bronze Age (fig. 39).

IRON AGE REMAINS IN AREAS B, D AND E

In addition to the Iron Age II remains from Area A, contemporary materials have been excavated in Areas B, C, D and E. The renewed excavations in 1993–1999 have not yet returned to Area C on the western edge of the high tell but excavations have been continued in Areas B. Iron Age materials in Area D were not evident in the 1983–1984 excavations but have been documented subsequently. Several phases of Iron Age II wall foundations were excavated in Area E, including a major structure indicated in Squares E1 and E9.

Area B

In Area B, the 1983–1984 excavations exposed six adjacent squares. In our first season, the area was cleaned up and excavations resumed in four of the squares, on the east and south sides (figs. 43–47). Square B9 was started in 1997 to connect the excavated areas to the edge of the tell, particularly to extend the Iron Age exposure to that area and explore any fortification walls that may be present. Many phases of Iron Age domestic architecture were encountered in the area during the 1983–1984 excavations. Additional walls and other features were added to the previously excavated sequence (figs. 43–45), particularly in the southern half of the area. Square B6 was the least

Fig. 43. General view of B1–3 after clearance in 1993, from the southeast.

disturbed and included a cross-wall that extended at an angle into B2 to the north. An oven was cleared in the southwest corner of a room formed by the intersection with a second wall that continued to the southeast, beyond the limits of the square (figs. 46, 47). The northeastern part of the area was badly disturbed by pits. Some of the pits contained exclusively Iron Age sherds but others contained pottery of Hellenistic–Ayyubid date as well. We concentrated our efforts on Square B2 in order to obtain a sequence of occupations in the area.

Our concentration on excavation in square B2 is intended to provide a benchmark area for Iron Age stratigraphy on the site (figs. 44, 48, 52–56), and provide a backbone for our ceramic analysis and also for the analysis of the zoological and botanical materials. Thus far, twelve occupation levels have been documented within eight phases defined by architectural remains. Good lines of stone foundations have been traced and portions of mudbrick walls were preserved to between 1 and 4 courses high. In many cases, the rebuildings were compacted close together in several superimposed layers of foundation stones and often the brickwork that can be traced over the foundations is preserved only by in the thickness of one brick or less. The complicated details of these difficult re-

mains will be presented in the final report but figs. 43–45 ilustrate the nature of the preservation and the rebuilding activity. Extensive pitting was also encountered in B2 (figs. 49, 52 and 53), but all pits seemed to have been dug during Iron Age II. This of course has made the interpretation of the area very complicated with only small segments of many walls remaining that are very difficult to connect. Several large ash layers help to pull the sequence together (figs. 54–56) and other features provide markers within the sequence.

In the 1998 season we apparently reached levels beneath the heavily pitted area and the outlines of a number of built structures began to appear. Some were very difficult to trace but became clearer as we proceeded. It became evident that we were dealing with silos or storage bins, many built with mudbrick sides that were probably located in a courtyard area outside of dwellings. Apparently fragments of these silos and storage structures had continued at higher levels but were terribly confused by later pitting (figs. 52 and 54–56), so that we were not clear on any of the details until the end of the 1998 season. Two bins are shown in the eastern half of the square in fig. 54. The one in the southeast corner (fig. 55), had the best preserved brick lining, probably because this

Fig. 44. General view of B2 east section at the end of the 1993 season, from the southwest. Stone wall foundations on the right and left are earlier phases of walls excavated in 1983–84. A long sequence of stone foundations, mudbrick walls, plastered floors and destruction layers are clear in the section.

Fig. 45. General view of Squares B2 and 3 at end of 1993 season, showing walls and large circular pit, from the east.

area had weathered over several seasons of excavation and became easier to see as a result. Another bin inside the arc of a larger bin began to emerge but its phasing was not yet clear at the end of the season. In the northeast corner another bin extended into the north and east sections. Surrounding bricks were difficult to trace in the thick clay material around the edge of the structure but may emerge after the soil has dried out (fig. 56).

The east section of Square B2 (figs. 44, 54 and 56) demonstrate the long sequence of layers of Iron II occupation in the Area. Fig. 43 shows the clearance of the area when we resumed excavation. Several house wall foundations angle to the east with one cross-wall near the section separating B1 and B2, and a stone pavement along the south balk of the same squares. The surfaces going with at least four phases of stone wall founda-

Fig. 46. Iron Age walls and oven in B6 with one wall extending into B2 to the south. General view of foundations exposed at the end of the 1983–1984 seasons, from the southeast.

tions and several phases of mudbrick walls are clear in the east section (fig. 44). Figures 54 and 56 show that a series of ash layers and rough surfaces continue for more than a meter below the stone foundations. The east section was not cut back to the section line at the southeast corner because of the many stones projecting into the balk. During this phase of occupation, a courtyard apparently existed in most of B2. Only occasional patches of stones and mudbrick indicated the remains of structures but they were broken by the series of pits. Only when we reached the silos illustrated in figs. 54–56 was the courtyard nature of the area substantiated. The details of the strati-graphy are very complicated because of the disruptions and will be presented in detail in the final report.

Fig. 47. View of B5, foreground, and B6, background, showing minimal clearance in 1993, from the west.

Fig. 48. East section of B2 at the end of the 1994 season, from the west. Fragmentary stone foundations exposed after long sequences of surfaces, possibly occupation floors, more than 1.00 m in depth.

As our corpus of Iron Age pottery is increasing and good closed groups are being collected, we are beginning to see some evidence of phasing within the Iron II ceramic inventory. In Area B, as in Areas A and D, the ninth and eighth centuries are well represented by a well-developed repertoire of red burnished forms (figs. 77, 78, 80–82).

Area D

A deep sounding in square D6 (figs. 61, 62) indicated a depth of Iron Age deposit on the lower tell. In the restricted area excavated in D6, a number of other walls and rebuildings were exposed but only in small segments. The wall foundation

Fig. 49. View of same level in B2 as in fig. 48, showing foundation remains at the end of the 1994 season, from the north; the east section is on the left.

Fig. 50. General view of the pits, pavement fragments and bottom of the ash pit excavated in the 1996 season, from the north.

DF10 did not extend very far north (figs. 57 and 58), before its continuation was destroyed by later building activities. A patch of gravel west of it indicated a street sloping up from the southwest corner. Two phases of a wall DF12 and 13 were excavated along the south balk (figs. 61, 62). Wall DF12 was the remains of a substantial mudbrick wall but with the limited exposure it is impossible

to understand how the two shaped stones of DF13 were originally used. The date of the pottery associated with Walls DF12 and 13 was Iron II. The most interesting object associated with this building phase is a well-preserved bronze piece of unknown function (fig. 63). It is a 56 mm shaft with four attached semi-circular plates. Though a handle could have been fitted into the central hole, this

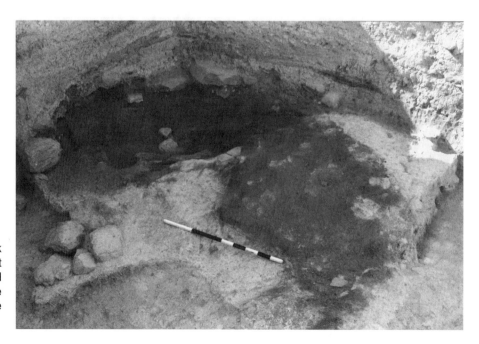

Fig. 51. Thick black ash pit in northeast corner of B2, cleared near the end of the 1996 season, from the northwest.

Fig. 52. View of B2 at the end of the 1997 season, showing pits and fragmentarily remains of structures, from the south.

would have produced a very small head for a weapon. This does not seem likely. It would seem that this object may have served as a tool of some sort or a furniture fitting that was intended to connect other parts at the four leaves to a framework connected at the shaft hole. The fitting could have been used in a piece of furniture or a specialized stand or supporting frame.

A major purpose of the excavations in Area D was to create an exposure of the Iron Age levels on the lower tell to correspond with the sequence being excavated in Areas A and B on the high tell. Most of the later remains in Area D were removed to reach the Iron Age levels. One of the ovens outlined in the middle of Square D7, probably Hellenistic in date, still remains to be clarified (figs.

Fig. 53. North section of B2 at the end of the 1997 season, from the southeast.

Fig. 54. East section of B2 at the end of the 1998 season, showing the remains of several silos extending into the sections on the north, east and south, from the west.

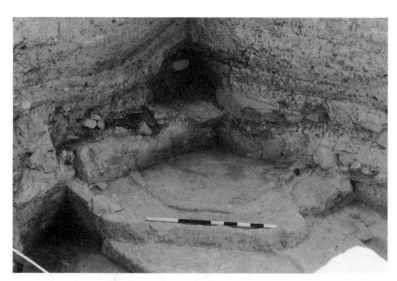

Fig. 55. Close up of brick-lined silos in southeast corner of B2, from the northwest.

Fig. 56. View of silo in northeast corner of B2 and pit against middle of the north section, from the west.

Fig. 57. Wall DF10 with gravel surface to the west, cleared in the 1994 sounding, from the north.

64–66 [upper right], 105–107). A heavy concentration of Iron Age sherds were pressed flat on a surface excavated along the north side of wall DF11 (figs. 58, 60). Similar sherd patches were found at higher levels but their association with later foundations was sketchy since they were cut in subsequent building operations. Though higher than wall DF10, wall DF11 could not be traced farther to the west and was not preserved near DF10.

The east section of D6 (figs. 59, 61 and 62), shows an abrupt change to a tight series of whitish clay layers for about one-half meter over wall DF11 and associated surfaces. The date of these layers was Iron Age II, but the ash layers and other patches of surfaces beneath wall DF11 contained pottery of the transitional phase between Iron I and II. The east section shows that the Iron II surfaces break before they reach the south section, indicating that the Iron II materials may have been cut down to a greater depth in this area. In contrast, figs. 64 and 65 indicate that little Iron II or Iron I–II transitional material was preserved at the north end of D7, where Early Bronze Age IV pottery was found inside what is apparently a pottery kiln (figs. 66, 67). This kiln may be similar to the kiln outlined but not yet excavated in D8 (fig. 109). Many ash layers and several additional ovens (in

Fig. 58. Same view, after additional excavations in 1997 uncovered wall DF11 and sherd scatter to the north, cleared in the 1997 season, from the west.

Fig. 59. View of same area and east section after 1998 excavations have removed the sections and adjacent areas of D6 and D7 down to the floor levels associated with wall DF11, from the west.

Fig. 60. Close up of patch of Iron II sherds north of wall DF11, from the west.

Fig. 61. 1997 view of east section of D6 with DF11 above test trench with mudbrick wall DF13 on the right at bottom of test trench, from the west.

Fig. 62. Bottom of test trench in 1994 with mudbrick wall DF12 and stones of wall DF13 against south section, from the north.

Fig. 63. Bronze fitting from Iron II context in D7.

the foreground of fig. 65) were encountered in the center of the area. It seems that the industrial character of this area has a very long history. So far only a small amount of Iron Age material has been excavated in Area D but hopefully, as excavations continue, more will be found to clarify the extent to which Iron Age material was removed by later building operations and the different depths to which Iron Age walls were founded.

Area E

Excavations were begun in Area E in 1995 with the intent of balancing our sequence in Area A by opening an exposure on the opposite side of the high tell (fig. 68). The highest occupation in the area, as elsewhere was Islamic and a substantial building was encountered (figs. 69, 70, 116 and 117). Ayyubid, Roman and Hellenistic re-

mains cut down into Iron Age II structures, as in Area A. Several layers of Iron Age architecture were encountered and remains of a substantial building were exposed in the lowest level.

The highest Iron II stone foundations were exposed in the southeast corner of E9 (figs. 71, 72). Beneath this an Iron Age II structure was excavated. In one building phase (fig. 73), several walls and a doorway were rebuilt a number of times and associated with an excellent collection of Iron II pottery. An unusual incised steatite stone bowl was found with this material (fig. 74). At the end of the 1999 season foundation stones of a major structure were just coming to light, with one of the walls measuring almost two meters in width (figs. 75, 76). These foundations seem still to date to the Iron II period. As the south balk in E4 was removed, a series of at least five architectural levels was observed that corresponded to most of the sequence excavated in E9. Since the exposure was very limited and the stone architecture tightly packed, little pottery was available to date comfortably the layers (fig. 187). Ayyubid, Roman, Hellenistic, and Iron II pottery was found in this exposure. A sounding in the room of the Ayyubid building also reached stone foundations of earlier structures (figs. 69 and 70). Though little pottery was preserved in the small exposure, the remains seem to belong to the large Iron Age structure exposed at the bottom of E9.

Fig. 64. General view of D6 and D7 at the end of the 1998 season, from the south.

Fig. 65. General view of squares D6 and D7 at the end of the 1999 season, from the south.

Fig. 66. Northern end of square D7 showing remains of Early Bronze Age IV kiln, from the west.

Fig. 67. Northern end of square D7 showing remains of Early Bronze Age IV kiln in lower left. Same view as fig. 66 but from the east.

Fig. 68. General view of Area D on low tell showing high tell and Area E in the background, from the northwest during the 1998 season.

EXTENT OF THE IRON AGE OCCUPATION

The information from the excavations in Areas A, B, D, and E indicate that the high southern tell at Qarqur may well have served as a citadel area in the Iron Age but occupation was not confined to the citadel but extended on to the extensive lower tell as well. If the Iron Age occupation covers all areas of both tells, then Tell Qarqur has to be considered a major city of that time period. If the Iron I remains indicated from different areas of the site but particularly from squares B2 and D6 prove to be indicative, Tell Qarqur may have been a major city for many centuries in the Iron Age.

IRON AGE POTTERY FROM AREA A, THE GATEWAY AREA, AND AREAS B AND D

Iron IIA

A fairly comprehensive selection of Tell Qarqur Iron IIA pottery forms are illustrated in figs. 30, 31, and 77 through 86. These have been collected from all areas of the tell. The Iron Age IIA tradition seems to have a long duration with minimal change, so at this point it is difficult to illustrate different chronological phasing in the existing inventory. Our field readings have given the designation Iron IIA to this body of material but exactly how that is to be defined within the tenth to eighth centuries B.C. needs to be determined precisely as we collect more materials from well-stratified contexts.

Most common in this inventory are platter-bowls and deep carinated bowls. A variety of other less common bowl forms, ring bases on a variety of forms, jars, jugs and juglets provide the remainder of the current inventory. The most distinctive surface treatment on these vessels is hand- or slow-turnette burnishing on a red surface or slip. The color range of the red burnished wares is medium to dark red to red-brown and dark brown. Some bowl rims indicated a range of profiles common in the eighth–seventh centuries B.C., but it is unclear where the line should be drawn since the wheel burnishing and lighter color ranges or colors ranging from pinkish red to orange that become common later in Iron II, are extremely rare. Only in the 1996–1998 seasons have larger collections of well-stratified pottery become available to make detailed analyses worthwhile and that task is just beginning. At this point, I am retaining the 918 B.C. date for the dividing line between Iron I and Iron II, in keeping with Mazzoni's sugges-

Fig. 69. Sounding beneath Ayyubid stone foundations in E1, from the west.

Fig. 70. Same, showing the lowest, possibly Iron Age wall encountered in the sounding.

Fig. 71. Possible remains of Iron Age wall in southeast corner of square E9, from the west.

Fig. 72. Possible remains of Iron Age wall in southeast corner of square E9, from the north.

tion (2000). Tentatively, I am considering Iron IC as a transitional phase between Iron I and Iron II. The establishment of Iron Age subdivisions will require considerable study, and will have to remain tentative until a workable body of ceramic material is available to provide divisions that can be used with confidence. The current indications are that Tell Qarqur illustrates an established Iron Age tradition, which covers five or six centuries. Basic color schemes and decoration types are included in our sample as well as a sampling of imported Cypriot wares and one Greek Cycladic cup sherd.

The current evidence does not allow us to document a development in profile or surface treat-

Fig. 73. Iron Age II foundations in E9, from the southwest.

Fig. 74. Incised steatite bowl fragments from Iron II levels in E9.

Fig. 75. Major stone foundations, probably of the Iron II period, encountered at the end of the 1999 season, from the southeast.

Fig. 76. Stone foundations in the south section of E9, from the east.

ment for the hallmark form, the red-burnished platter-bowl. The corpus of well-stratified pottery is not yet large enough to provide a line of development in square-ended, round-ended or other related platter-bowl rim forms (fig. 78: 1–19 and fig. 77), or in a shift in the color range from darker browns to red-browns to lighter shades of red and pink or in a development in burnishing techniques, from hand to wheel burnishing. A range of variations occurs for each feature but a pattern is not yet clear. There seems to be a close overlap between burnished and plain bowl forms (fig. 80), but again no noticeable pattern has yet been recognized in their associated contexts. We have a good sampling of carinated bowls (single-angled (fig. 79: 16–18) or double-angled (fig. 79: 20–25, and fig. 82) that have been connected with a variety of Neo-Assyrian bowl forms (Adachi 1997). They seem to be present throughout Iron II and are not concentrated late in the sequence.

Fig. 77. Platter and plain bowl sherds.

Fig. 78. Plain ware Iron II bowl, handle and lamp sherds.

Fig. 79. Variety of Iron II plain and profiled bowl sherds.

Fig. 80. Double and single angle Iron Age II bowl sherds.

A variety of wine storage jar rims (figs. 19, 30 and 31), are present as well as a variety of jar rims (figs. 79: 23, 26, 27; 83: 1–10; 84: 1–10 [top row and left four sherds in the second row]), krater rims (fig. 83: 13, 14; 84: 11, 12, 15–20 [last two sherds in the second row and all of the third row with the exception of the middle sherd]), and a variety of heavier store jars (fig. 84: 18 [center sherd in the bottom row] and 84: 59 [all of the rim sherds]). A hole-mouthed cooking pot with ribbon handles at the shoulders (fig. 83: 18, 19), seems to be characteristic of Iron Age II. So far, few good stratigraphic contexts are present to provide any precision in illustrating a typological development for any of these forms. Individual sherds of Cypriot vessels (figs. 83: 11; 86: 4 [third from the left in the top row], 18–21 [three sherds in the middle of the third row], 28 [the fifth sherd from the left in the third row], 33, 34 [the last two sherds in the bottom row]), include black-on-red juglets and jugs, white-painted jars and flasks, and other jugs, and one Greek, Cycladic cup sherd with pendant concentric semi-circle decoration (fig. 79: 15) fit in the basic time range that we have indicated but similarly so far do not provide additional precision in dating. A small selection of painted pottery is illustrated on fig. 83: 1, 3, 7, 8, 13–15 and the remaining sherds not specified as Cypriot imports above in fig. 86. Most of this decoration consists of painted bands with a range of colors from red-orange to brown to black. Typical bichrome painted bands of varying widths are common.

It is obvious that some pottery forms have a long period of use, when the pottery from the lowest levels we have reached in Area B (fig. 88), are compared with those illustrated in figs. 30, 31, 77–86. The circumflex handles, krater shapes, krater rims and painted decoration indicate an eleventh century date. Some of the rim forms, however, continue into Iron II contexts and red–burnished platter-bowl forms are already present. After raising questions and providing the basic documentation available, it is clear that we need to build a much larger corpus of well-stratified ceramic forms to achieve clarification concerning these ceramic materials and to position them correctly

with the ceramic inventories from sites within a 100 mile radius of Qarqur.

One key to understanding the sequence may be in the smaller jar forms, which have been found in larger number in the last few seasons. A basic representation of club-shaped and other bowl rims with eighth century parallels is now available and careful analysis of their provenience and association with other forms may provide evidence for phasing within the sequence. A variety of simple profile bowl rims for large and small bowls characteristic of the period are represented on fig. 81, and on fig. 79: 1–13. A disconcerting fact, however, is that the ware and surface colors represent the same varieties present in the platter-bowls and carinated bowls. So far we have very few sherds that are clear indicators of the seventh and sixth centuries B.C., such as sherds with close wheel-burnishing or spaced wheel-burnishing and light red to pinkish surface colors and only one example of a black-burnished variant of the common red-burnished bowl form, (fig. 81: 11, fourth sherd from the left in the second row).

Iron I

During the 1997 season, Iron I pottery began to appear in the sherd readings (figs. 87–90). As excavation continued it became clear that we did not have a clear break but common Iron II forms continued side by side with the new forms and decoration types. The pottery readings also provided the indication of a shift in the red-burnished tradition. Forms commonly found later with red-burnished finish were present, as illustrated on fig. 88: 2 and 9, but more detailed work needs to be done to determine any change in the frequency of the plain (fig. 88: 4 and 6) and red-burnished wares. If a change in frequency is supported by the detailed analysis that is now underway, we should be able to provide valuable evidence for a transition from Iron I to Iron II ceramic traditions. This analysis will also show any change and frequency of forms characteristic of Iron I, like the circumflex handle (fig. 88: 5 and 89: 3, 6, 7, 10, on the left), and the use of specific painted decoration: specifically parallel painted bands on vessel body and rim (figs. 89: 1–5, 9, top row and left

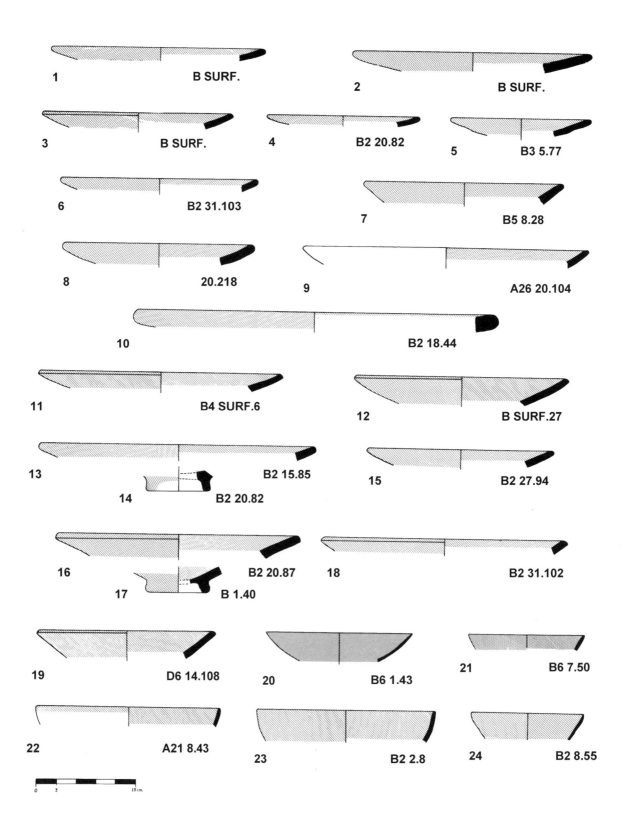

Fig. 81. Pottery drawings for the Iron Age II platter bowls and other red-burnished bowls.

Drawing Figure	Sherd Number	Area	Plot	Locus	Basket	Form	Exterior	Color	Interior	Color	Ware	Color	Inclusions	Surface Treatment	Height in mm.	Dia. in mm.	Thick ness
81 : 01	TQ93-0005	B	SURF		8	B-004	2.5YR5/8	Red Burnt	2.5YR5/8	Red	2.5YR5/6 05YR4/3 2.5YR5/6	Red Red Brown Red	Fine Lt. Med. White Black	Wheel Burnish	18	320	8
81 : 02	TQ93-0024	B	SURF		29	B-006	2.5YR5/8	Red	2.5YR5/8 7.5YR8/2	Red Pink White	10YR8/2	White	Fine Large Med. Black Sand Mica Tan Clay		29	360	13
81 : 03	TQ93-0055	B	SURF		26	B-004	10YR4/8	Red	10YR4/8	Red	05YR5/6	Yellow Red	Fine Med. Red Brown Sand	Hand Burnish	23	290	9
81 : 04	TQ93-0071	B	2	20	82	B-004	10YR4/6	Red	10YR4/6	Red	2.5YR6/4 10YR7/3 2.5YR6/4	Lt. Red Brown Vr. Pale Brown Lt. Red Brown	Fine Med. Lt. Med. Brown Black Sand	Lt. Hand Burnish	15	230	7
81 : 05	TQ93-0016	B	3	5	77	B-004	05YR6/4	Lt. Red Brown	10R5/8	Red	05YR5/6	Yellow Red	Fine Lt. Med. White Sand Clay Brown Sand	Lt. Hand Burnish	26	210	9
81 : 06	TQ93-0067	B	2	31	103	B-004	2.5YR3/6	Dark Red	2.5YR3/6	Dark Red	10YR8/2 10yr7/3 10YR8/2	White Vr. Pale Brown White	Very Fine Lt. Black White Mica Sand Clay	Lt. Hand Burnish	18	300	9
81 : 07	TQ93-0018	B	5	8	28	B-006	2.5YR5/8	Red	2.5YR5/8 7.5YR8/2	Red Pink White	10YR8/2	White	Fine Large Med. Black Sand Mica		31	300	13
81 : 08	TQ93-0007	B	2	20	218	B-004	10R3/4	Dusky Red	10R3/4	Dusky Red	2.5YR5/8	Red	Fine Med. Large Med. Red Brown Sand	Hand Burnish	31	290	12
81 : 09	TQ93-0065	A	26	20	104	B-004	10YR8/2	White	10YR3/3	Dkk. Brown	10YR8/1	White	Fine Med. Large Med. Brown White Sand	Wash Hand Burnish Inside	27	430	9
81 : 10	TQ93-0075	B	2	18	44	B-095	2.5YR5/6	Red	7.5YR8/2	Pink White	7.5YR4/0	Dk. Gray	Fine Med Large Med. Heavy Black White Mica		26	550	23
81 : 11	TQ93-0006	B	4	SURF	6	B-004	05YR6/4	Lt. Red Brown	05YR6/3	Lt Red Brown	7.5YR6/8 7.5YR5/4 7.5YR6/8	Red Yellow Brown Red Yellow	Fine Med. Large Med. Straw Brown Sand	Spaced Burnish	27	370	9
81 : 12	TQ93-0003	B	SURF	SE	27	B-020	10R4/6	Red	10R4/6	Red	05YR6/6	Red Yellow	Fine Med. Large Heavy Multi Color Sand	Hand Burnish	41	320	10
81 : 13	TQ93-0009	B	2	15	85	B-004	2.5YR5/8	Red	2.5YR5/8	Red	05YR8/3	Pink	Med. Lt. Tan Sand	Double slip	22	420	11
81 : 14	TQ93-0096	B	2	20	82	BB-09	2.5YR4/6	Red	2.5YR4/6	Red	10YR8/3	Vr. Pale Brown	Fine Med. Large Med. Brown Multi Color Sand		30	100	11
81 : 15	TQ93-0008	B	2	27	94	B-004	2.5YR4/8 05YR7/4	Red Pink	2.5YR4/8	Red	7.5YR6/6	Red Yellow	Small Med. Large Med. Multi Color Sand	Wash Lt. Burnish In Spaced Ring Burnished out	24	280	10
81 : 16	TQ93-0001	B	2	20	87	B-004	2.5YR3/6	Dk. Red	2.5YR3/4	Dk. Red Brown	7.5YR7/3 05YR7/1 7.5YR7/3	Pink Lt. Gray Pink	Fine Med. Large Med. Heavy Multi Color Sand	Hand Burnish	34	370	13
81 : 17	TQ93-0025	B		1	40	BB-09	05YR6/8	Red Yellow	05YR6/8	Red Yellow	05YR7/3 7.5YR7/2 05YR7/3	Pink Pink Gray Pink	Fine Med. Med. Tan White Brown		38	100	12
81 : 18	TQ93-0030	B	2	31	102	B-020	2.5YR3/6	Dk. Red	2.5YR3/6	Dk. Red	7.5YR6/8 10YR7/4	Red Yellow Vr. Pale Brown	Fine Med. Large Med. Heavy	Hand Burnish	21	370	10
81 : 19	TQ93-0004	D	6	14	108	B-020	05YR5/6	Yellow Red	2.5YR4/8	Red	7.5YR6/8 10YR7/4 7.5YR6/8 7.5YR6/8	Red Yellow Vr. Pale Brown Red Yellow Red Yellow	Fine Med. Large Med. Heavy Multi Color Sand Multi Color Sand		40	290	10
81 : 20	TQ93-0017	B	6	1	43	B-086	2.5YR5/8 10YR6/6	Red Brown Yellow	2.5YR5/8	Red	2.5YR3/6	Dk. Red	Fine Med. Lt. White Sand Shell	Wheel Burnish Radial Burnish Out	42	220	4
81 : 21	TQ93-0070	B	6	7	50	B020	2.5YR5/8 7.5YR8/0	Red White	2.5YR5/8 7.5YR8/0	Red White	7.5YR8/0	White	Some Fine Black Few Corse White	Hand Burnish Close In Spaced Out	35	180	5
81 : 22	TQ93-0074	A	21	8	43	B-086	05YR3/1 2.5YR5/8 10YR7/6	Vr. Dk. Gray Red Yellow	5YR5/8 05YR7/4	Yellow Red Pink	05YR6/4	Lt. Red Brown	Med. Large Lt. White Gray	Hand Burnish	27	280	5
81 : 23	TQ93-0027	B	2	2	8	B-085	2.5YR3/6 2.5YR5/6	Dk. Red Red	2.5YR3/6	Dk. Red	2.5YR6/6 7.5YR7/2 2.5YR6/6	Lt. Red Pink Gray Lt. Red	Fine Med. Lt. Multi Color Sand Pottery Granuals	Hand Burnish	47	270	7
81 : 24	TQ93-0064	B	2	8	55	B-086	05YR6/4 05YR5/8	Lt. Red Brown Yellow Red	05YR6/4 05YR5/8	Lt. Red Brown Yellow Red	05YR6/3	Lt. Red Brown	Fine Lt.		38	170	4

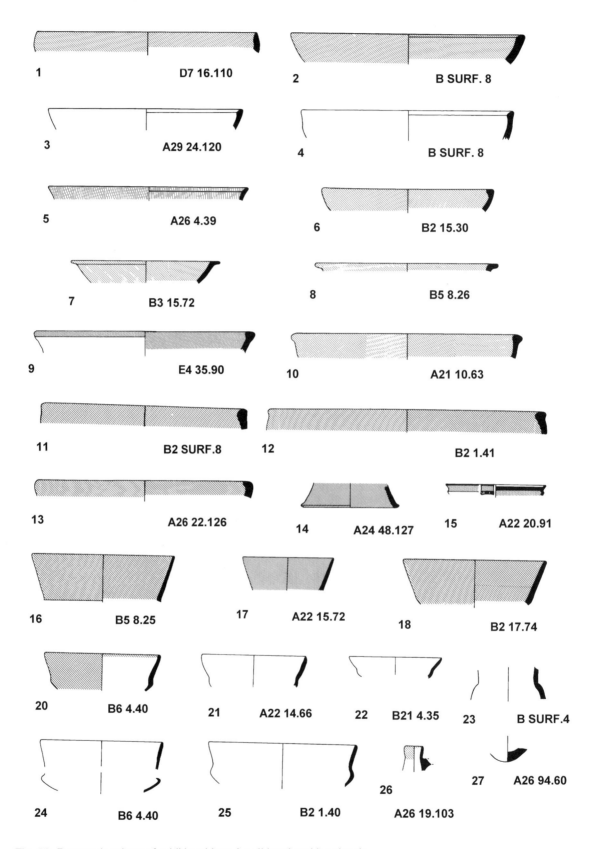

Fig. 82. Pottery drawings of additional Iron Age II bowl and jar sherds.

Drawing Figure	Sherd Number	Area	Plot	Locus	Basket	Form	Exterior	Color	Interior	Color	Ware	Color	Inclusions	Surface Treatment	Height in mm.	Dia. in mm.	Thick ness
82 : 01	TQ93-0057	D	7	16	110	B-0129	10R4/8	Red	10R4/8	Red	7.5YR6/6	Red Yellow	Fine Med. Large Med. Multi Color Sand	Hand Burnish	30	340	9
82 : 02	TQ93-0066	B	SURF		8	B-025	10R4/8	Red	10R4/8	Red	05YR7/4	Pink	Fine Med. Large Med. Heavy Multi Color Sand	Hand Burnish	44	360	12
82 : 03	TQ93-0068	A	29	24	120	B-031	10R6/6 05YR7/3	Lt. Red Pink	10R6/6 10R6/3	Lt. Red Pale Red	05YR6/8 05YR5/1 05YR6/8	Red Yellow Gray Red Yellow	Fine Med. Fine Straw Black White Sand	Spaced Burnish	31	300	7
82 : 04	TQ93-0288	B	SURF		8	B-025	2.5Y4/6	Red	2.5Y4/6	Red	5YR7/6 10YR7/2	Red Yellow Lt. Gray	Many Fine Black	Hand Burnish In/Out	44	320	9
82 : 05	TQ93-0075	A	26	4	39	B-101	05YR2.5/1	Black	05YR2.5/1	Black	05YR3/1	Vr. Dk. Gray	Med. Med. White Sand	Lt. Burnish In.	20	310	5
82 : 06	TQ93-0022	B	2	15	30	B-093	10R4/8	Red	10R4/8	Red	2.5YR6/3 10R6/2 2.5YR6/3	Lt. Red Brown Pale Red Lt. Red Brown	Fine Med. Med. Black White Sand	Hand Burnish	34	240	7
82 : 07	TQ93-0019	B	3	15	72	B-099	2.5YR4/6	Red	2.5YR4/6	Red	05yr6/4	Lt. Red Brown	Fine Med. Large Med. Heavy Multi Color Sand	Hand Polish	34	230	7
82 : 08	TQ93-0073	B	5	8	26	B-100	05YR5/6 05YR3/2	Yellow Red Dk. Red Brown	05YR5/6 05YR3/2	Yellow Red Dk. Red Brown	05YR6/3	Lt. Red Brown	Fine Med. Large Med. Multi Color Sand	Hand Polish	12	280	7
82 : 09	TQ97-0090	E	4	35	90	B-098	10YR8/4	V. Pale Br.	2.5YR4/6	Red	10YR4/1 10YR7/3	Dk. Gray V. Pale Br.	Some Fine Black		34	340	8
82 : 10	TQ93-0048	A	21	10	63	B-107	10R5/8	Red	10R5/8	Red	7.5YR5/6 10YR5/1 7.5YR5/6	Str. Brown Gray Strong Brown	Vr. Lt. Fine Gray Sand	Lt. Burnish	36	320	7
82 :11	TQ93-0029	B	SURF		8	B-105	10R4/8 05Y8/1	Red White	10R4/8 10R4/8	Red White	05YR8/2 2.5Y8/2 05YR8/2	Pink White White Pink White	Fine Lt. Lt. Straw Brown Sand	Flakey Red Slip On White Slip	31	320	9
82 : 12	TQ93-0018	B	SURF	1	41	B-106	05YR5/8	Yellow Red	05YR5/8	Yellow Red	05YR7/2 05YR6/1 05YR7/2	Pink Gray Gray Pink Gray	Fine Med. Large Med. Heavy Multi Color Sand	Hand Burnish	34	215	8
82 : 13	TQ93-0041	A	26	22	126	B-115	05YR5/4 05YR4/2	Red Brown Dk. Red Gray	05YR6/4	Lt. Red Brown	7.5YR3/0 05YR6/6	Vr. Dk. Gray Red. Yellow	Fine Med. Med. White Sand	Hand Burnish	24	340	10
82 : 14	TQ97-0086	A	24	48	127	BB-15	7.5YR5/4	Brown	10YR8/4 7.5YR5/4	V. Pale Br. Brown	10YR7/2	Lt. Gray	Some V. Fine Black		36	150	5
82 : 15	TQ95-0072	A	22	20	91	B-102	7.5YR7/4 2.5YR5/6	PINK Red	2.5YR4/8 5YR3/2	Dk. Red Brown	5YR8/1	White			14	150	4
82 : 16	TQ93-0026	B	5	8	25	B-134	2.5YR3/4	Dk. Red Brown	2.5YR3/4	Dk. Red Brown	2.5YR4/2	Weak Red	Fine Lt. Black White Sand	Hand Burnish In Vertical Burnish Out	70	220	6
82 : 17	TQ95-0029	A	22	15	72	B-112									48	140	6
82 : 18	TQ93-0023	B	2	17	74	B-112	2.5YR4/6	Red	2.5YR4/6	Red	05YR6/4	Lt. Red Brown	Fine Med.	Hand Burnish	66	220	9
82 : 19	TQ93-0015	B	6	4	40	B-081	10R4/4	Weak Red	10R4/4 05YR8/3	Weak Red Pink	05YR7/4	Pink	Fine Med. Med. Multi Color Sand		54	180	7
82 : 20	TQ95-0012	A	5	17	36	B-079									46	160	6
82 : 21	TQ95-0010	A	22	14	66		7.5YR6/6	Red Yellow	7.5YR6/6	Red Yellow	5YR8/1 7.5YR4/0	White Dk. Gray	Some Fine Black		29	160	4
82 : 22	TQ93-0049	A	21	4	35	Jug	7.5YR7/3	Pink	7.5YR7/4	Pink	7.5YR7/4 7.5YR7/0	Pink Lt. Gray	Lt. Med. Fine Med. Brown White Sand		47	135	8
82 : 23	TQ93-0061	B	SURF		4	B-084	2.5YR4/6	Red	2.5YR4/6	Red	2.5YR3/6	Dk. Red	Fine Med. Lt. Black Brown Sand	Hand Polish	41	240	5
82 : 24	TQ93-0078	B	6	4	40	B-084	2.5YR4/6	Red	2.5YR4/6	Red	2.5YR3/6	Dk. Red	Fine Med. Lt. Black Brown Sand	Hand Polish	24	240	3
82 : 25	TQ93-0063	B	SURF	1	40	B-080	7.5YR6/4	Lt. Brown	05YR6/6	Red Yellow	05YR6/4	Lt. Red Brown	Fine Med. Med. Multi Color Sand	Hand Burnish Out	64	230	6
82 : 26	TQ93-0038	A	26	19	103	J-042	7.5R4/6 7.5YR8/3	Red Pink	05YR7/6	Red. Yellow	05YR7/6	Red. Yellow	Fine Med. Large Med. Heavy Multi Color Sand	Band Painted	36	30	4
82 : 27	TQ93-0054	A	26	94	60	BB-17	10YR8/2	White	10YR7/2	Lt. Gray	10YR7/2 10YR6/1	Lt. Gray Gray	Fine Med. Lt.		23	65	12

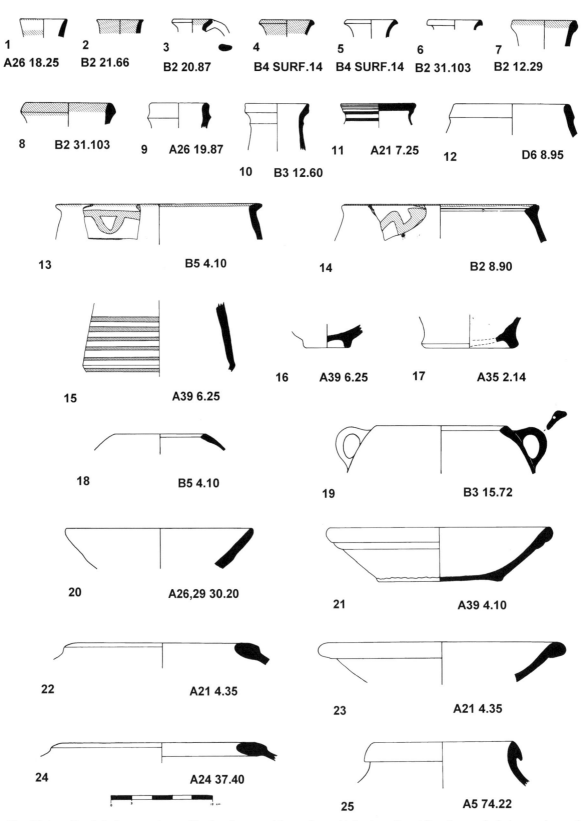

Fig. 83. Iron II painted wares, jar and krater rims, cooking pots and later Iron II and Persian period storage jar and bowl profile drawings.

Drawing Figure	Sherd Number	Area	Plot	Locus	Basket	Form	Exterior	Color	Interior	Color	Ware	Color	Inclusions	Surface Treatment	Height in mm	Dia. in mm	Thickness
83 : 01	TQ93-0088	A	26	18	85	J-0041	05YR7/6 10R4/6	Red Yellow Red Paint	05YR7/6	Red Yellow	2.5YR6/6	Lt. Red	Fine Med. Lt. Med Multi Color Sand	Painted Bands	27	70	7
83 : 02	TQ93-0086	B	2	21	66	J-043	2.5YR4/6	Red	2.5YR4/8	Red	7.5YR7/3	Pink	Fine Med. Med. Multi Color Sand	Hand Burnish	20	70	6
83 : 03	TQ93-0081	B	2	20	87	J-048	10YR8/4 10R4/6	V. Pale Brown Red Paint	10YR8/4 10R4/6	V. Pale Brown Red Paint	05YR7/6	Red Yellow	Fine Med. Large Heavy Multi Color Sand	Red Paint	38	62	5
83 : 04	TQ93-0085	B	4	SURF	14	J-059	2.5YR4/6	Red	2.5YR4/6	Red	2.5YR6/8 2.5YR4/3 2.5YR6/8	Lt. Red Red Brown Lt. Red	Fine Lt. Black Sand	Hand Burnish	22	80	4
83 : 05	TQ93-0084	B	4	SURF	14	J-058	Red	Red	Red		Red		Fine Med. Med. Multi Color Sand		26	80	4
83 : 06	TQ93-0087	B	2	31	103	J-058	10R5/8	Red	10R5/8	Red	10R5/8 7.5YR7/6 10R5/8	Red Red Yellow Red	Fine Med. Med. Multi Color Sand		15	80	3
83 : 07	TQ93-0058	B	2	12	29	J-064	05YR7/6 2.5YR5/8	Red Yellow Red Paint	05YR7/6	Red Yellow	7.5YR7/3	Pink	Lt. Med. Med. Heavy Multi Color Sand	Painted Bands	37	100	7
83 : 08	TQ93-0059	B	2	31	103	J-063	05YR7/4 2.5YR5/8	Pink Red Paint	05YR7/4 2.5YR5/8	Pink Red Paint	05YR6/6	Red Yellow	Fine Med. Med. Heavy Black White Sand	Red Bands	31	140	7
83 : 09	TQ93-0198	A	26	19	87	J-021	Red. Yellow Yellow	Red. Yellow	Red. Yellow Red. Yellow	Red. Yellow	Red. Yellow White		Many Med. Black Plain Some Coarse Red		36	80	8
83 : 10	TQ97-0108	B	3	12	60	J-076									60	90	7
83 : 11	TQ94-0018	A	21	7	25	J-079									31	110	2
83 : 12	TQ93-0050	D	6	8	95	J-038	7.5YR7/3	Pink	7.5YR7/4	Pink	7.5YR6/6	Red. Yellow	Med. Fine Med. Black White Sand	Blackened	48	170	8
83 : 13	TQ93-0011	B	5	4	10	J-089	10YR8/2 05YR6/6	White Red Yellow Pt.	10YR8/2	White	05YR6/6 2.5Y7/4 05YR6/6	Red Yellow Pale Yellow Red Yellow	Fine Med. Large Med. Multi Color Sand	Red Paint	51	310	7
83 : 14	TQ93-0010	B	2	BAULK	90	J-090	05YR7/4 2.5YR4/8	Pink Red Paint	05YR7/4	Pink	7.5YR6/6	Red Yellow	Fine Med. Large Heavy Black Sand Multi Color Sand	Red Paint	55	290	9
83 : 15	TQ95-0024	A	39	6	25	BS									102	210	10
83 : 16	TQ95-0016	A	39	6	25	BB-16									32	170	10
83 : 17	TQ95-0018	A	35	2	14	BB-09									46	140	4
83 : 18	TQ93-0090	B	5	4	10	J-062	10YR8/2	Black	10YR8/2	Black	10YR8/2 10YR3/2 10YR8/2	Black V. Dk. Gray Brown Black	Med. Large Med. Shell White Sand		23	135	4
83 : 19	TQ93-0098	B	3	15	72	J-062	05YR7/2 05YR5/4	Pink Gray Red Brown	05YR5/2	Red Gray	2.5YR3/6	Dk. Red	Fine Med. Large Med. Heavy White Calcite		68	190	5
83 : 20	TQ94-0017	A	=26-29	30	20	B-017	05YR7/4	Pink	05YR7/4	Pink	05YR6/6	Red. Yellow	Fine Med. Large White Brown Sand White Sand		58	280	14
83 : 21	TQ95-0003	A	39	4	10	B-103 BB- J-104									78	332	9
83 : 22	TQ93-0037	A	21	4	35	B-104	7.5YR7/3	Pink	7.5YR7/4	Pink	7.5YR7/4 7.5YR7/0	Pink Lt. Gray	Fine Med. Lt. Brown White Sand		30	290	10
83 : 23	TQ93-0051	A	21	4	35	B-104	05YR7/4	Pink	05YR7/4 10YR8/3	Pink V. Pale Brown	7.5YR6/3	Lt. Brown	Med. Large Fine Med. Heavy Red Brown Sand		58	365	11
83 : 24	TQ97-0008	A	24	37	40	J-104	10YR8/3	V. Pale Brown	10YR8/3	V. Pale Brown	10YR8/3	V. Pale Brown	Many V. Fine Black		27	320	8
83 : 25	TQ95-0050	A	5	74	22	J-078	10YR6/3	Pale Brown	10YR6/3	Pale Brown	10YR7/2	Lt. Gray	Some Med. White		64	204	9

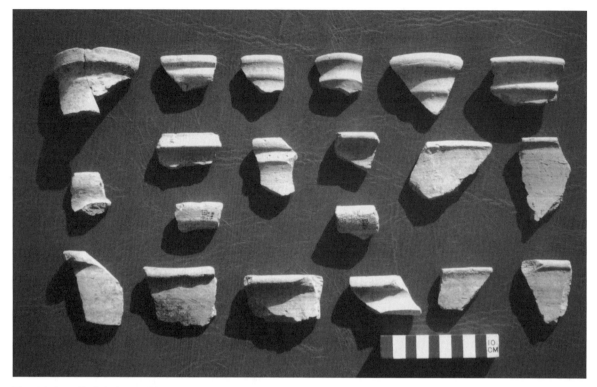

Fig. 84. Iron II plain jar and krater rim sherds.

Fig. 85. Large and medium sized store jar sherds.

Fig. 86. Variety of Iron II painted sherd, local and Cypriot imported sherds.

Fig. 87. Photograph of transitional Iron I–Iron II pottery from B2.

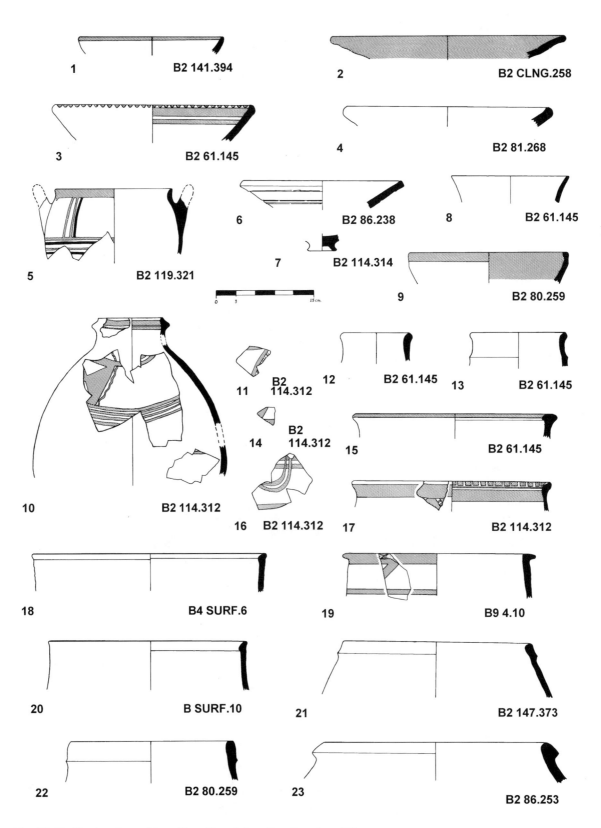

Fig. 88. Profile drawings of transitional Iron I–Iron II pottery from B2.

Drawing Figure	Sherd Number	Area	Plot	Locus	Basket	Form	Exterior Color		Interior Color		Ware Color		Inclusions	Surface Treatment	Height in mm	Dia. in mm	Thickness
88 : 01	TQ97-0108	B	2	141	394	B-087	7.5YR7/4	Pink	7.5YR7/4 7.5YR5/4	Pink Brown	10YR4/1 10YR7/3	Dk. Gray Pink	Many Fine Black		27	220	9
88 : 02	TQ97-0029	B	2	CLNG	258	B-001	7.5YR7/4 5YR6/6	Pink Red Yellow	5YR6/6	Red Yellow	10YR7/3	V. Pale Br.	Few Fine White		37	350	9
88 : 03	TQ96-0047	B	2	61	145	B-087	7.5YR8/4	Pink	7.5YR7/6	Red Yellow	7.5YR7/6	Pink	Many Fine Black		45	300	10
88 : 04	TQ97-0005	B	2	81	268	B-097	10YR7/3	V. Pale Br.	10YR7/3	V. Pale Br.	10YR7/3	V. Pale Br.	Some Med Gray		33	310	14
88 : 05	TQ97-0001	B	2	119	321	B-135									105	180	6
88 : 06	TQ96-0048	B	2	86	238	B-030									24	44	9
88 : 07	TQ97-0109	B	2	114	314	BB-14									24	44	9
88 : 08	TQ96-0049	B	2	61	145	B-113									40	180	6
88 : 09	TQ97-0007	B	2	80	259	B-092	7.5YR6/4	Lt. Brown	5YR5/6	Yellow Red	10YR7/3	V. Pale Br.	Some Fine Gray		47	240	8
88 : 10	TQ97-0110	B	2	114	312	J-065									118	240	9
88 : 11	TQ97-0111	B	2	114	312	BS									44	240	50
88 : 12	TQ96-0044	B	2	61	145	J-055	5YR7/6	Red Yellow	5YR7/6	Red Yellow	7.5YR7/2	Pink Gray	Many Fine Black Few Fine White		42	100	6
88 : 13	TQ96-0046	B	2	61	145	J-057	7.5YR8/4	Pink	5YR7/6	Red Yellow	10YR7/2	Lt. Gray	Many Fine Black Some Med White		50	140	6
88 : 14	TQ97-0112	B	2	114	312	BS									27	240	25
88 : 15	TQ96-0045	B	2	61	145	J-087	10YR8/3	V. Pale Br.	10YR8/3	V. Pale Br.	10YR8/3	V. Pale Br.	Some Fine White Some Fine Red	Paint on Rim	37	300	9
88 : 16	TQ97-0113	B	2	114	312	BS									88	240	92
88 : 17	TQ97-0097	B	2	114	312	J-093	5YR8/4 PAINT:	Pink	5YR7/6 PAINT:	Red Yellow	7.5YR7/3	Pink		Paint Out and In. Rim	47	270	6
88 : 18	TQ93-0293	B	4	SURF	6	J-092									54	350	9
88 : 19	TQ93-0272	B	9	4	10	J-088	10YR8/3	V. Pale Br.	10YR8/2	White	10YR8/2 7.5YR7/4	White Pink	Some Fine Black		66	260	12
88 : 20	TQ93-0294	B		SURF	10	J-091									74	300	8
88 : 21	TQ97-0082	B	2	147	373	J-038	7.5YR7/6	Red Yellow	7.5YR7/6	Red Yellow	7.5YR7/6 10YR7/3	Red Yellow V. Pale Br.	Many Med Gray Many Fine Black		75	280	8
88 : 22	TQ97-0094	B	2	80	259	J-013	7.5YR7/4	Pink	7.5YR7/4	Pink	7.5YR7/4	Pink	Many Med White Many Med Gray		61	250	8
88 : 23	TQ96-0050	B	2	86	253	J-111									60	380	14

Fig. 89. Photograph of transitional Iron I–Iron II and Iron I pottery from B2 and D6–7.

Fig. 90. Photograph of additional transitional Iron I–Iron II and Iron I pottery from B2 and D6–7.

two sherds in the second and third rows); the use of bichrome decoration, 88: 5; decorated panels on jars, 88: 10 and kraters 88: 11, 14, 15, 17 and 19; and swags spreading down from handles on store jars (fig. 88: 16). Krater rims like fig. 88: 18 and 20, continue into Iron II contexts (figs. 83: 13

and 14; 86: 11, 12, 15, 16, 19, 20), as do the jar rims like fig. 88: 21, 22, which are quite common in Iron II contexts (figs. 83:12 and 85: 3, 4, 7–10 [right two sherds in the top row and right four sherds in the second row]). The ware color for this transitional period is primarily in a range of orange-pink hues. The last season provided earlier examples with darker, red-brown paint (fig. 90), earlier cup forms (fig. 90: 3, 4 [right two sherds in the top row]); and a krater with geometric decoration. These examples came from Area D and seem to indicate twelvth century materials. A small faience Bes amulet was found in this context as one of the few non-ceramic artifacts of this part of the sequence (fig. 91).

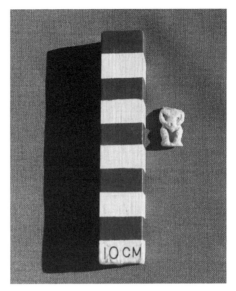

Fig. 91. Faience Bes figurine from transitional Iron I–Iron II locus in B2.

OCCUPATION REMAINS OVERLYING THE IRON AGE LEVELS

Islamic Materials in Area A

Islamic materials have been encountered to some degree in all areas of the site and most of these remains date to the Ayyubid period. In the gateway area, a tower and associated wall with a doorway east of it were excavated in 1983–1984 and subsequent seasons (figs. 8, 10–13, 23–25, 35 and 36). The tower and associated layers and fills were found up to 0.35 m above the Iron Age levels associated with the gateway. The lowest stones of the tower foundations were only 0.35 m above the Iron Age stone-paved street, F78 (figs. 35, 36).

In square A10 and the test trench which extends down the slope from Area A, stone robbing, pitting and dumping of stones were encountered but in the lowest trench patches of walls and a grouping of circular ovens were found very close to the surface (fig. 92). Excavation was limited in depth in this area except were the pits cut down to a depth of almost two meters. No follow-up excavations have been carried out on the Islamic remains in this area either by removing them to reach earlier levels or by exposing a broader area at this elevation. Farther south, below the edge of the tell, a meter wide trench for irrigation pipes (fig. 92), also encountered Islamic materials including many stone wall foundations and a circular kiln. The Islamic pottery from Tell Qarqur Area A is charac-

terized by a variety of glazed wares (fig. 93) and an extensive repertoire of incised pottery in coarse, dark brown cooking pot-like wares (fig. 94). Very few glazed sherds from secure or unsecured levels seem as early as the Ummayad or Abassid periods. Typical glazed or incised wares of those periods are extremely rare at this point in the excavations.

Islamic Materials in Area D

A situation similar to that in Area A seems to hold true in Areas B and D where later materials were encountered. The topographic map of the tell (fig. 4) gives the location of the excavated areas and fig. 68 shows the high tell in the distance and Area D in the foreground on the lower tell. A portion of an Ayyubid building was excavated in Area D in 1993 (figs. 96–98). Portions of two walls and a paved area were excavated, with a doorsill preserved as part of the foundations of wall DF1 (figs. 96, 97). No secure floors were preserved so close to the surface, a maximum of 0.40 m down. Portions of wall DF1 were covered by the section between Squares D6 and D7 but this and a greater portion of the intersecting wall DF2 to the northwest were excavated in 1997 when the balks were removed. The north balk of square D7 was also

Fig. 92. Ovens, walls and other features of Islamic occupation found near the surface in A40, from the north.

removed to expose a third wall, DF3. Wall DF3 in the north balk of D7 also showed remains of a doorsill and part of a second area paved with flat stones.

Evidence of several rebuildings were clear but again only a few floor patches were preserved. Though we are assigning an Ayyubid date to the building on the basis of several coins in the area and the preponderance of associated pottery, the date is not as secure as we would like. A good collection of late Byzantine coins, dating in the eleventh through thirteenth centuries, an Ayyubid coin and a coin of the First Crusade, were found primarily in this building in Area A, in the building close to the surface in E1 and E12, and in the upper levels of B9. A selection of six coins is shown here (figs. 103–108). Professor William Fulco, S.J, who is preparing a detailed final report, has supplied the following information. Three coins are different follis of Michael IV, dated around A.D. 1040 from squares on different parts of the site: A26 (figs. 99, 100), D6 (figs. 101, 102) and E12 (fig. 103: 1 = 104: 1). An E9 follis of an earlier Byzantine ruler, Romanus III, dates around A.D. 1037 (fig. 103: 2 = 104: 2) and another follis of the middle of the eleventh century A.D. (fig. 103: 3 = 104: 3) is in a style that is similar to the previously mentioned coins. The last illustrated coin is

Fig. 93. View of trench that was cut as part of an irrigation project across part of the low tell that extends south beyond the main portion of the high southern tell, from the north.

Fig. 94. Islamic glazed and incised wares from various areas at Tell Qarqur.

Fig. 95. Islamic incised wares on cooking pot type wares from various areas at Tell Qarqur.

Fig. 96. General view of Islamic walls and pavement in D7, 1993 excavations from the south.

Fig. 97. View of Islamic walls DF1–3 fully exposed after the excavation of three sections in Area D, from the southeast.

Fig. 98. Intersection of walls DF2 and 3, from the southwest.

Fig. 99. Late Byzantine follis attributed to Michael IV, about A.D. 1040, from A26, locus 2, from the 1993 season, obverse.

Fig. 103. 1. Late Byzantine follis attributed to Michael IV, about A.D. 1040, from E12, locus 4, from the 1998 season, obverse. 2. Late Byzantine follis attributed to Romanus III, about A.D. 1037, from E9, locus 1, from the 1998 season, obverse. 3. Late Byzantine follis of the middle of the eleventh century A.D., from E5, locus 2, from the 1993 season, obverse. 4. Follis of the First Crusade from B9 minted in Edessa and attributed to Baudouin I, about A.D. 1097–1100.

Fig. 100. Late Byzantine follis attributed to Michael IV, about A.D. 1040 , from A26, locus 2, from the 1993 season, reverse of same coin.

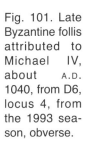

Fig. 101. Late Byzantine follis attributed to Michael IV, about A.D. 1040, from D6, locus 4, from the 1993 season, obverse.

Fig. 102. Late Byzantine follis attributed to Michael IV, about A.D. 1040, from D6, locus 4, from the 1993 season, reverse of same coin.

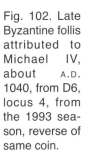

Fig. 104. 1. Reverse of Late Byzantine follis attributed to Michael IV, about A.D. 1040, from E12, locus 4, from the 1998 season. 2. Reverse of Late Byzantine follis attributed to Romanus III, about A.D. 1037, from E9, locus 1, from the 1998 season. 3. Reverse of Late Byzantine follis of the middle of the eleventh century A.D., from E5, locus 2, from the 1993 season. 4. Reverse of Follis of the First Crusade from B9 minted in Edessa and attributed to Baudouin I, about A.D. 1097–1100.

Fig. 105. General view of D7–D6 with two ovens in foreground, from north, taken in 1997.

Fig. 106. View of ovens in D7 during the 1998 season,
from the north.

Fig. 107. General
view of D7–D6 show-
ing the ovens in D7 at
the end of the 1998
season, from the
south.

Fig. 108. View of oven in D8, from northwest in the 1993 season.

a follis from B9, dating to the First Crusade, around A.D. 1097–1100 (fig. 103: 4 = 104: 4). It was minted in Edessa under Baudouin I.

Islamic Materials in Area B

In Area B, Ayyubid materials were encountered in 1997 when we opened a new square, B9, to the east of the main area of excavation to carry this exposure over to the edge of the tell (fig. 112). Ayyubid pottery was fairly consistent in the first 0.40 m below the surface and at that depth a number of complete or nearly complete vessels were found (figs. 113–115). Several wall foundations and an oven in the north balk were attributed to this period. Several phases of the Ayyubid period were preserved. The tops of Iron Age II stone wall foundations and portions of mudbrick walls be-

Fig. 109. Kiln in D8, beneath stone pavement and oven in fig. 108, from the southwest.

Fig. 110. Close up view of oven in the center of D6, from the west.

gan to appear between 40–50 cm beneath the surface.

Islamic Materials in Area E

The extended view of Area E from the west in the 1998 season (fig. 116), shows a substantial building of the Ayyubid period in squares E1, 12 and 9. The scree of stones showing in the north section of E9 (fig. 120), was present over all three squares and, as was the case almost everywhere on the tell, plant and animal disturbances were so great that good floor surfaces were not preserved except in limited patches. Patches of white mortar

Fig. 111. View of oven in the center of D6 after sectioning, from the west.

Fig. 112. Foundations of several Islamic walls close to the surface in B9, from the southeast.

were preserved against the south face of wall EF3, the 1.80 m–wall in E12 (fig. 119). This wall extended into the north balk and formed a room with EF1 and EF2 in square E1 (figs. 69, 117). A block of cement with white limestone tesserae was found in the area indicating the floor surface that must once have existed on the floor of this or a nearby room.

The pottery close to the surface in squares E1, E12 and E9 was very mixed, with Ayyubid as the latest represented pottery. A portion of a human face from a figurine (fig. 118) was found in the stones of the north–south wall but very close to the surface (fig. 117). The date of the fragment is uncertain. One would expect a late Hellenistic or Early Roman date, but the chin, lips and nose could

Fig. 113. Small decorated Islamic pitcher from B9, side view.

Fig. 114. Reconstructed Islamic jug from B9, side view.

also be considered to be similar to figurines of Neo-Assyrian date. A fragment of a bronze fibula and a number of beads also date to the Iron Age but again are not from stratigraphically secure contexts.

Two additional phases of stone architecture were found in E1, the lowest of which may be Iron Age II (figs. 69, 70). Stones beneath the Ayyubid surfaces in E12 proved to be the end of a wall fragment that extended north–south along the east balk of E9 (figs. 71, 120). Though not conclusive, the date of this wall fragment seems to be Roman.

Hellenistic through Byzantine Remains

Except for the Roman tower in square A24, the possible Hellenistic room in A22, and the ovens in Area D, few architectural remains of these periods have been encountered so far in the excavations at Tell Qarqur. The best-preserved room was in A22, where a good floor was found associated with the walls AF303, 308, and 309. That floor was associated with a doorway in AF309 and the single large stone that had served as the doorsill. At a lower level in this room, an oven was found at the intersection of walls AF308 and AF309 (fig. 15).

In squares D6–D8, we encountered around 0.40 and 0.65 m of earth between the Ayyubid and Iron Age levels. The intervening material was very broken and only patches of stones were preserved from building remains of the intervening periods. At about 0.80 to 1.00 m below the surface we encountered a number of circular ovens in the area,

Fig. 115. Small decorated Islamic juglet from B9, side view.

several of these are illustrated in figs. 105–108, 110 and 111, and possibly a kiln in area D8 fig. 109. This kiln is apparently a two-chambered structure but we have barely started removing the collapsed material covering its remains and it is possible that it may date considerably earlier than ovens we have mentioned. We have barely started clarifying the apparent industrial nature of this complex. The ovens were between 0.50 and 0.90 m in diameter with walls ranging from 0.10 to 0.20 m thick. In most cases the ovens were placed on a footing of large flat sherds of storage jars and similar sherds in most cases were built up along the

Fig. 116. Extended view of Area E during the 1998 season, from the west.

Fig. 117. The upper two phases of Ayyubid architecture in E1, from the west.

Fig. 118. Fragment from the face of a molded terracotta figurine.

outside of the oven (figs. 106, 108). The dates of the ovens are still uncertain, particularly since another kiln was found about a meter to the northeast in D7 and dates to the Early Bronze IV (figs. 66, 67). The ovens were fairly well preserved to heights of between 0.30 and 0.50 m but associated wall remains were extremely fragmentary.

It is not yet clear whether all of the ovens date to the same period. First and second century Roman coins were found in the area as well as a good repertoire of Roman and Hellenistic pottery. The area unfortunately was cut up too badly to provide a good stratigraphic sequence but does provide us with evidence of fairly continuous occupation through these periods. A basic inventory of Byzantine and Roman pottery have been collected and Hellenistic pottery is exceptionally well represented both with black glazed wares (fig. 121) that seem to continue from the Persian period sequence, and red glazed wares (fig. 122) that continue into the Roman period.

Fig. 119. Ayyubid structure in E12 with only fragments of contemporary floors preserved, from the west.

Fig. 120. Portion of a Roman wall foundation in E9, from the southwest.

Persian Period Remains

Scattered Persian period materials have been found at Tell Qarqur, particularly in Area A. Persian period rebuildings associated with the gateway have been included earlier to keep then in context with the Iron Age materials into which or over which they were built. On the east side of the Iron II gateway, an oven and a tumble of stones west of wall AF303 was associated with Persian Period pottery (figs. 16, 17). On the west side, evidence for rebuilding was also noted. This evidence is too scanty to be sure of the architectural configuration of the gateway in this phase, and several alternative reconstructions are possible. It is possible that wall AF310 did not continue south

Fig. 121. Hellenistic pottery with black glaze decoration from all areas of Tell Qarqur.

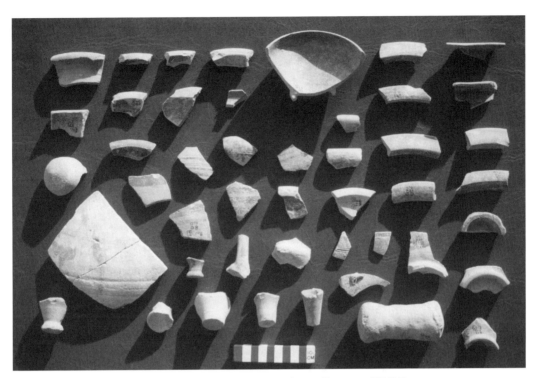

Fig. 122. Hellenistic pottery with red glaze decoration from all areas of Tell Qarqur.

and the single chambered gateway was replaced by buttresses flanking a gateway door (figs. 22, 24). On the other hand it is unclear how this apparent buttress relates to wall AF310. A well-preserved wall surface on the south face of the buttress indicates a possible doorway in AF310 connecting the western room with the main chamber of the gateway. Little more can be said other than that the date of this rebuilding is possibly indicated by the presence of Persian period pottery.

Some ceramic forms and wares of this period are clearly identifiable, but others need to be reexamined when a better-stratified corpus becomes available. A few bowl and jar forms are illustrated on fig. 83: 21, 23 and 25. The small corpus of Persian period pottery has yet to be examined in comparison with the Iron II ceramic materials and the excellent corpus of third- to first-century B.C. Hellenistic pottery that has been collected. The most representative items of the period are the terracotta horse and rider figurines and characteristic female figurines. A good collection of such figurines has been found in Area A and a representative sample is illustrated in figs. 123–127.

Fig. 123. Head and body fragments of Persian period horse and rider terracotta figurines.

Fig. 124. Head and body fragments of Persian period horse and rider, and female terracotta figurines.

Fig. 125. Female figurines of the Persian period.

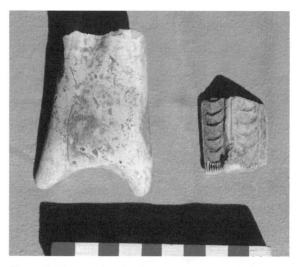

Fig. 126. Traces of red paint are preserved on the front legs of a Persian "horse and rider" figurine and the lower portion of a robed figurine.

PRE IRON AGE REMAINS: MIDDLE BRONZE AGE II, EARLY BRONZE AGE IV AND EARLIER OCCUPATIONS

Middle Bronze Age II

Middle Bronze Age pottery was associated with the three steps of the earlier stairway AF321 encountered in Square A9 (fig. 42). At the northwest corner of square A9, additional stones indicated another stone feature, possibly a still earlier stairway but the stones were so badly disrupted by later pitting that no pattern could be discerned. The ash layers and destruction debris covering the lower levels of stairs AF321

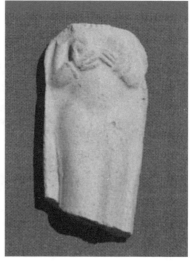

Fig. 127. Female terracotta figurines of the Persian period, one naked and one robed.

Fig. 128. Middle Bronze Age sherds primarily from square A9.

and the stone feature AF322 in the southwest corner were Middle Bronze II. Many wall lines are evident in the heavy concentration of stones between the stairway and the gateway, and may be the remains of wall foundations of the Middle Bronze Age (fig. 39). Here, outside the gateway, Middle Bronze remains are evident, while inside the gateway almost all evidence of this period of occupation has been removed in the squares we have excavated.

Figure 128 illustrates the pottery associated with these ash layers in A9. Middle Bronze Age pottery has been found on many portions of the site. A large number of Middle Bronze Age sherds were also found in Area D but contemporary architectural remains had been removed by later building. The sherds shown in fig. 130 and the profile drawings on fig. 129 include sherds from all areas of Tell Qarqur to show a greater range of typical forms of this time period. A Middle Bronze II jar lid was found on the surface of the tell (fig. 131).

Early Bronze Age IV B in Area A

The 1993–1999 seasons of excavation focused on trying to access the extent and depth of the Iron Age remains in Area A. As excavations continued below gravel layers, some of the foundation levels and construction fills, and moved to underlying materials, the percentage of Bronze Age ceramics that were recovered increased dramatically. A consistent though small component of Iron Age sherds made it difficult to draw the line between the Early Bronze and Iron Age occupation levels. The expected depth of occupation, possibly several phases of the Iron Age occupation to mirror the extent of the Iron Age occupation in Area B, did not materialize and instead it became clear that the underlying remains were Early Bronze Age. Any intermediate levels of Iron Age I to Middle Bronze Age were apparently removed in the area when the gateways and associated surfaces were constructed or removed by building operations.

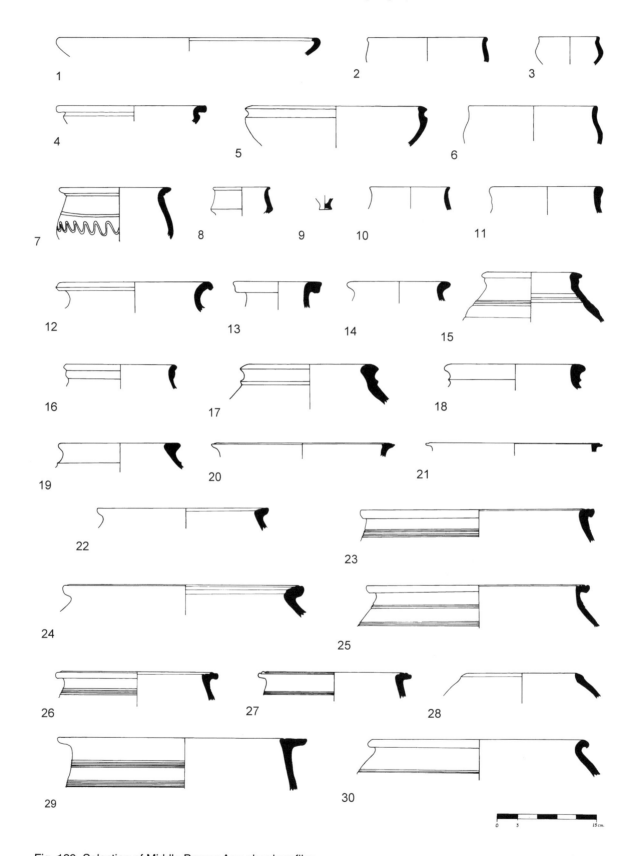

Fig. 129. Selection of Middle Bronze Age sherd profiles.

Drawing Figure	Sherd Number	Area	Plot	Locus	Basket	Form	Exterior	Color	Interior	Color	Ware	Color	Inclusions	Surface Treatment	Height in mm.	Dia. in mm.	Thickness
129 : 01	TQ95-0015	A	10	1	8	B-117	7.5YR5/4	BROWN	7.5YR4/6	STRONG BROWN	10YR7/2	LT.GRAY	MANY MED BLACK	PLAIN	28	240	6
129 : 02	TQ95-0290	D	7	2	41	B136	10YR8/2	WHITE	10YR8/2	WHITE			MANY MED BLACK FEW COARSE RED		37	180	7
129 : 03	TQ93-0045	D	7	18	31	B-075	10YR8/2	WHITE	7.5YR7/4	PINK	10YR8/2	WHITE	MANY FINE BROWN		42	90	4
129 : 04	TQ94-0016	D	6	31	180	B-111	2.5Y8/2	WHITE	10YR8/3	V.PALE BR.	7.5YR7/4	PINK	MANY FINE MULTI		27	220	8
129 : 05	TQ97-0002	A	9	CLNG	55	B-110	2.5YR8/2	WHITE	2.5YR8/2	WHITE	10YR7/1	LT. GRAY	MANY FINE BLACK		60	260	6
129 : 06	TQ93-0039	D	6	5	80	B-041	7.5YR6/4	LT.BROWN	7.5YR7/6	RED.YELLOW	7.5YR6/4	LT.BROWN	MANY FINE WHITE MANY FINE BROWN		55	190	5
129 : 07	TQ97-0077	A	24	53	157	J-083	10YR8/4	V. PALE BR.	7.5YR7/6	RED.YELLOW	10YR7/1	LT. GRAY	MANY FINE BLACK		77	160	8
129 : 08	TQ93-0196	D	SURF		1	B-40a	10YR8/2 7.5YR8/4 5YR7/6	WHITE PINK RED.YELLOW	10YR8/2 7.5YR8/4	WHITE PINK	10YR8/2	WHITE	MANY FINE BLACK	PLAIN	40	80	6
129 : 09	TQ97-0107	A	39	32	18	BB-28	10YR8/2	WHITE	10YR8/2 7.5R5/8	WHITE RED.YELLOW	10YR7/3	V.PALE BR.	FEW MED BLACK	PAINT OUT	18	18	4
129 : 10	TQ94-0009	A	26	19	56	B-074									35	117	6
129 : 11	TQ93-0283	D	SURF		3	J-056	5YR6/6	RED.YELLOW	5YR6/6	RED.YELLOW	10YR7/6	YELLOW	MANY FINE BLACK	INCISED RIM PAINT IN/OUT/RIM	39	160	7
129 : 12	TQ93-0253	A	29	1	1	J-114	2.5Y8/3	PALE YELLOW	2.5Y8/3	PALE YELLOW	2.5Y8/3	PALE YELLOW	MANY MED BLACK		46	210	16
129 : 13	TQ97-0006	A	9	70	111	J-077	2.5YR7/2	LT.GRAY	2.5YR7/2	LT.GRAY	2.5YR7/2	LT.GRAY	FEW MED WHITE MANY FINE BLACK		41	110	8
129 : 14	TQ97-0013	A	9	36	73	J-082	7.5YR7/3	PINK	7.5YR7/3	PINK	7.5YR7/3	PINK	MANY FINE BLACK		26	150	8
129 : 15	TQ93-0201	D	SURF		12	J-031	2.5Y8/3 2.5Y8/2	PALE YELLOW WHITE	2.5Y8/3	PALE YELLOW	2.5Y8/3	PALE YELLOW	MANY MED BLACK MANY MED WHITE	PLAIN, COMB IN. STRAIGHT&WAVY	75	130	5
129 : 16	TQ93-0206	B	SURF		12	J-034	10YR8/3	V.PALE BROWN	10YR8/3	V.PALE BROWN	10YR8/3	V.PALE BROWN	MANY MED BLACK	PLAIN	37	140	5
129 : 17	TQ93-0200	D	SURF		12	J-032	10YR8/3	V.PALE BROWN	2.5Y7/3	PALE YELLOW	2.5Y8/2	WHITE	MANY MED BLACK	PLAIN, COMB INCISED BAND	58	182	10
129 : 18	TQ93-279	D	SURF		13	J-086	10YR7/4	V.PALE BR.	10YR7/4	V.PALE BR.	10YR7/4	V.PALE BR.	MANY MED BLACK		36	190	7
129 : 19	TQ97-0003	A	9	56	97	J-084	10YR8/4	V. PALE BR.	10YR8/4	V. PALE BR.	10YR8/4	V. PALE BR.	MANY FINE BLACK		38	180	4
129 : 20	TQ93-0251	A	26	1	4	J-098	7.5YR8/6	RED. YELLOW	7.5YR8/6	RED. YELLOW	7.5YR8/6	RED. YELLOW	FEW FINE WHITE	INCISED RIM	20	260	7
129 : 21	TQ93-0280	D	SURF		5	J-097	5YR6/6	RED.YELLOW	5YR6/6	RED.YELLOW	10YR7/6	YELLOW	MANY FINE BLACK	INCISED RIM PAINT IN/OUT/RIM	13	250	6
129 : 22	TQ93-267	B	2	27	80	J-094	7.5YR7/4	PINK	7.5YR7/4	PINK	7.5YR7/4	PINK	MANY FINE BLACK		32	250	9
129 : 23	TQ93-276	D	SURF		12	J-099	10YR8/3	V.PALE BR.	10YR8/3	V.PALE BR.	10YR8/3	V.PALE BR.	MANY FINE BLACK	INCISED RIM&EXT	48	330	7
129 : 24	TQ93-274	D	SURF		8	J-095	10YR8/3	V.PALE BR.	10YR8/3	V.PALE BR.	10YR8/3	V.PALE BR.	MANY FINE BLACK SOME MED BLACK	INCISED RIM	48	350	10
129 : 25	TQ93-0278	D	SURF		13	J-099	5YR7/4	PINK	10YR8/2	WHITE	5YR7/4	PINK	MANY FINE BLACK SOME MED RED SOME MED WHITE		62	330	7
129 : 26	TQ93-0275	D	SURF		12	J-032	10YR8/3	V.PALE BR.	10YR8/3	V.PALE BR.	10YR8/3	V.PALE BR.	MANY FINE BLACK	INCISED RIM&EXT	42	210	8
129 : 27	TQ97-0002	A	9	56	37	J-096	10YR8/2	WHITE	10YR8/2	WHITE	10YR8/2	WHITE	FEW FINE BLACK		36	200	9
129 : 28	TQ93-0263	A	21	10	67	J-075	10YR3/3	DK. BROWN	10YR5/2	GREY BROWN	10YR3/2	V. DK. GREY. BR.	FEW MED RED		35	160	6
129 : 29	TQ97-0008	A	9	36	93	J-100	5YR6/4	LT.RED.BR.	5YR6/4	LT.RED.BR.	10YR7/3	V.PALE BR.	MANY FINE BLACK FEW MED WHITE		75	380	10
129 : 30	TQ93-0282	D	7	SURF	117	J-106	10YR6/6	BR.YELLOW	5YR7/8	RED.YELLOW	10YR6/6 5YR7/8	BR.YELLOW RED.YELLOW	MANY FINE BLACK SOME FINE WHITE	INCISED	54	160	10

Fig. 130. Middle Bronze Age sherds from various areas at Tell Qarqur.

A test trench alongside the Iron Age street reached wall foundations and one or more phases of a doorsill constructed of large flat paving stones at a depth of 1.20 m below the street (fig. 132). We expanded the exposed area without destroying the Arab period tower and associated construction (fig. 133), and gradually exposed a portion of the building associated with this door sill (figs. 134–140). Patches of the lowest gravel layer ran over the destruction debris of the Early Bronze Age (fig. 135). Other gravel patches were associated with fragments of Early Bronze wall foundations (fig. 161).

The stratigraphic situation was somewhat different between A26–29 to the north and A22 to the southeast. A depth of 20–40 cm destruction debris and fallen walls were preserved over the latest Early Bronze Age foundations in A26–29. In A22 most of this debris and the latest Early Bronze levels had been removed by later construction activity. The nature of the construction sequence and the tight phasing of the Early Bronze Age levels was identical in both A22 and A26–

29. Also, the absolute levels of the lowest floors reached in the two separated areas are identical.

Beneath the lowest gravel layer in A26–29 the outline of several wall alignments began to appear and also a second paved doorway in the southeast corner, fig. 138 on the left. The brickwork that was encountered could, with patience, be articulated and represented in one location at least twelve courses of brick (approximately 12 cm thick by

Fig. 131. Middle Bronze Age jar lid, surface find.

Fig. 132. Stone doorsill in corridor A, 1993 exposure, from the southeast.

40 cm × 40 cm) from a wall that had fallen on its side (figs. 136–140). Considerable burning had created heavy gray and black ash layers. Many superimposed clay layers were found within a bracket of wall remains that were inconsistent in their evidence for rebuilding but fairly consistent in superimposed locations (figs. 137–140). It is difficult to separate layers that may have been deposited at the same time in a single destruction from layers from different destruction events. At least 12 layers were excavated in the area and at least four structural phases, including one with a small circular oven between ash layers and a larger oven in the lowest layers. We have not attempted an architectural plan at this point because any rendering would be very incomplete. The wall remains and foundations are very shallow and all the lines and doorways for different phases have not yet been excavated completely. The remaining walls need to be removed systematically to finalize the preliminary plans.

The building consisted of mudbrick superstructure on stone foundations and only where we reached the stone foundations did the actual building plan start to become clear. A 0.70 m thick wall ran along the south balk between the two doorways with stone sills. One entered 1.00 m wide

Fig. 133. Removal of balk between A26 and A29 in progress as excavations move to levels below the Iron Age stone paved street in 1994, from the northwest.

Fig. 134. Corridor A shown with doorsill against brick-work and destruction on the left, from the north.

Fig. 135. Remains of lowest gravel surface on lower left, on top of destruction debris with fallen brickwork in A29, from the east.

Fig. 136. Outlines of brick from fallen brick-work in center, show-ing courses of brick-work from collapse of a wall, from the east.

Fig. 137. Fallen brickwork, in lower right, major ash layer and destruction debris in center. Brickwork of walls associated with corridor B and stone doorsill in upper left corner, from the north.

Fig. 138. Same location as Fig. 126 after additional excavation to remove ash layer over series of floors in center, from the north.

Fig. 139. Same, after additional clearance of some of the walls associated with corridor B has been taken down to the foundation stones, from the north.

Fig. 140. General view of corridors A and B and main room with many floor levels showing after the removal to a major ash layer in center and the remains of a small oven, from the north.

Fig. 141. Deep excavation in A29 in 1993 showing one of a series of pits that cut down to Early Bronze IV layers, from the west.

corridors inside the doorways but the length of each corridor is still unclear. A room, apparently 3.5 m east west and 2.00 m north-south extended between the corridors. Destruction has been such that no doorway has been found so far which connected either the western or eastern corridor with the room between them. The west wall of the western corridor is under the Iron Age street and the east wall has not yet been carried down to its foundations for its full length (figs. 132, 134). A pit apparently destroyed part of the west wall of the eastern corridor (figs. 137–140), but a wall could be traced by a plaster line against the east balk and turned into another doorway in that direction. The finds associated with this structure and its many ash layers were consistently Early Bronze Age IVB.

Fig. 142. Destruction debris in "vetch kitchen," from the south.

Fig. 143. General view of "vetch kitchen," from the east.

We had great difficulty articulating brick for the northern part of the room though bricky material was encountered in a stretch about 0.50 m south of the north balk. The deep pits encountered in the 1993 season had reached down to this depth and it is unclear how much has been destroyed (fig. 141). At the end of the 1997 season we did reach stone foundations on the west side of this stretch so we

may be close to clarifying this wall and hopefully access to the room from the south.

The third phase was better preserved than the later phases and provided a benchmark that allowed us to separate it from the rebuildings and changes in plan that were preserved in the shallow remains above. One room of this third construction phase, locus 125 and associated loci, was

Fig. 144. Close up of vetch grains and sherds on floor of room, from the west.

completely filled with broken vessels (figs. 142–144), and an estimated 10 liters of "bitter vetch" seeds (fig. 144). Paleoethnobotanist Dr. Julie Hansen of Boston University identified the seeds and indicated that they were most likely a food resource in the past, although humans no longer eat them. The large amount of vetch with only traces of other grains in this deposit is unusual and indicates that this was most likely a separate crop, which was being processed for consumption when

Fig. 145 Early Bronze Age IVB chalice from the "vetch kitchen."

Fig. 146. Early Bronze Age IVB small spouted juglet from the "vetch kitchen."

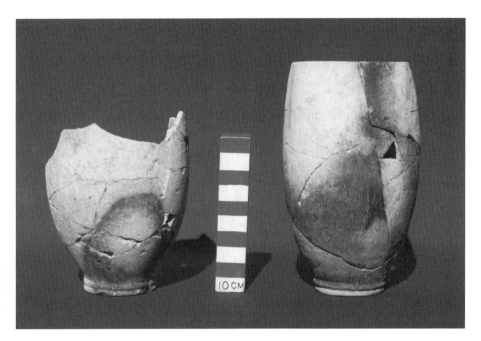

Fig. 147. Reconstructed, plain ware chalices, one complete, one incomplete.

Fig. 148. Reconstructed storage jar with loop-handle at rim.

it burned. The ceramic inventory of the kitchen provides an excellent group of about twenty-seven reconstructable vessels, including cups, bowls, a spouted jar, medium sized storage vessels and cooking pots. A selection of reconstructed vessels: chalices, a small decorated spouted jar and a 40 cm high jar are illustrated on figs. 145–148. The broken vessels were compacted into several rough layers within heavily burnt debris about 0.20–0.25 m thick. An oven was found in the southwest corner of this kitchen room.

The room in this phase is roughly square and measures about 2.35 m on a side. Though most of the lines of the interior faces of the walls are preserved, only the east wall is well enough preserved to measure its thickness of 0.45 m. The walls of the higher phases may have been thicker, as much as 0.95 m, but they are not as well preserved. Both upper phases have doorways on the east and west ends of the southern wall, leading to corridors that flank a room in between. Because of the breaks in the west and north walls, it is unclear at this point where the doorways had been. The western doorway of the third phase has been cleared, but we have not yet completed the excavation of the room east of the kitchen or any doorway leading to the south from that room (fig. 151). The orientation of the walls of the second phase was shifted slightly

Fig. 149. Sectioning of oven in southwest corner of "vetch kitchen."

Fig. 150. General view of Early Bronze IVB building cleared down to the floor of the "vetch kitchen," from the west.

clockwise from the lower phases. Evidence of a fourth phase is preserved in the northwest.

The highest preserved Early Bronze Age architectural remains were preserved in the northeast corner of A22. A small segment of a stone wall foundation, and several bricks of its superstructure extended into the sections at the northeast corner, on the left beneath the meter stick in figs. 156 and 157. Beneath his wall, a complex of walls was moderately well preserved in the northern part of the square (fig. 156). They were faced with whitish-cream colored clay plaster. What seems to be a block of brickwork in the southeastern part of the square may be the remains of a badly weathered brick wall that could not be clearly articulated (fig. 157). Many patches of plaster from walls and floors were preserved but were difficult to trace. Only small patches of plastered floor surfaces could be traced in most of the square but fallen wall plaster left fairly long curved or zigzag lines. The east–west wall segment in the northern part of the square was the best preserved and had been plastered and replastered many times during its use. The plaster often sloped down to the contemporary floor surfaces but these were very patchy and tracing any individual plaster layer over even a portion of the wall surface was usually impossible because of the preservation (figs. 154–

Fig. 151. Room east of the "vetch kitchen," down to intermediate floors in 1998, from the north.

Fig. 152. General view of Area A from the northwest, showing A22 on the far right, at the end of the 1999 season.

156). In one phase a complete jar was found smashed on the floor near this wall (fig. 155).

A number of large stones formed a doorsill in the east–west wall (fig. 154), and in the foreground of fig. 156. This wall segment was connected with a north–south wall and preserved about 0.40 m higher than the preserved floor, which extended into the west section. They intersected near the west section but the continuation to the south was destroyed. At the end of the 1997 season floors were becoming easier to trace, as indicated by several floor levels that were exposed as steps for demonstration (fig. 156). As these floors were traced we had the distinct impression that a vertical wall surface lay very close but just inside the north balk and this area may be a corridor similar to the two

Fig. 153. Early Bronze IV remains in A22 in foreground separated from A21 and A24 to the west by Hellenistic wall AF303, from the east.

corridors exposed in A26–29 about 6 m to the northwest. An Early Bronze Age wall segment in A21 seems to line up with the northern walls and doorway just discussed but apparently was cut off when AF305, one of the earlier phases of the Iron Age gateway, was constructed. The construction methods, material and pottery found in squares A26, 29, A6, 7 and A21, 22, 24 are clearly the same, and also the same as the Early Bronze Age building in E4. The exact phasing and orientation of the remains in Area A need to be clarified by carrying the excavation of A6, A24, A21 and two additional new squares down to the same depth. This should show whether one or more buildings are present at any point in the sequence of occupation.

In squares A6, 7 and 21, 24, the meter-wide north–south section between the eastern and western squares was reestablished in 1997 to help trace and document the stratigraphic layers, and then was almost completely removed in the 1999 season (fig. 158). Early Bronze IVB levels began in this area beneath the series of Iron Age gravel layers. The excavated remains of three fragmentary wall foundations are contemporary with the building remains mentioned above in A26, 29 and A22 (figs. 158, 159). The preserved depth of Early Bronze IV B occupation decreased considerably

Fig. 154. General view of the Early Bronze IV occupation in A22 showing wall AF401 and associated walls, floors and doorway, from the east.

Fig. 155. Smashed jar on floor against mud-brick wall AF401, from the north.

as we moved from the northern part of the area to the south, and the gravel pavements, which sloped down in that direction, were thicker to the south.

Early Bronze Age IVA in Area A

A significant change in the nature of the Early Bronze Age occupation was encountered in A24 at the end of the 1998 season. The line of the top preserved edge of a mudbrick wall was evident beneath the almost two meter-wide stone wall foundation of the earlier phase the Iron Age gateway but on a slightly different orientation (AF305 on the plan fig. 8, fig. 18, as well as on the left side of fig. 152 and at the top of fig. 158). A series of floor layers were excavated extending from the face of this wall around the top of what seems to be a massive Early Bronze IVA mudbrick column, covered with a yellowish-white plaster surface that had been renewed many times (fig. 159). The pillar measures 1.7 m in diameter and seems to indicate the presence of monumental architecture. This major change between levels may demonstrate a stratigraphic break between Early Bronze Age IVB, and IVA, since the earlier phase may be contemporary with the Ebla Palace G. A test trench on the west side of the column was excavated for almost a meter, and, though very weathered, the

Fig. 156. Walls AF401, AF430 and stone sill in doorway with several floor layers partially cleared on the north side, from the west.

Fig. 157. General view of A22 at end of the 1997 season showing several mud-brick walls and stone foundations, from the northwest.

Fig. 158. Squares A24, A21, A6 and A7 at the end of the 1998 season, showing the earlier phase of the Iron Age gateway in the foreground and two portions of Early Bronze Age IVB walls between the Roman tower and the Early Bronze Age IVA level of the massive mud-brick column, from the south.

plaster facings could be traced for most of that depth (figs. 160, 161).

Debris from a major destruction filled the area of the test trench but no floor level was evident after the first 0.30 m. Further to the west in A6, 7, considerable mudbrick collapse was also encountered. Here, we have the remains of several phases of mudbrick walls above the level of the massive

column. The stratigraphy of the area is very complex because of the later intrusions. The Iron Age gravels apparently covered the Early Bronze Age IVB materials that remained after intervening materials had been removed from A6, 7. In A6, a considerable amount of the Early Bronze Age IVA material had been removed as well.

Fig. 159. Massive Early Bronze IVA mudbrick column after 1998 excavations, from the east.

Fig. 160. General view of center portion of Area A at the end of the 1999 season, after removal of most of the balks in the area, from the southeast.

Early Bronze IV Excavations in Area E

A small portion of an important Early Bronze Age IVB building was exposed in Area E over several seasons (fig. 162). Excavation proceeded to deeper levels in E4 after portions of stone foundations were removed along the south balk, associated with levels beneath the Islamic, Roman and Iron Age remains. A thick layer of Early Bronze Age IV destruction debris covered the whole area of Square E4. The initial exposures reached this destruction layer and encountered areas of very heavy black ash deposits, fallen and intact brickwork, and white clay plaster lines where the plaster facing of the brick walls had fallen at various angles and had been cut in the excavation. In the destruction debris, primarily on the north side of the square E4 and in E5, a large number of egg-

Fig. 161. Same area shown in fig. 160, also from the 1999 season but seen from the southeast.

shaped projectiles were found (fig. 163), similar to those found at Tell Braq (Matthews 1996: and fig. 4) and elsewhere.

A portion of a room bounded on the south by a brick wall with plaster facing, EF10, was excavated. The face of EF10 was virtually on the line of the face of the south section and a low bench, about 0.50 m deep, extended along most of its exposed length (fig. 164). The plaster on the wall was well preserved over most of its northern face and had been renewed a number of times. In places where the heat from heavy burning focused on sections of the wall, the plaster was damaged and difficult to follow. The wall was cleared to a maximum height of 1.00 m and turned in at a corner 1.20 m from the north balk and parallel to it, possibly at a doorway. Wall EF10 proved to be 1.00 m thick and at least three building phases could be

Fig. 162. Area E from the west during the 1997 season, showing square E1 to the right and E4 to the left.

Fig. 163. "Sling stones" from upper destruction layers of Early Bronze Age IV destruction in E4.

discerned (figs. 164, 165 and 181, 183, 187 and 188). It extended slightly to the east, into the east balk where it made a corner with wall EF12. This wall was revealed in the east section in 1999.

The northern wall, EF11 (figs. 165 [on the left], 184 and 186), was in effect a series of at least four wall foundations, but more excavation is needed to tie the different phases of the walls of

Fig. 164. South section of E4 with badly burnt plaster face of wall EF10 near the line of the section and remains of mudbrick structure on the left, from the north.

Fig. 165. East section of E4 in the background showing destruction layers between walls EF10 on the right and EF11 on the left, from the west.

Fig. 166. Fragments of reconstructable "incense burner" found together with many pottery and metal artifacts in destruction debris of Early Bronze Age IV building in E4, from the east.

this room together. Fragments of facing plaster were traced at various points along the lower portions of its south face. The face of the lowest phase of the wall was parallel to the north balk and about 0.50 m south of it. The lowest course is of narrow flat stones, with a second course set in somewhat from the southern line. A few stones fill in between this course and a second course of narrow flat stones, again set in almost 0.20 m from the south edge of the lower course. Two additional courses of stone stand above the third course from the bottom and seem to be set in still further to the north so that the highest stones seem to be about 0.40 m from the southern face at the bottom of the wall. The E4 room was more then 3.50 m, in a north–south direction and bounded on three sides by walls, on the north, south and east. As excavations progressed it was clear, as is indicated in the

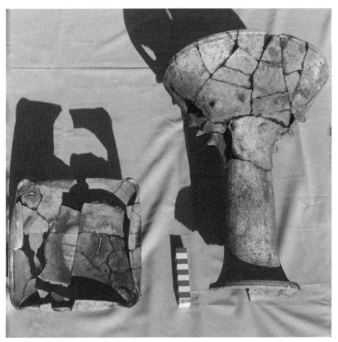

Fig. 167. Reconstructed "incense burner" and four spouted lamp from Early Bronze Age IV destruction in E4.

east balk in fig. 165, that the floor of the eastern section of the room was paved with mudbrick. Some type of bench, platform or altar structure that was frequently rebuilt took up the west side of the excavated portion of the room (figs. 164, 165, 181–183).

The destruction debris of the Early Bronze Age IV building was filled with a variety of objects (figs. 167, 171–180 and 190) primary in the initial phase that was encountered in 1995 and 1997. A 1.20 m tall "incense stand" was reconstructed from scattered fragments (fig. 166) and pieces of at least three large, 0.40 m square four-spouted lamps were found, the most complete of these is illustrated in fig. 167. Bronze pins, a piece of a bronze knife blade, a twisted and partially melted bronze figurine, and a 1.6 by 1.8 cm sheet of gold weighing about 20 grams were

Fig. 168. Body and rim fragments of very coarse pottery crucibles found in the Early Bronze Age IV destruction debris of E4.

Fig. 169. Pouring spout fragments of very coarse pottery crucibles found in the Early Bronze Age IV destruction debris of E4.

Fig. 170. Foot and body fragments of coarse pottery crucibles found in the Early Bronze Age IV destruction debris of E4.

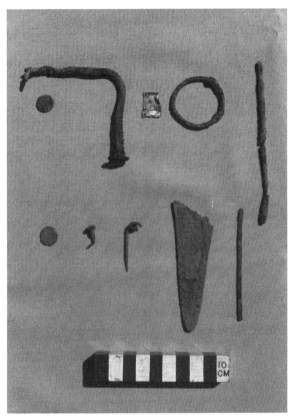

Fig. 171. Selection of metal artifacts from various areas and periods at Tell Qarqur, including knife blade fragment and piece of gold foil from E4.

found in the destruction debris (fig. 171). The most interesting object is an over-sized, terracotta female figurine (figs. 174, 175). The typical bird-like face, applied clay decoration for hair, breasts,

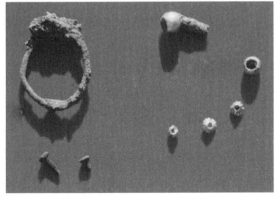

Fig. 172. Small metal items from the Early Bronze Age destruction level in E4; a copper ring, small nails, a gold tipped pin fragment and four gold beads.

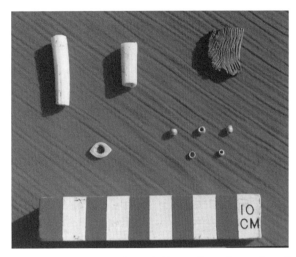

Fig. 173. Collection of special items from Areas A and E; five gold beads and an inlay for the eye of a statue from Area E and a piece of an incised lapis lazuli inlay and two cowry shells from Area A.

eyes, headpiece, and necklaces are typical for such figurines found in Early Bronze Age contexts at many Syrian sites and similar in style to figurines from Hama, Tell Mardikh and the Euphrates Valley, from Mari in the east to the Amuq in the west (Badre 1980). The figurine was found in four fragments scattered in the destruction.

The 1998 season added five gold beads (fig. 173) found in the heavy fraction of the flotation debris and fragments of a drinking straw, a knife blade, a pin, pin fragments, small nails, a bead and a ring (fig. 176). In 1999 from E3 a pin and two long needles were added to the list of Early Bronze IV objects from Area E (fig. 177). A shell eye inlay, possibly from a small statue, was found south of the last phase of the platform exposed in the 1998 excavations (fig. 173: 4). A cylinder seal was found with fragments of many small bowls, cups and animal bones. It depicted the sun god Shamash rising from the mountains between two doors of a gateway (fig. 180). The seal dates to the Akkad period (Collon 1990: 85–87 and plates 24: 169–25: 177). Expedition paleozoologist Susan Arter noted that there was an unusually high concentration of young sheep and goats, under a year old, in this room. Figures 178 and 179 show a small collection of pottery vessels. The pottery assemblage is similar to that found in the destruction of the

Fig. 174. Oversized female figurine from Early Bronze Age IV destruction in E4.

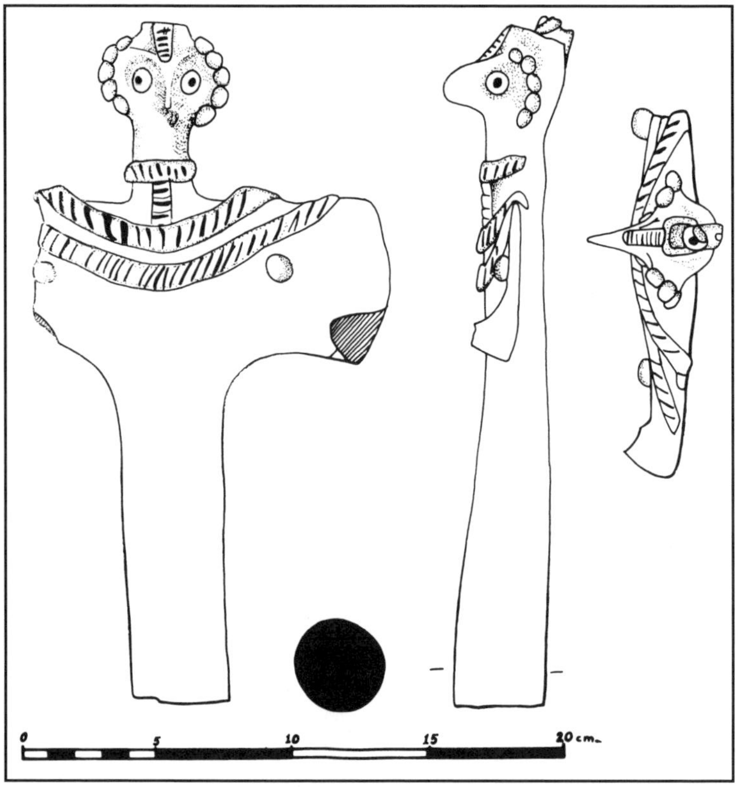

Fig. 175. Drawing of oversized female figurine from Early Bronze Age IV destruction in E4.

building(s) in A22 and A26, 29 (figs. 145–148 and 198–206). The painted and incised cups and the four spouted lamps place this material clearly in the Amuq J (Braidwood and Braidwood 1960), Hama J4–1 (Fugman 1958) and Tell Mardikh II B2 (Matthiae 1981) horizon.

Though the area is extremely interesting, it is still premature to characterize its function until we

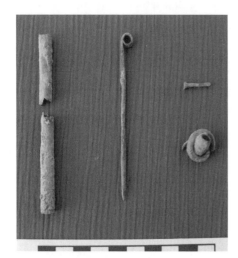

Fig. 176. Early Bronze Age IV copper/bronze objects: a straw, pin with rolled-over head, small nail, small ring and bead from destruction in E4.

Fig. 177. Early Bronze IV copper/bronze needles and pin from E3.

Fig. 178. Selection of pottery from Early Bronze Age IV destruction in E4.

Fig. 179. Selection of characteristic Early Bronze Age IV sherds from E4.

Fig. 180. Cylinder seal found in E4, showing the sun god rising on the mountains of the east with the dawn holding one of the doors of the gateway.

sor Heather Lechtman at the Massachusetts Institute of Technology. The analysis showed that two were made of unalloyed copper, one of a low tin–arsenic bronze and one of a silver–copper alloy. Many sherds of thick, course, footed vessels have been reconstructed to large pieces but not to complete vessels. They seem to be portions of several crucibles (figs. 168–170). Among the pieces are base fragments with pointed or flat feet as well as a clay ridge that supported the body of the vessel on the underside. The sides of the vessel were about 12–15 cm high and pieces of at least two pouring spouts were found. Beads of metal were found on the interior surface of some of the sherds and layers of material adhering to the surface of many sherds may be residue from the manufacturing process. Many of the sherds show signs of a second pottery coating, particularly on the bottom surfaces, indicating the reuse of the vessels over a period of time. Metalworking and other craft activities are well known in Near Eastern temple areas but we need more evidence before we can provide a secure identification of the function of this building.

are able to open a larger exposure. The altar like mudbrick structure and the rich collection of objects indicates the possibility of a major building, possibly a temple. Making this identification less certain is the obvious and continued practice of secondary metal working in the area. We have mentioned the large number of copper/bronze objects found in Area E. Four of these have been analyzed by a Boston University graduate student, Karan Méligne, under the supervision of Profes-

Fig. 181. View of earlier phases under wall EF10, south section of E4 and mudbrick structure after removal of some bricks, from the north.

Fig. 182. View of possible altar in foreground showing plastered surfaces and outline of several buttresses and a niche. Wall EF10 is on the left and excavation of the lowest level is just beginning in the background, from the west.

Fig. 183. View of "altar" after floor going with buttresses and niches were cleaned, from the west.

Fig. 184. View of superimposed phases of north wall of Early Bronze IVB building in E4, from the south.

Fig. 185. View of small mudbrick pillars exposed in lowest level of E4, in test area near the east balk, from the west.

The fourth, lowest level at first looked as if it belonged to a very different type of structure, but some of the walls continued down with the same basic configuration and the materials found in this layer were very similar to the repertoire found in the higher levels. The heavy, footed vessels, possibly used as crucibles for metal working as indicated above, continued to be found in quantity, as well as several sections of large four–spouted lamps and many bronze items in various states of preservation. The unusual feature exhibited in this lowest phase was five circular pillars, between 35 and 50 cm in diameter (fig. 185). The floor of this phase has not yet been reached and we cannot yet say whether the brick platforms to the west continue into this layer.

In 1999 we concentrated on expanding the area of excavation around this Early Bronze Age IV building by removing the south and west balks, and opening a new square on the east (fig. 191). The overlying, compact series of architectural remains are mentioned on p. 23. A shaped, vertical stone was found 0.65 m west of the Early Bronze Age IV mudbrick wall (figs. 287, 188 and 191). It had been plastered around the sides and may have served as a pillar in a doorway, though no traces of the western side of a doorway has yet been

Fig. 186. General view of E4 at the end of the 1998 season, from the northeast.

Fig. 187. View of possible pillar west of wall EF10, after excavation of the south balk of E4, from the north.

Fig. 188. View of "pillar," wall EF10 and associated destruction debris at the end of excavations in 1999, from the east.

found. The stone clearly belongs to a later phase of the building than any we had previously excavated. Important objects included a goblet (fig. 189) and a fenestrated axe head, found underneath the goblet (fig. 190). Also found were a bronze ring, a gold covered pin head, four more gold beads (fig. 172), and a number of pieces of rough-shaped bronze. Fenestrated axe heads of similar size and proportions have been found at numerous sites in Early Bronze Age IV and Early Middle Bronze Age contexts (Philip 1990: 65–67 for his type 2 fenestrated axe).

The new square on the east, E3, sloped steeply to the northwest. We had to excavate quite deep along the south balk to reach undisturbed materials. As we started excavating at the highest level preserved in the southeast corner, and continued stratigraphically through the sequence in the area, we found considerable mudbrick wall remains. Unfortunately, only very short segments of these walls were preserved in the square but they showed up very nicely in the section. The pottery indicates that a good sequence of Iron Age architecture will be encountered when excavation proceeds eastward. At the end of the 1999 season, a substantial mudbrick wall began to appear on the line of the north wall of the Early Bronze Age building in E4

Fig. 189. Early Bronze Age IV chalice on top of fenestrated axe head in destruction debris of southern extension of E4, from the north.

(fig. 191). Large sections of storage jars were found fallen on the floor to its south, including a base section of a storage jar and a large section of another storage jar with irregular horizontal ridges (fig. 192). This wall is more than a meter higher than the wall in E4. This, together with the high rebuilding associated with the pillar in the south balk of E4, indicates that the building continued in use for a longer period of time than was previously evident. More excavation is required to allow us to understand the phasing and dating of this Early Bronze Age IV building.

Only a few human terracotta figurines have been found during the course of excavations. In addition to the oversized female figurine from the Early Bronze IV building in Area E mentioned above, only two typical figurines of the second half of the third millennium B.C. with parallels in the Euphrates Valley and elsewhere were found (fig. 193). The fragment of a seated figurine (fig. 194), conforms to the type of a seated man holding a scepter over one shoulder. This figurine type dates to the beginning of the second millennium.

Three cylinder seal impressions on pottery vessels were found in Early Bronze Age IVB contexts in Area A. Two seals were impressed on the exterior surface of the rim. The ware of the vessels resembles cooking pot ware and the form with short, near vertical stance is commonly found with deeply combed surface (fig. 205: 17). This vessel form was found with seal impressions in Palace G at Tell Mardikh (Mazzoni 1992). One of these impressions has a very simple geometric weave pattern (fig. 195) and the other shows several quadrupeds and a stick-figure human figure (fig. 196). The third impression, on the shoulder of a jar, is uneven and broken but shows several human figures and a quadruped. It is difficult to understand the additional fill decoration and the one additional figure of the scene shown in fig. 197. This impression is an example of Akkadian glyptic

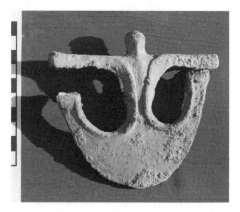

Fig. 190. Fenestrated bronze axe found in latest destruction debris in E4.

Fig. 191. General view of squares E3 and 4 at the end of the 1999 season, showing the line of the south wall of the Early Bronze Age IV building extending into E3 with storage jars smashed on late floors of this building, from the northeast.

style, possibly representing a mythological scene (Collon 1990: 21–36 and figs. 131–149).

THE EARLY BRONZE AGE IVB POTTERY TRADITION AT TELL QARQUR

An excellent corpus of Early Bronze IVB and IVA pottery is now available, particularly from Areas A and E. An overview of this material is illustrated on figs. 198–206. The plates of profile drawings in figs. 198 and 203 were assembled from scattered sherds from everywhere on the tell. These have been supplemented with photographs of selected sherds and vessels. The Early Bronze IVB assemblage corresponds very well with Amuq J and the later levels of Hama J. A large number of plain–simple wares are present, like the many typical chalice rim fragments and bases; a sampling of these are shown in fig. 198: 5–7, 9–15, 17, 20–22, etc. and in the photographs (figs. 99–201). Painted bands are very common in various patterns, sometimes with horizontal combing on the paint or incised into the fabric of the vessel. Several unpainted sherds also include one or more incised wavy horizontal lines. Only a few painted jar rims are shown on the drawings in fig. 203: 8 and 10. A selection of plain ware jar and jug rims,

with and without attached handles from shoulder to rim, are illustrated on fig. 202. A variety of typical painted body and base sherds are shown on fig. 204. The paint is a range of colors from black to brown, depending on the firing of the vessel.

Figures 199 and 200 illustrate the fact that these decorated chalice sherds are found in large quantities. They occur with many variations in a simple format of painted and/or incised decoration. The ongoing analysis is looking at the stratigraphic contexts of the variations in cup forms and wares, and variations in painted and incised decoration. The limited number of reliable stratified loci encountered so far through the entire sequence complicates this examination. We have not yet exposed very much of the Early Bronze Age IVB level and the latest pottery is found mixed in later contexts.

Figure 201 illustrates a variety of base profiles found on cups and goblets. Some features, like the ribbing on figs. 201: 6 and 7, seem to be indicators for different phases, but most do not yet provide a clear pattern. The repertoire of patterns is limited and has excellent parallels at many sites from the Euphrates to the coast. The jar in fig. 203: 8 is a fairly complicated combination of horizontal bands, incised wavy lines and a net pattern, very much within the basic decorative tradition. Simple

Fig. 192. Late Early Bronze Age IV storage jar body sherd with irregular horizontal ridges, from E3.

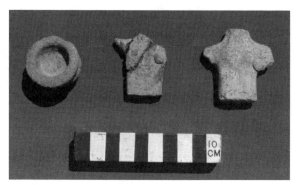

Fig. 193. Early Bronze Age figurines and miniature vessel from various areas at Tell Qarqur.

vertical painted lines, sometimes paired and sometimes wavy, occur frequently. Also well represented are knobbed, vertical lines, usually in pairs, crossed by horizontal lines. This pattern is known on complete or reconstructible vessels from Ugarit, Hama, Ebla and other sites.

Preliminary study of the pottery indicated a series of markers for the end of the period. These include the bowl and jar rims, and bases with double or triple grooves (figs. 198: 32, 36, 37 and 40–42; 201: 6 and 7; 203: 1, 2 and 14; and 205, and 206: 1–6), triangular folded-over rims (figs. 198: 32, 34, 35 and 38, 39), and the cup rims with the triangular–sectioned rim (fig. 198: 16). Characteristic simple rolled-over rims of store jars are shown on fig. 203: 11–13 and 206: 7–15 are also contemporary. The gray-burnished jar well known in Early Bronze Age III–IV contexts in the Euphrates Valley, is also present here (fig. 203: 9). Handles are rare but typical examples of the common circular-sectioned handles are shown on figs. 198: 23; 202: 1–5 and 203: 6 and 7. Flat bases are characteristic of the assemblage on many cup, bowl and jar forms. The variety of painted decoration in this assemblage, illustrated on figs. 199, 200 and 204, has already been noted. It seems to continue until the end of the Early Bronze Age sequence. There is some indication of change in the tradition at the end of the period but we are looking for detailed substantiation of this as more material is excavated.

In Square E3, a large section of a horizontally-ribbed body portion of a storage jar (fig. 192) and the base of a second large storage jar were found on a high floor, apparently associated with the Early Bronze Age building in E4. A jar with similar decorative treatment was found in the Amuq, in what Braidwood called the second mixed range (Braidwood and Braidwood 1960: fig. 361), which consists of materials from mixed context where later building activities cut into earlier layers so as to make their stratigraphic attribution uncertain. A post-J attribution for this storage jar seems clear. In another high floor of the Early Bronze IV building in Area E, the cup (fig. 189) found over the fenistrated ax head (fig. 190) has a slightly flaring rim that does not seem to be common on cups

Fig. 194. Middle Bronze I–II figurine fragment showing seated individual holding "scepter."

Fig. 195. Early Bronze Age IV Cylinder seal impression on rim of jar, showing geometric weave pattern.

Fig. 196. Early Bronze Age IV Cylinder seal impression on rim of jar, showing several quadruped and a human stick figure.

Fig. 197. Early Bronze Age IV Cylinder seal impression on the shoulder of a storage jar.

earlier in our sequence. One of the objectives of future excavation seasons will be to obtain a stratified sequence to verify specific variations in detail and appropriate dates for phases of the sequence. I have tried to provide detailed illustrations of the material to make it available for basic comparisons while studies and excavations continue.

EARLY BRONZE IVA–EARLY BRONZE I, AND EARLIER POTTERY IN IRON AGE CONSTRUCTION FILLS AND STRATIFIED CONTEXTS IN A26 AND A29

A series of markers are emerging for what we are now calling Early Bronze IVA. There is no indication that the red-black burnished wares that are well represented in secondary context are present in this assemblage. For the time being I are equating this horizon with Tell Mardikh IIB1, but whether this is appropriate or whether I should be labeling this material Early Bronze III is not yet certain. Heavily burnished cups with simple profiles showing a slight depression below the rim are most common. These cups range in size from small to quite large and range in color from red-orange to dark gray-brown (figs. 198: 1; 207: 2, 3 and 7; and 208). The corrugated cup, well-known as earlier in the Amuq I, J sequence than the chalice forms mentioned above, the earlier levels in Hama J and Tell Mardikh IIB1 are also quite common (figs. 198: 2, 14 and 209). Simple band painted cups and jars are present, but are not very elaborate (fig. 198: 10, 11, 17 and 20–22).

In squares A26 and A29, the construction fills immediately beneath the stone paved street and associated gravel layer provided a ceramic glimpse into the history of the site, which was not so obvious elsewhere. An excellent corpus of early third millennium B.C. pottery was present, as well as pottery of Uruk, Ubaid, and Neolithic date. Most of the typical forms of "Khirbit Kerak" ware, also called red-black burnished ware, are represented on fig. 210, and the color range from yellow to orange to red and black and gray surfaces is typical for this type of pottery. The rim profiles, molded and ribbed surface exterior treatment,

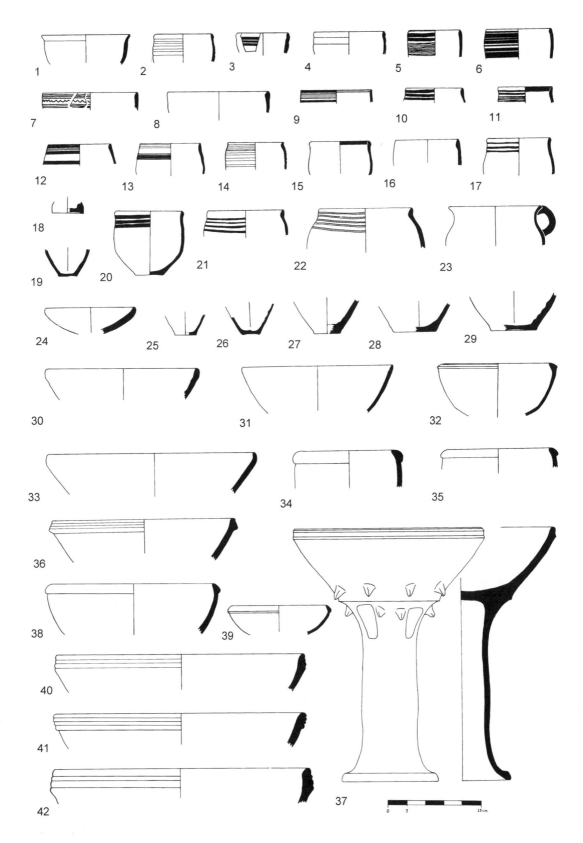

Fig. 198. Early Bronze Age IV pottery drawings.

Drawing Figure	Sherd Number	Area	Plot	Locus	Basket	Form	Exterior	Color	Interior	Color	Ware	Color	Inclusions	Surface Treatment	Height in mm.	Dia. in mm.	Thickness
198 : 01	TQ97-0078	A	29	68	178	B-062	7.5YR7/6	RED.YELLOW	7.5YR7/6	RED.YELLOW	10YR7/2	LT.GRAY	SOME FINE BLACK		49	140	5
198 : 02	TQ93-0266	A	21	2	20	B-064	10YR8/4	V.PALE BR.	10YR8/4	V.PALE BR.	10YR8/4	V.PALE BR.	MANY FINE BLACK		42	90	4
198 : 03	TQ96-0003	A	22	48	165	B-036	2.5Y8/3; PAINTED STRIPES: 10YR5/6; 7.5YR3/0	PALE YELLOW; YEL. BROWN; V.DK.GRAY	10YR8/4	V.PALE BROWN	10YR7/2	LT.GRAY	MANY MED BLACK	WASH BAND PAINTED	30	80	5
198 : 04	TQ95-0063	A	39	9	47	B-053	10YR8/4	V.PALE BROWN	10YR8/4	V.PALE BROWN	10YR8/3	V.PALE BROWN	SOME MED BLACK	PLAIN	40	110	4
198 : 05	TQ97-0079	A	29	79	195	B-053	10YR8/2; STRIPES 10YR4/1	WHITE; DK. GRAY	10YR8/2	WHITE	10YR8/2	WHITE	SOME FINE BLACK		40	80	4
198 : 06	TQ93-0273	D	SURF		3	B-065	10YR8/2; STRIPES: 10YR5/1	WHITE; GRAY	5YR8/3	PINK	10YR8/2; 5YR8/3	WHITE; PINK	FEW FINE BLACK		47	100	5
198 : 07	TQ97-0015	A	29	71	179	B-053	10YR7/3; PAINT 7.5YR5/4	V.PALE BR.; BROWN	10YR7/3	V.PALE BR.	10YR7/3	V.PALE BR.	MANY FINE BLACK		29	150	5
198 : 08	TQ93-0184	A	26	7	34	B-053	7.5YR7/4; PAINTED STRIPES: 5YR4/1	PINK; DK.GRAY	7.5YR7/4	PINK	10YR7/2	LT.GRAY	MANY FINE BLACK	MUTI-BAND OUT PAINTED RIM	34	190	4
198 : 09	TQ93-0287	D	8	8	63	B-068	2.5YR4/6; 5YR7/4	RED; PINK	5YR7/6; 2.5YR3/6	RED.YELLOW; DK. RED	2.5YR5/6	RED	V. FEW FINE, V. FINE MULTI-COLOR SAND		19	110	4
198 : 10	TQ97-0076	A	22	72	238	B-052	10YR8/2; STRIPES 10YR4/1	WHITE; DK. GRAY	10YR8/2	WHITE	10YR8/2	WHITE	SOME FINE BLACK		23	90	5
198 : 11	TQ97-0093	A	29	81	233	B-071	10YR8/3; STRIPES 10YR4/1	V.PALE BR.; DK. GRAY	10YR8/3	V.PALE BR.	10YR8/3	V.PALE BR.	SOME FINE BLACK		20	90	5
198 : 12	TQ95-0080	E	4	2	7	B-053	10YR8/3; STRIPES 5YR5/6; 5YR2.5/1	V.PALE BR.; YELLOW RED; BLACK	10YR8/3	V.PALE BR.	10YR7/2	LT. GRAY	SOME FINE BLACK	PAINTED BANDS LT. COMBED BNDS	33	100	5
198 : 13	TQ95-0081	E	4	2	7	B-067	2.5Y8/3	PALE YELLOW	2.5Y8/3	PALE YELLOW	10YR8/4	V. PALE BR.	SOME MED BLACK		49	100	5
198 : 14	TQ93-0264	A	21	10	67	B-066	10YR8/2	WHITE	10YR8/2	WHITE	10YR8/2	WHITE	FEW FINE BLACK		40	90	5
198 : 15	TQ95-0073	A	22	24	108	B-070	10YR7/3	V.PALE BR.	10YR7/3; 7.5YR7/4	V.PALE BR.; PINK	10YR7/3	V.PALE BR.	MANY FINE BLACK		51	90	4
198 : 16	TQ93-0032	A	21	10	63	B-071	2.5Y8/2; 10YR7/1	WHITE; LT. GRAY	10YR8/3	V.PALE BR.	10YR8/3	V.PALE BR.	MANY FINE BROWN		40	120	6
198 : 17	TQ97-0013	A	22	65	180	B-069	10YR8/3; STRIPES 10YR4/1	V.PALE BR.; DK. GRAY	10YR8/3	V.PALE BR.	10YR8/3	V.PALE BR.	SOME FINE BLACK		58	100	4
198 : 18	TQ93-0160	A	29	25	118	BB-10	2.5Y8/3	PALE YELLOW	2.5Y8/3	PALE YELLOW	2.5Y8/3	PALE YELLOW	MANY FINE BLACK; MANY FINE BLACK	PAINT IN/OUT	20	40	9
198 : 19	TQ96-038	A	22	48	165	BB-12	10YR7/3	V.PALE BR.	7.5YR8/2	WHITE	10YR7/3	V.PALE BR.	MANY FINE BLACK		42	31	5
198 : 20	TQ97-0075	A	22	65	180	B-069; BB-13	10YR8/3; 7.5YR7/6	V.PALE BR.; RED.YELLOW	10YR8/3	V.PALE BR.	10YR8/3	V.PALE BR.	FEW MED BLACK		45	100	6
198 : 21	TQ96-0030	A	22	43	165	B-076	10YR8/3; STRIPES: 5YR4/1	V.PALE BR.; DK.GRAY	5YR7/6	RED.YELLOW	10YR8/2	WHITE	SOME FINE BLACK		37	120	6
198 : 22	TQ93-0259	A	21	10	65	B-076	10YR8/2; STRIPES 10YR6/6	WHITE; BR. YELLOW	10YR8/2	WHITE	10YR8/2	WHITE	SOME FINE BLACK		64	150	6
198 : 23	TQ96-0041	A	22	50	164	B-078	10YR5/2	GRAY. BR.	10YR4/2	DK.GRAY.BR.	10YR4/2	DK.GRAY.BR.	SOME MED WHITE		62	140	5
198 : 24	TQ96-0040	A	22	50	164	B-017	10YR7/3	V.PALE BR.	10YR7/3	V.PALE BR.	10YR7/3	V.PALE BR.	SOME MED BLACK		40	140	9
198 : 25	TQ96-0001	A	22	48	165	BB-12	10YR8/4	V.PALE BROWN	10YR8/4	V.PALE BROWN	10YR7/2	LT.GRAY	FEW FINE BLACK	PLAIN	35	35	3.5
198 : 26	TQ96-0039	A	22	48	165	BB-13	10YR7/4	V.PALE BR.	7.5YR7/6; 10YR7/4	RED.YELLOW; V.PALE BR.	10YR7/4	V.PALE BR.	FEW FINE BLACK		51	31	3
198 : 27	TQ97-0064	A	22	78	195	BB-12	10YR7/2	LT. GRAY	10YR7/2	LT. GRAY	10YR7/2	LT. GRAY	SOME FINE WHITE		41	70	7
198 : 28	TQ96-0034	A	22	48	165	BB-11	7.5YR8/4	PINK	10YR8/4	V.PALE BR.	10YR8/4	V.PALE BR.	MANY MED BLACK; FEW MED RED; FEW MED WHITE		48	67	7
198 : 29	TQ96-0032	A	22	48	165	BB-23	10YR7/3	V.PALE BR.	10YR7/3	V.PALE BR.	10YR6/3	PALE BROWN	SOME FINE BLACK; FEW MED WHITE		60	70	7
198 : 30	TQ96-0005	A	22	50	164	B-017	5YR3/1; 7.5YR3/3	V. DARK GRAY; DK BROWN	7.5YR3/0	V. DARK GRAY	10YR8/3	V. PALE BROWN	MANY MED BLACK	PLAIN, C.P.WARE	50	240	9
198 : 31	TQ97-0070	A	22	82	204	B-086	2.5YR5/6	RED	2.5YR5/6	RED	2.5YR5/8	RED	MANY FINE WHITE	SMEARED WASH IN/	76	240	6
198 : 32	TQ93-0013	D	8	8	81	B-124	10YR7/3	V. PALE BROWN	10YR7/4	V. PALE BROWN	10YR7/3	V. PALE BROWN	MANY MED BLACK	PLAIN	32	160	8
198 : 33	TQ97-0103	A	39	37	202	B-089	7.5YR5/3	BROWN	7.5YR5/3	BROWN	7.5YR5/3	BROWN	SOME MED BLACK		71	330	9
198 : 34	TQ93-0285	D	7	17	154	B-120	5YR7/3	PINK	5YR7/3	PINK	5YR7/3	PINK	MANY FINE BLACK		57	140	10
198 : 35	TQ93-0205	A	21	10	66	B-023	10YR7/3	V. PALE BROWN	10YR7/4	V. PALE BROWN	10YR7/3	V. PALE BROWN	MANY MED BLACK	PLAIN	32	160	8
198 : 36	TQ93-0254	A	29	25	118	B-122	10YR8/2	WHITE	10YR8/2	WHITE	10YR8/3	V.PALE BR.	MANY FINE BLACK; FEW FINE WHITE		70	290	15
198 : 37	TQ97-0073	E	4	21	75	B-121; BB-27		V. PALE BR.				V. PALE BR.		PLAIN	400	300	15
198 : 38	TQ93-0261	A	21	10	65	B-023	10YR8/4	V. PALE BR.	10YR7/6	YELLOW	10YR7/2	LT GRAY	MANY FINE BLACK		75	260	11
198 : 39	TQ93-0250	D	SURF		1	B-119	10YR8/2	WHITE	2.5Y8/2	PALE YELLOW	10YR8/2	WHITE	FEW FINE BLACK		44	150	6
198 : 40	TQ94-0002	A	21	7	33	B-126	10YR8/2	WHITE	10YR8/2	WHITE	10YR8/2	WHITE	MANY FINE BLACK		55	400	8
198 : 41	TQ97-0088	A	29	72	180	B-125	10YR8/3	V.PALE BR.	10YR8/3	V.PALE BR.	10YR8/3	V.PALE BR.	MANY FINE BLACK		53	400	16
198 : 42	TQ95-0075	A	29	71	158	B-127	10YR8/3	V.PALE BR.	10YR8/3	V.PALE BR.	10YR8/3	V.PALE BR.	MANY FINE BLACK		50	420	12

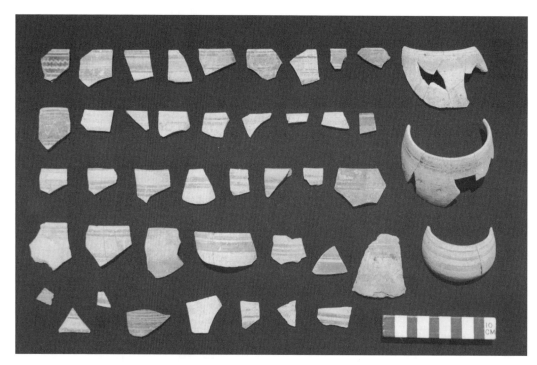

Fig. 199. Early Bronze Age IV pottery.

Fig. 200. Early Bronze Age IV pottery.

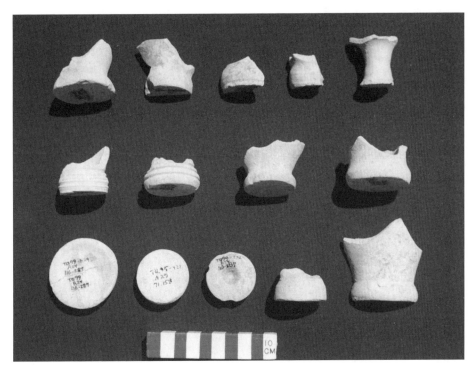

Fig. 201. Early Bronze Age IV pottery.

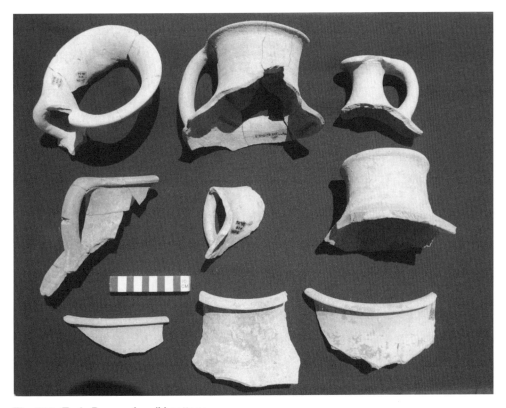

Fig. 202. Early Bronze Age IV pottery.

Fig. 203. Additional Early Bronze Age IV pottery from Area A.

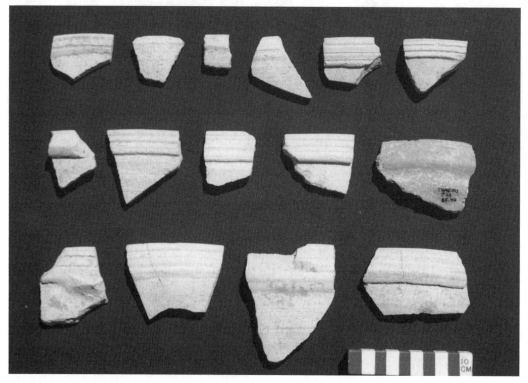

Fig. 204. Additional Early Bronze Age IV pottery from Area A.

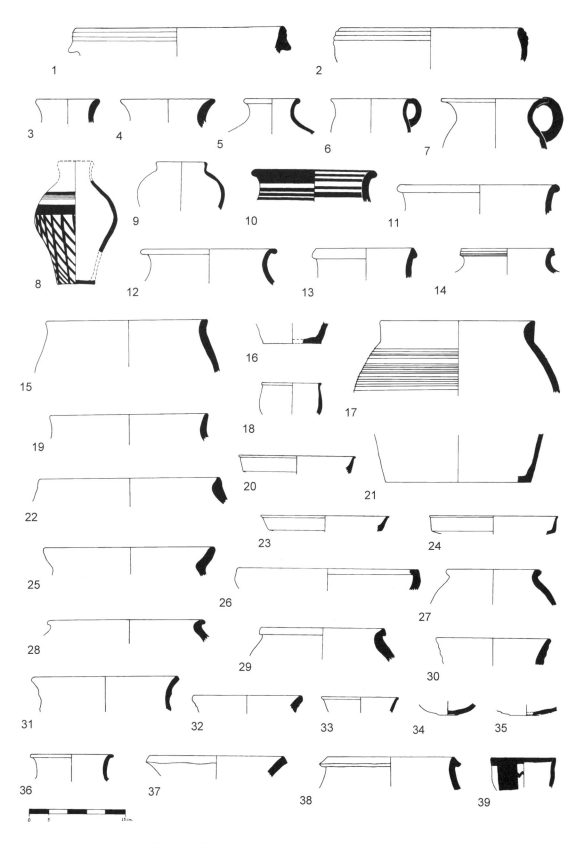

Fig. 205. Early Bronze Age IV and earlier pottery.

Drawing Figure	Sherd Number	Area	Plot	Locus	Basket	Form	Exterior	Color	Interior	Color	Ware	Color	Inclusions	Surface Treatment	Height in mm.	Dia. in mm.	Thick ness
205 : 01	TQ93-0256	A	29	26	121	B-126	8.5YR8/3	PALE YELLOW	8.5YR8/3	PALE YELLOW	8.5YR8/3	PALE YELLOW	MANY FINE BLACK	PLAIN	35	320	13
205 : 02	TQ93-0192	A	29	16	73	B-029	5YR7/6 10YR7/2	RED.YELLOW LT. GRAY	5YR7/8 5YR7/6 5YR5/6	RED.YELLOW RED.YELLOW RED.YELLOW	5YR7/6 10YR7/2	RED.YELLOW LT. GRAY	MANY MED BLACK	PLAIN	55	280	11
205 : 03	TQ95-0013	A	22	14	65	J-040	7.5YR3/3	DK BROWN	10YR7/3	V PALE BROWN	10YR7/1	LT. GRAY	MED. MED. BLACK AND WHITE	PLAIN	35	100	8
205 : 04	TQ93-0188	D	7	18	72	J-022	10YR7/2 5YR6/6	LT. GRAY RED.YELLOW	10YR7/2 5YR6/4	LT. GRAY LT.RED.BROWN	10YR7/2	LT. GRAY	MANY MED BLACK FEW MED WHITE	PLAIN	45	140	12
205 : 05	TQ97-0069	A	22	82	204	J-047	10YR7/3	V.PALE BR.	10YR7/4	V.PALE BR.	10YR7/4	V.PALE BR.	SOME FINE BLACK	PLAIN	55	77	4
205 : 06	TQ93-0255	A	29	25	119	B-077	10YR8/2	WHITE	10YR8/2	WHITE	10YR8/2	WHITE	MANY FINE BLACK	PLAIN	52	120	4.5
205 : 07	TQ97-0067	A	22	82	204	J-068	5YR7/6	RED.YELLOW	10YR6/3	PALE BROWN	10YR6/3	PALE BROWN	FEW MED BLACK FEW MED WHITE	PLAIN	75		8
205 : 08	TQ95-0061	E	4	2 1	7 8	BB-25	7.5YR7/4	PINK	10YR8/4	V. PALE BROWN	10YR8/2	WHITE	FEW FINE BLACK	PAINTED AND INCISED OUT	[185]	[128]	9
205 : 09	TQ95-0082	E	4	2	7	J-080	5Y6/1	GRAY	5Y7/1	LT. GRAY	5Y7/1	LT. GRAY	FEW FINE BLACK	SP. BURN. OUT	70	75	5
205 : 10	TQ93-0262	A	21	10	66		10YR5/2 STRIPES: 5YR5/3 5YR4/2	GRAY.BR. RED.BR. DK.RED.BR.	10YR5/2	GRAY.BR.	10YR5/2	GRAY.BR.	SOME FINE BLACK FEW FINE WHITE	RESERVED SL. IN AND OUT	50	180	17
205 : 11	TQ97-0053	A	22	78	195	J-049	10YR7/4	V.PALE BR.	10YR7/4	V.PALE BR.	10YR7/4 10YR5/2	V.PALE BR. GRAY BROWN	FEW FINE FLACK	PLAIN	38	240	16
205 : 12	TQ93-0265	A	21	11	77	J-050	5YR6/6	RED.YELLOW	7.5YR7/4	PINK	7.5YR7/2	PINK.GRAY	MANY FINE WHITE	PLAIN	49	200	6
205 : 13	TQ96-0031	A	22	48	165	J-066	10YR8/2	WHITE	10YR8/2	WHITE	7.5YR7/4	PINK	FEW FINE BLACK FEW FINE WHITE	PLAIN	50	100	12
205 : 14	TQ93-0202	A	26	26	139	J-035	2.5Y8/2	WHITE	2.5Y8/2	WHITE	2.5Y8/2	WHITE	MANY MED BLACK	PLAIN, RIDGED RIM	40	140	9
205 : 15	TQ94-0004	A	-3	19	47	J-103	7.5YR3/2 7.5YR4/2	DK.BROWN DK.BROWN	7.5YR3/2 7.5YR4/2	DK.BROWN DK.BROWN	10YR5/2	GRAY.BR.	MANY MED WHITE	PLAIN	82	250	8
205 : 16	TQ97-0066	A	22	78	195	BB-25	5YR6/6	RED.YELLOW	7.5YR7/4	PINK	7.5YR7/2	PINK.GRAY	FEW FINE BLACK	PLAIN	34	90	8
205 : 17	TQ97-0092	A	22	65	180	J-044	10YR4/2	DK.GRAY.BR.	7.5YR6/4	LT.BROWN	10YR5/2	GRAY. BR.	MANY MED WHITE MANY MED QUARTZ	PLAIN	113	240	11
205 : 18	TQ94-0015	A	26	56	74	B-073	2.5Y7/2	LT.GRAY	10YR6/3	PALE BROWN	2.5Y7/2	LT.GRAY	SOME FINE BLACK	PLAIN	50	90	6
205 : 19	TQ93-0190	A	29	21	99	J-026	7.5YR3/3	DK BROWN	10YR7/3	V PALE BROWN	10YR7/3	V PALE BROWN	FEW FINE WHITE	PLAIN, C.P.WARE	42	240	9
205 : 20	TQ95-0011	A	22	14	66	B-108	5YR6/6	RED YEL.	7.5YR6/6	RED YEL.	10YR7/3 5YR3/1 10YR7/3	V. PALE BROWN V. DK. GRAY V. PALE BROWN	MED. FINE SAND MED. LT. STRAW	PLAIN	23	200	8
205 : 21	TQ96-0033	A	22	48	165	BB-02	10YR8/4	V.PALE BR.	10YR8/4	V.PALE BR.	5YR7/6	RED.YELLOW	MANY MED BLACK FEW FINE WHITE	PLAIN	75	230	10
205 : 22	TQ94-0003	A	26	57	76	J-107	7.5YR3/2 7.5YR4/2	DK.BROWN DK.BROWN	7.5YR3/2 7.5YR4/2	DK.BROWN DK.BROWN	10YR5/2	GRAY.BR.	MANY MED WHITE MANY FINE MICA	PLAIN	45	280	10
205 : 23	TQ95-0010	A	22	14	66	B-108	7.5YR6/6	RED.YELLOW	7.5YR6/6	RED.YELLOW	5YR8/1 7.5YR4/0	WHITE DK./ GREY	SOME FINE BLACK	PLAIN	29	180	8
205 :24	TQ95-0083	A	29	13	58	B-108	10YR8/2	WHITE	10YR8/2	WHITE	10YR5/3	BROWN	MANY FINE GRAY FEW MED WHITE	PLAIN	24	200	6
205 : 25	TQ97-0011	A	22	65	180	J-108	10YR6/3	PALE BROWN	10YR6/3	PALE BROWN	10YR4/1	DK. GRAY	SOME FINE BLACK	PLAIN	48	260	13
205 : 26	TQ93-0168	A	29	19	92	B-050	5YR7/4	PINK	5YR7/4	PINK	10YR7/2	LT.GRAY	MANY MED BLACK SOME COR. WHITE	PLAIN	30	250	13
205 : 27	TQ94-0005	A	-3	19	47	J-102	7.5YR8/4 10YR8/3 5YR5/6	PINK PL. BROWN V.PL.BROWN	7.5YR5/4	BROWN	2.5YR6/6 7.5YR6/2	LT. RED PINK. RED	LT. M.-M.F. SAND LT. F.-MF. STRAW	RESERVED SL. AND COMBED, BURN. BELOW RIM	55	150	6
205 : 28	TQ93-0154	A	26	22	127	J-039	5YR4/4 7.5YR8/0	RED.BROWN WHITE	5YR4/4 7.5YR8/0	RED.BROWN WHITE	2.5Y8/3 5YR3/1	PALE YEL. V.DK.GRAY	MANY MED BLACK	PLAIN	34	240	12
205 : 29	TQ93-0191	D	8	16	84	J-022	7.5YR6/4 7.5YR5/4	LT BROWN BROWN	7.5YR6/4	LT BROWN	10YR7/3	V. PALE BROWN	SOME COR. WHITE MANY FINE BLACK	ZIG-ZAG RESERVE SLIP OUT	46	190	15
205 : 30	TQ93-0288	A	29	19	92	J-054	1GLEY2.5/N	BLACK	5YR5/6	YEL. RED	2.5Y2.5/1 10YR3/1 10YR5/8	BLACK V.DK.GRAY YEL. BROWN	M. V.C. LT. SAND LT. FINE STRAW	CLOSE H.B. OUT OVER AND TOP IN	43	180	10
205 : 31	TQ93-0289	A	26	2	124	J-061	5YR6/6 1GLEY 2.5/N	RED. YEL. BLACK	5YR5/8	YEL. RED	5Y5/1 5YR6/6	GRAY RED YEL.	M. FINE SAND M. HVY. SAND	CLOSE H.B. OUT OVER AND TOP IN	55	230	8
205 : 32	TQ93-0290	A	29	22	197	J-052	5YR4/6	YEL. RED	2.5YR2.5/6	RED	7.5YR7/6 7.5YR3/1 7.5YR7/6	RED YEL. V. DK. GRAY RED. YEL.	LT. FINE STRAW	CLOSE H. B. OUT AND IN	29	170	11
205 : 33	TQ93-0291	A	21	8	52	B-109	10YR8/1	WHITE	10YR8/1	WHITE	10YR8/1	WHITE	FEW V. FINE BLACK	PLAIN	24	120	4
205 : 34	TQ93-0014	A	26	22	126	BB-26									18	33	6
205 : 35	TQ93-0162	A	21	11	76	BB-08	10YR7/2	LT. GRAY	10YR7/2	LT. GRAY	10YR7/2	LT. GRAY	FEW COR.RED MANY FINE BLACK	PLAIN	14	54	5
205 : 36	TQ93-0292	A	29	21	99	J-050	10YR7/1	LT. GRAY	7.5YR7/2	PK. GRAY	2.5YR6/6	LT. RED	LT. MED. SAND FINE MED. SAND	FINISHED ON SLOW WHEEL	43	130	5
205 : 37	TQ95-0084	A	29	45	116	B-094	5YR7/4	PINK	5YR7/4	PINK	10YR6/3	PL. BROWN	HV. M. & L. STRAW LT. F. SAND	PLAIN	34	220	11
205 : 38	TQ95-0085	A	35	6	41	J-067	2.5Y8/3	PALE YELLOW	10YR8/3	V.PALE BROWN	7.5YR8/4	PINK	MANY FINE WHITE	PLAIN	48	200	10
205 : 39	TQ97-0107	E	4	1	27	B-063	2.5Y8/2 7/5YR3/1	PALE YELLOW PAINT V.DK.GRAY	2.5Y8/2	PALE YELLOW	2.5Y8/2 7.5YR7/6	PALE YEL. RED.YELLOW	FINE V.LT.SAND	STRAW WIPED WHEEL FINISHED PAINTED DECOR.	44	100	6

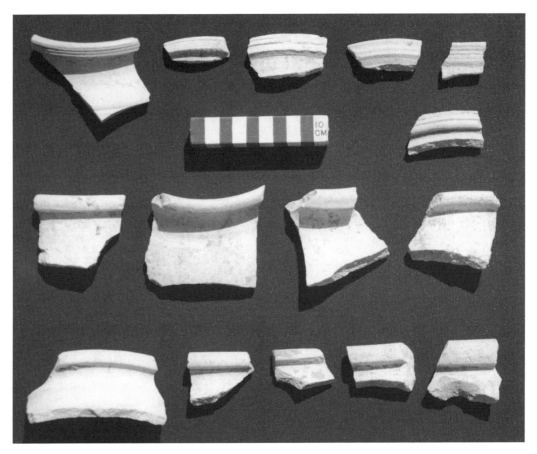

Fig. 206. Additional Early Bronze Age IV pottery from Area A.

knobs, lids, and incised decorations indicate that the Qarqur material is in the mainstream of this tradition.

Also common in the Amuq (Amuq H) and elsewhere in Early Bronze Age II–III is a variety of reserved-slip ware (fig. 211). It is present in a variety of color ranges but with a greater use of incised wavy line or smeared wavy line decoration than is illustrated in Amuq. The Amuq phase G cyma-recta cups and very shallow ring bases are well illustrated at Qalat el Mudig in the Orontes Valley, about 40 km south of Qarqur (Collon and Zaqzuq 1972: fig. 4) and at Tell Hadidi in the Euphrates Valley (Dornemann 1990: 87, 88 and plate 20: 8–14) are also present at Tell Qarqur. We have given an Early Bronze Age II date to these forms at Tell Hadidi and contemporary north Syrian sites. The beveled rim bowls, or chaff-faced ware of Amuq, known through Early Bronze Age

I contexts in Syria are present as well as the distinctive combed ware that is contemporary at Tell Hadidi (Dornemann 1988: 1–5 and 26–29). Some red burnished forms and incised wares are also indicative of the first half of the third millennium B.C. Typical Chalcolithic painted sherds are present as well as Neolithic dark-faced burnished wares, some which have the typical thumb nail impressed decoration of Amuq A and B. Tell Qarqur is a high tell and clearly represents a site with a very long history of occupation. Figures 172: 18–38 and 212 illustrate a selection of representative sherds mentioned above from Early Bronze Age II through Neolithic.

When we excavated the square to the north of the Early Bronze Age IV building in E4 to see if the building continued in that direction, we found that it did not. The north wall of the building extended into the balk between E4 and E5. Square

Fig. 207. Early Bronze Age IVA pottery from Area A.

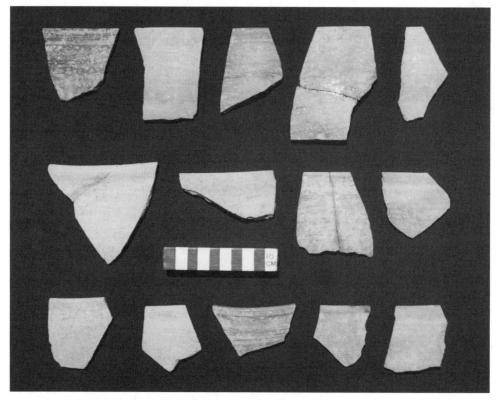

Fig. 208. Additional Early Bronze Age IVA pottery from Area A.

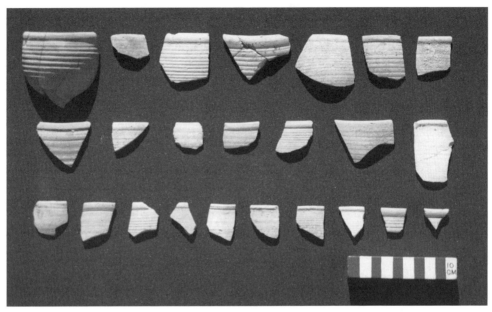

Fig. 209. Early Bronze IVA corrugated cup sherds.

Fig. 210. Red-Black burnished ware, (Khirbet Kerak ware) from Iron Age construction fills in A29.

Fig. 211. Early Bronze II–III sherds from store jars decorated with reserved slip and incised patterns from Iron Age construction fills in A29.

Fig. 212. Sherds for Early Bronze II, I, Chalcolithic and Neolithic periods from Iron Age construction fills in A29.

E5 (fig. 213) contained no architectural elements and is a promising location for examination of the earlier levels on the site. The earliest pottery assemblage that we reached in E5 was earlier than what we have seen elsewhere so far in Area E, and may be Early Bronze IVA.

Fig. 213. View of E5 showing disruptions of stratigraphy by plant and animal intrusion, outside, to the north, of the Early Bronze Age IV building in E3–4, from the north.

PRELIMINARY ANALYSIS OF BOTANICAL AND ZOOLOGICAL REMAINS

Paleobotanical Samples

Analysis of the zoological and botanical remains is ongoing. Professor Julie Hansen, Chair of the Department of Archaeology at Boston University, has been analyzing the paleobotanical materials with the assistance of her students. Ms. Alexia Smith, one of her students has recently taken on the study of the Tell Qarqur paleobotanical materials as part of her Ph.D. dissertation. The analysis of the botanical remains has concentrated on Area B, but the numbers of samples is very large and processing is very time consuming. A preliminary list of identified plant remains compiled by Professor Hansen and her students are as follows:

Ficus carica	Fig
Vitis, vinifera	Grape
Vitis, orientalis	Grape
Pyrus communis	Pear
Malva	Mallow
Vicia faba	Broad bean

Astragalas sp.	Milk vetch
Vicia ervilia	Bitter vetch
Vicia sp.	Vetch
Trifolium sp.	Clover
Triticocum sp.	Wheat
Triticum sp.	Wheat
Triticum aestivum	Bread wheat
Triticum turgidum dicoccum	Emmer wheat
Triticocum monococcum	Einkorn wheat
Hordeum sp.	Barley
Hordeum vulgare	Barley
Lolium sp.	Rye grass
Secale cereale	Rye
Polygonum sp.	Buckwheat
Phalaris sp.	Canary grass
Rumex sp.	Dockweed
Acer sempervirens	Maple
Quercus coccifera	Kermes Oak
Quercus trojana	Oak (half evergreen)

On pages 81–83, I mentioned the large concentration of carbonized "bitter vetch" seeds found in an Early Bronze IV building in Area A (fig. 144). Portions of the deposit are shown *in situ* in figs. 142 and 143.

Paleozoological Samples

An extensive collection of animal bones has been accumulated over the years. Susan Arter, the expedition paleozoologist, has completed a basic analysis of these remains, her phase I analysis, and is beginning a more detailed study as phase II. Her report of the phase I analysis of materials from the 1993 through 1998 season follows in the appendix.

CONCLUSION

The seven seasons of excavation at Tell Qarqur between 1993 and 1999 have been very productive in the information that has been obtained and clearly indicate the archaeological importance of the site. Though the focus of the excavation has been on specific questions and periods, it is clear that Tell Qarqur was a significant site over a very long period of time. This report is intended to provide an overview of what has been found by the expedition, including a basic representation of ceramic inventories of the different periods, illustrations of all of the important objects, and summaries of the paleozoological and paleobotanical remains. Since the site has been rebuilt so many times over such a long period, many levels are badly disturbed. Only as we continue our excavation can we solidify the sequences we have so far only outlined and tie down solid, detailed stratigraphic pottery sequences that will be valuable for comparative purposes. The potential is clear and the basic outline which is now available will provide direction on where future efforts are best focused.

NOTES

1. The representatives from our Directorate of Antiquities and Museums for the five seasons must be acknowledged for their assistance: Kurwan Marwan, Said El Said, Labib Sebai, Dr. Hana Qudeier, Mariam Bshesh and Salam Qonta. Nasib Salibi of the Damascus office was always most helpful and congenial but sadly passed away recently. Our guard Taha Yassine has been very diligent with his son Arab in watching over the site for many years, and Ibrahim Younis, OSJ has helped us with housing and logistics all these years.

2. Financial support was also received from the following: Robert Benson, Burton and Charlotte Cohn, Carolyn Cox, Virginia Howbert, Winston Lindberg, Russel and Shirley Sherman, Lowrie Lee Sprung, and Michael and Neathery Fuller.

3. Staff participating during the seven seasons were the following: Dr. Kathleen Nash, Associate Director, Area B supervisor (1993, 1996, 1997, 1998); Dr. Lee Maxwell, Associate Director, Area A supervisor, ceramicist for Classical and Islamic materials, and surveyor (1995–2000); Dr. Deirdre Dempsey, epigrapher and plot supervisor (in the field in 1997, 1998); Dr. Brian Schmidt, epigrapher; Dr. Julie Hansen, paeleoethnobotanist (in the field in 1998); Susan Arter, paleozoologist (1994, 1995, 1997, 1998); Rita Sabbagh Khachadourian, assistant ethnobotanist and artist (1996–2000); Donald Mitchell, surveyor (1993); Barabara Pritzkat, surveyor (1995); Andy Laird, photographer, (1997); Anne Grace Bollinger Pondevie, registrar, (1997); Square supervisors: Dr. Maxwell Miller (1993, 1994), Dr. Donald Wimmer (1993, 1994), Dr. Jean Nijhowne (1996), Eric Jensen (1997, 1999, 2000), Wade Clack (1995), Lauren Markley (1995, 1999), Karen Arter (1995), Maggie Mc Hugh (1998), Rebecca Schulthisie (1997), Jonathan Gimmel (1998, deceased), Nathan Maughan (1997, 1998), Jennifer McCormac (1993), Elizabeth Mc Intosh (1993), Lisa Pham (1993), Dr. Lynn Tatum (1993), Hiroaki Watenabe (1993), Sarah Scott (1997), Timothy Gerdes (1997), Christian Rasmussen; (1999), Warren Wood (1999), Maggie Reinbold (1999), Sarah Graff (1995–2000), Britt Hartneberger (1997), Jeff Nelson (1998), Dr. Harald Schoubye (1998), Jennifer Wexler (1998), Linda Wheatley Irving (1999), Salem Abdel Ghafour (99, 2000), and Raniah Ghafour (2000).

4. The length of each excavation season was as follows: July 3–August 12, 1993; May 28–June 29, 1994; July 1–August 10, 1995; May 27–June 27, 1996; June 23–August 7, 1997; June 14–July 20, 1998 and June 1–July 30, 1999.

5. A topographic survey of the northern *ghab* and the *rouj* was undertaken in 1983 and 1984. The expedition director, Dr. John Lundquist, kindly provided this data to us when excavations resumed in 1993, which has formed the basis of our topographic documentation on the site.

Appendix

Summary Report on the Phase I Analysis of Zooarchaeological Material

SUSAN ARTER

INTRODUCTION TO THE ANALYSIS OF THE TELL QARQUR FAUNAL MATERIALS

Archaeological animal bones are among the most durable and ubiquitous artifacts recovered from Near Eastern tell sites. Identification and analysis of these remains yield important evidence of the role animals played in the diets of past peoples and can be used to reconstruct animal-based subsistence economies in ancient societies (Uerpmann 1973). These data also reveal information about past environments. When viewed in conjunction with historical data, contextual site information, ceramic data, and other artifactual sources the faunal material can contribute significantly to our understanding of ancient lifeways and human cultural development.

Documentation of the types and proportions of animals utilized, their age at death, and the proportional representation of skeletal elements, among other criteria, provide a means for reconstructing animal husbandry practices associated with the distribution and consumption of animal-based resources. The data serve as means for identifying the production and procurement of animal resources associated with distinct occupational periods while monitoring socioeconomic shifts associated with changes in site function and political affiliations over time.

Analyses have been conducted on archaeological animal bone assemblages from Neolithic and early village deposits to later prehistoric Near Eastern sites in Turkey, northern Syria, Iran, Iraq,

and the southern Levant (Bokonyi 1973; Clason 1979–1980; Hesse 1986; Wattenmaker and Stein 1986; Uerpmann 1882; Zeder 1985, 1990; Zeder and Arter 1999). Zooarchaeological research currently underway at Tell Qarqur involves the first systematic study of animal remains from a major urban site in Syria's fertile Orontes River Valley.

Tell Qarqur is strategically situated at a crossroads between the ancient centers of Damascus and Hama in the south and Ebla and Aleppo in the north, and Mesopotamia in the east to Ugarit on the Mediterranean coast. Analysis of the faunal material should help reveal the extent to which animal products such as meat, milk, and wool, and muscle for transport and traction would have contributed to local and regional economies in ancient times. There resources are known to have served as assets in the payment of tributes or as a means of solidifying alliances in response to changing regional hegemonies.

FAUNAL SAMPLING AND ANALYTICAL PROCEDURES

Close to 90,000 animal bone fragments have been recovered from Tell Qarqur during six excavation seasons from 1993–1998. Analysis of the bone material follows Zeder's (1990) two-stage analytical system designed to maximize zooarchaeological data retrieval in the most efficient way. Conducted in the field, the first stage is quantitative and involves identifying, counting, and weighing all faunal specimens by species where possible, such as *Ovis aries* (Sheep), to a

Table 1. Stage 1 Analysis: Distribution of Faunal Specimens

Excavation Seasons	# Bones Analyzed	# Bones from Secure Priority Contexts
1993–1994	3,750	1,010
Iron IIA		724
Hellenistic		101
Byzantine		185
1995	10,196	178
Iron IIA		178
1996–1998	43,443	3,411
EB IV		1,755
Iron IIA		1,656
Total	**57,389**	**4,599**

less specific sub-family level such as caprinae (Sheep/Goat) to the least identifiable level of size and class such as Medium Sized Mammal. This process provides an overview of all faunal material recovered, documents the quantity of bone refuse coming from different sectors of the site, and insures that no unusual specimens are overlooked.

Stage 2 analysis is a qualitative study conducted on bone material from stratigraphically secure primary and secondary trash deposits and building collapse. Procedures involve detailed analysis of specimens distinguishable to the level of subfamily or better. Up to 30 attributes are recorded for each of these bones including species, element, side, weight, breakage, sex, age, pathologies, human and animal modifications, burning, and weathering. Measurements are taken following von den Dreisch (1976) and information about butchery marks recorded. Counts and weights of unidentifiable Large, Medium, and Small Sized Mammal elements are recorded by skeletal part (Head, Axial, and Limb) and incorporated into an overall body of data to provide a complete representation of specimens from controlled contexts.

Stage 1 analysis of the Tell Qarqur was initiated during the final two weeks of the 1994 excavation season. Due to the large quantity of backlogged material from the 1993 and 1994 seasons, an estimated 36,000 bones, it was decided that contrary to standard procedures bone from these two seasons would be inventoried and samples from stratigraphically secure loci would undergo the first stage of analysis. Standard procedures were resumed during subsequent seasons resulting in the stage 1 analysis of 57,389 bones from the 1993–1998 seasons. Of these, 4,599 specimens were recovered from stratigraphically secure, high priority contexts (Table 1). Soil matrices from these deposits were sieved through 1/4-inch hardware mesh.

OVERVIEW OF THE FAUNAL DATA BY PERIOD

Occupational debris from the Early Bronze to Late Arabic periods are represented at Tell Qarqur. Faunal remains from stratigraphically secure contexts have been recovered from the Early Bronze Age IVB, Iron Age IIA, Hellenistic, and Byzantine periods. Data summarized in Tables 2–4 reflect variations in types and numbers of animals from the Early Bronze Age to the Byzantine period. Figs. 215 and 220 reflect the types and percentages of animals recovered from the Early Bronze Age and Iron Age periods. Variations in the distribution and proportions of fauna reveal shifts in animal exploitation strategies within and between these periods. The number of identifiable faunal specimens from the Hellenistic and Byzantine periods are insufficient to warrant discussion (figs. 215 and 216).

The remains of domesticated sheep, goat, cattle, and pig are commonly recovered from Near Eastern tell sites. Sheep and goats in particular have traditionally served as the standard fare in most urban contexts and Tell Qarqur is no exception. However, there are notable differences in the percentages of these animals during the Early Bronze and Iron Age periods, which can be attributed to changes in sociopolitical circumstance and site function.

Major Contributors: Early Bronze Age IV

Zooarchaeological remains from stratified, priority Area A and E loci totaled 1,755. Among these, 438 specimens were identifiable, 432 of which represent dietary remains. Domesticated animals account for 78% of the identifiable food remains. Caprids (sheep, goat, and indistinguishable sheep/goat) represent the majority of all domesticates, followed by cattle and pig (fig. 217).

Among the 119 identifiable specimens recovered from Area A, 118 were dietary remains. Domesticated animals account for 69.5% of these. Caprids account for nearly three-quarters of all domesticated fauna and cattle, close to one-quarter. Pig bones make up a very small percentage of the domesticates. Among the ten distinguishable caprid elements, all were identified as sheep, signaling an emphasis on the consumption of mutton versus goat meat and possibly milk and/or wool production. Beef also served as a significant source of meat in this sector of the site.

Identifiable remains from Area E, Square E4, total 317 of which 314 represent dietary refuse. Domesticates account for 80% of all dietary remains. Caprid bones account for nearly all domesticated animals bone refuse recovered from this area and reflect a notable drop in the representation of cattle remains compared to Area A. Pigs bones remain scant in Area E and among the distinguishable caprid remains the ratio of sheep to goat was relatively even. These data suggests more restricted consumer access to sheep and goat meat with minimal consumption of beef and pork. Variations in the distribution of domesticates in Areas

Table. 2. Stage 1 Analysis: Number of Qarqur Fauna by Period and Type of Animal.

Period	Bos	Equid	Caprid	Pig	Canid	Deer	Rodent	Bird	Reptile	Fish	Crab	LMam	MMam	SMam	Unid	Total
EB IV	36	0	292	7	2	27	1	22	18	28	3	141	1153	9	16	1755
Iron IIA	184	15	466	104	6	7	0	35	5	41	5	441	1225	11	12	2557
Hellenistic	3	0	13	1	0	0	0	1	0	3	0	15	61	4	0	101
Byzantine	4	0	20	7	0	0	2	1	0	0	0	31	120	0	0	185
Total	227	15	791	119	8	34	3	59	23	72	8	628	2559	24	18	4598

Table 3. Distribution of Domesticated Animals by Period in Percentages Based on Number of Bones.

Period	Caprid	Bos	Pig	Total Number
EB IV	87	11	2	335
Iron IIA	62	24	14	753
Hellenistic	76	18	6	17
Byzantine	64.5	13	22.5	31

A and E are reflected in fig. 218. A larger sample size is needed to confirm differences in the consumption of sheep, goats, and cattle between these two areas, particularly from Area A.

Minor Contributors

The identification and relative proportions of nonstandard food animals such as deer, bird, turtle, fish, and crab can reveal important information about animal exploitation and ecology over time. Elevated proportions of these fauna may reflect efforts of consumers to supplement urban provisioning systems, or may reflect hunting activities conducted by the elite, and can highlight differences in status among site occupants. The percentage of nonstandard food animals including deer, bird, turtle, fish, and crab account for a significant 22% of all Early Bronze Age fauna. As with the domesticates, variations exist between the proportions of minor contributors in Areas A and E.

A considerable 30.5% of the all identifiable specimens from Area A were nonstandard fauna. Turtle and fish represent the majority of these specimens, followed by bird, deer, and crab.

Within Area E, the number of minor contributors remains significant but drops to 20% of all identifiable specimens. Figure 219 reflects the proportions of these animals by Area. In Area E the most predominate specimens are deer, bird, and fish followed by turtle and crab.

The majority of specimens in Area E were deer elements; however, the elevated number of specimens in Area E inaccurately reflect the relative proportion of meat provided by these animals. The majority of Area E deer elements were antler fragments. Recovery of antler fragments within archaeological contexts can not always be attributed to hunting activities and may instead reflect the procurement of shed antlers. The only way to confirm that antlers were directly procured as a result of hunting is if they are recovered still attached to the skull. Though less well-represented, postcranial deer bone fragments were recovered from Area E and confirm that a portion of the deer elements from this area do reflect food refuse from hunted animals.

Variations in the proportions on nonstandard animals between Areas A and E highlight the differences in the procurement of minor contributors between these two sectors of the site. However, a larger sample size is required to reliably assess intrasite variations in the procurement of these resources.

Major Contributors: Iron Age IIA

Zooarchaeological remains from controlled, priority contexts in Areas A, B. and D total 2,558 of which 869 bones (34%) were identified (fig. 220). Of these, 848 represent dietary refuse. Domesticated animal remains account for 86% of all Iron Age food debris. Among these, sheep and goat

Table 4. Distribution of Nonstandard Animals by Period in Percentages Based on Number of Bones.

Period	Dear	Boar	Bird	Reptile	Fish	Crab	Total Number
EB IV	28	0	23	17	29	3	97
Iron IIA	8	1	37	5	44	5	94
Hellenistic	0	0	25	0	75	0	4
Byzantine	0	0	100	0	0	0	1

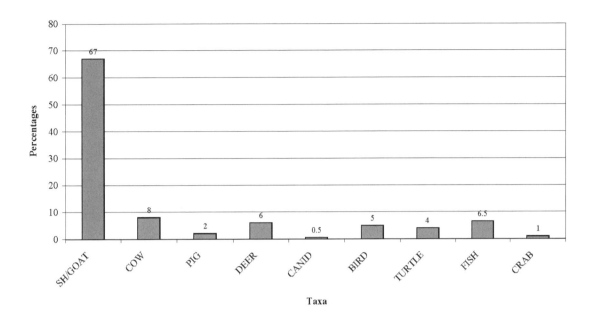

Total number of specimens = 434

Fig. 214. Tell Qarqur Early Bronze Age Identifiable Fauna.

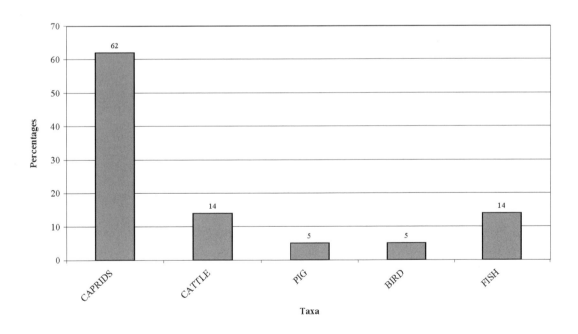

Total number of specimens = 21

Fig. 215. Tell Qarqur Hellenistic Period Identifiable Fauna.

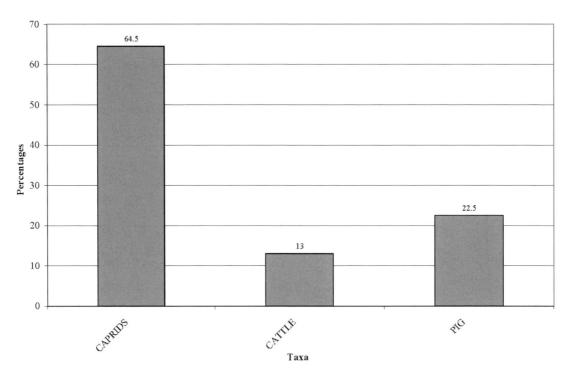

Total number of specimens = 31

Fig. 216. Tell Qarqur Byzantine Period Identifiable Fauna.

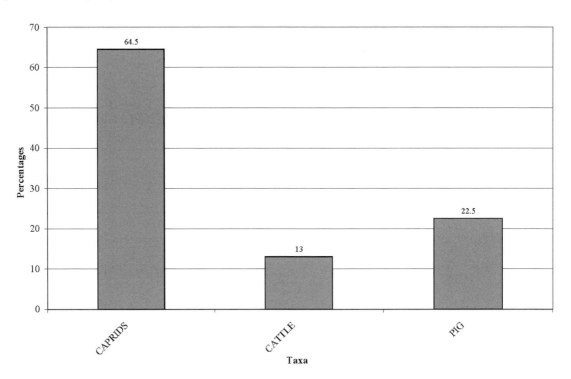

Total number of specimens = 31

Fig. 217. Tell Qarqur Early Bronze Age Domesticated Fauna.

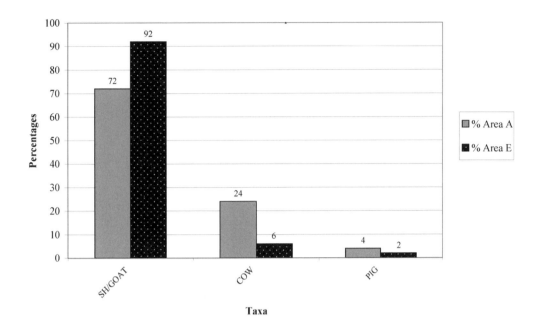

Number of specimens from Area A = 82
Number of specimens from Area E = 253

Fig. 218. Tell Qarqur Early Bronze Age Identifiable Fauna from Areas A and E.

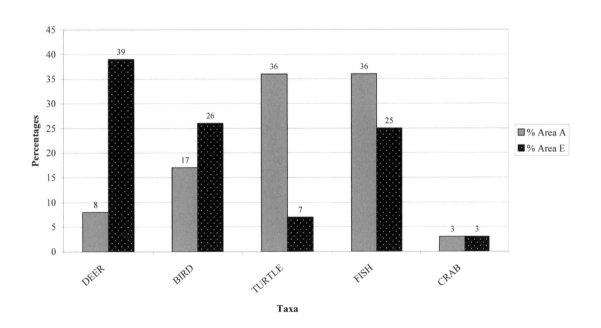

Number of specimens in Area A = 36
Number of specimens in Area E = 61

Fig. 219. Tell Qarqur Early Bronze Age Nonstandard Fauna from Areas A and E.

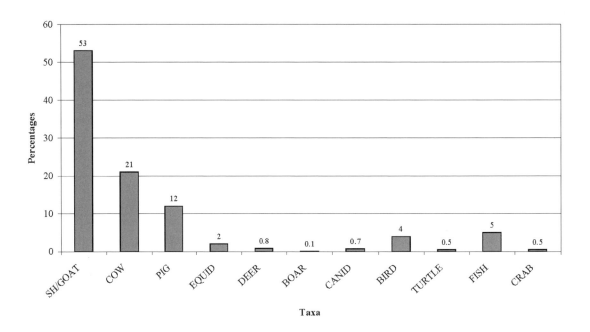

Total number of specimens = 869

Fig. 220. Tell Qarqur Iron Age Identifiable Fauna.

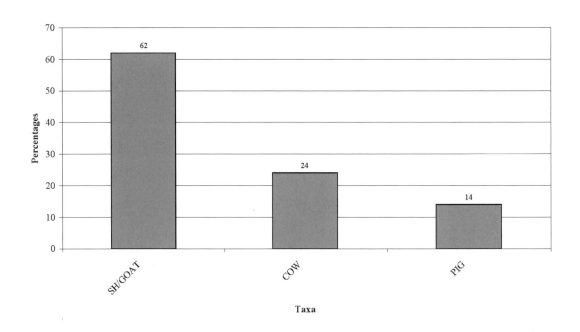

Number of specimens = 753

Fig. 221. Tell Qarqur Iron Age Domesticated Fauna.

remain the predominate meat resource, though cattle and pigs play an increasingly important role during the Iron IIA period (fig. 221). Together, cattle and pig remains account for 38% of all domesticates represented and reflect a major reliance on these animals for food, and in the case of cattle/cow, possibly for milk or for traction in agricultural pursuits. The presence of equid (*Equus. sp.*) and canid (*Canidae*) remains suggest that horses, mules, or donkeys, and dogs were also kept during the Iron IIA period.

Specimens recovered from various squares in Area A totaled 316. Of these 63 (20%) were identifiable, including 62 fragments of food refuse. Domesticated animal stock account for 83% of these specimens, nearly two-thirds of which were caprids, followed by cattle and to a lesser extent pig.

Bone samples from Area B, Square B2, produced 1,657 specimens. Among these, 634 (38%) were identifiable, 617 of which represent food debris. Domesticates account for an overwhelming 93% of the identifiable food refuse. The proportions of caprid, cattle, and pig remains mirror those recovered from Area A. Sheep bones outnumber those of goats by a ratio of 2.5:1.

Area D bone specimens were recovered from Squares D6 and D7 and totaled 583. Identifiable specimens accounted for 172 (30%) of these, 169 of which represent food remains. Sheep, goat, cattle, and pigs remain the major contributor with caprids accounting for just over 76% of all specimens from this Area. Although caprids were predominant, cattle and pig bones account for 39%, nearly half, of all domesticated animal resources recovered. Three equid fragments were also recovered from this area.

Figure 222 reflects the similarity in the proportions of major contributors recovered from these different sectors of the site. It also illustrates the important role cattle and pigs played during this period especially when compared to the Early Bronze Age fauna (fig. 223).

Minor Contributors

While the proportions of major contributors remain constant across the site, the ratio of domesticates to nonstandard fauna vary considerably. Overall, specimens including deer, wild boar, bird,

turtle, fish, and crab account for 14% of the Iron IIA period dietary refuse. By area the percentages of nonstandard contributors range from 17% in Area A, to 7% in Area B. to 24% in Area D. The types of animals also vary by area (fig. 224). Area A reflects comparable proportions of deer, bird, turtle, fish and crab elements. Birds account for the majority of specimens in Area B followed by fish and to a much lesser extent by deer, wild boar, turtle, and crab elements. Within area D fish remains are predominant, followed by bird, deer, and crab. These data are intriguing yet larger samples are required for each area before these patterns can be substantiated.

Interpretation of Early Bronze Age IV Faunal Materials

The 1997 and 1998 excavation seasons produced the first secure, stratified Early Bronze period faunal samples, making this is the first summary of fauna from this period. Although only 432 identifiable dietary specimens have been recovered from controlled priority contexts, a distinct pattern of meat consumption has begun to emerge. Overall, a high proportion of the dietary remains can be attributed to domesticated animals ranging from 69.5% in Area A, to 80% in Area E. Caprids accounted for 72% of all domesticates in Area A, and 92% of all domesticates in Area E, suggesting that consumption of caprids was more highly focused in Area E, while cattle played a more important dietary role within Area A. Nonstandard food animals account for 29.5% of all identifiable specimens recovered from Area A and 20% from Area E.

Data from Area A indicate greater access to beef and exploitation of nonstandard culinary fare in this sector of the site and may be attributed to elevated socioeconomic or political status. The fauna also reflect the ability of the region to sustain cattle which require more water and richer pasturage than goats, the availability of riverine fauna, and access to deer in the adjacent coastal Jebel Ansariyah range. The presence of additional species of wild fauna identified from mixed strata during Phase I analysis indicates that Tell Qarqur's inhabitants had access to an even broader range of animals. Included among identifiable Area A fauna recovered from unreliable contexts were hedgehog, mustelid (a small weasel-like animal) wild boar, elk, gazelle, ibex, fox, wolf, and bear remains.

In Area E, caprids account for nearly all domesticated fauna recovered. Beef consumption drops considerably and pigs fall to 2% of all domesticates represented. The restricted focus on caprids would indicate employment of a standardized provisioning system. However, the variability in the age of the caprid specimens suggests that an alternative culling strategy may have been employed. Many of the sheep/goat bones from this area of the site belonged to young animals. The relative age of these animals ranges from over three years to under three months. A minimum of nine to twelve animals were aged under ten months, eight of which were under twelve weeks old. The specimens fall both within and outside of the age range expected of a meat-based husbandry strategy whereby animals are culled at twelve to eighteen months, the point at which they reach their maximum growth levels for fodder and care invested (Reading 1981).

The broad range of ages represented by these specimens suggests employment of herding strategies other than meat maximization for urban provisioning. Efforts focused on maximizing herd security for example would result in the culling of a good portion of males aged six to twenty-four months, approximately sixty percent, and females of various ages including young animals and older less productive ewes (Reading 1981). It is also possible that the data reflect herding strategies, which favored milk or wool production.

The very young animals under ten months, many twelve weeks or less at the time of death, may represent sacrificial animals or the remains of tender young animals. Clarification of the function of this portion of the site and closer examination of the age and sex ratios during stage 2 analysis of the Area E material will help clarify the nature of animal production, distribution, and consumption.

Domesticated animal bone refuse from controlled loci in the lowest levels of Square E4 from the 1998 season revealed some other interesting features. A good portion of the bone fragments from a locus of mudbrick and plaster collapse was stained green. Destruction debris in the same area consisted of burned mudbrick collapse, plaster, carbonized material, slag, and numerous objects including an incense burner, spouted lamps, bronze artifacts and green bone. The majority of discolored bones were found amidst the unburned brick and plaster collapse. Burned, carbonized, and calcined bone were recovered from the destruction debris along with a less sizeable amount of green bone.

Green discoloration results from two post-depositional processes that act on bone and other artifacts. Greenish-blue staining occurs when bones come into contact with corroded copper alloys. Corrosion products generated by deteriorating metal alloys such as bronze can migrate and stain associated organic materials (Sease 1994), and can thoroughly penetrate the bone when sufficient moisture is introduced. Greenish-yellow staining occurs when bones come in contact with algae bloom associated with sewage waste.

The majority of affected bone was recorded only as green, though a small number of bones recovered from the destruction debris were noted as yellowish green. Preliminary data indicate the discoloration resulted from contact with sewage waste however, it is unclear whether bronze artifacts recovered among the destruction debris may have produced sufficient corrosive products to affect the bone. Bits of slag and fragments of course, footed vessels with pouring spouts were also found among the burned debris and may have been associated with manufacturing activities. If smelting had occurred on-site it may help explain the presence of the green-stained bones. Simple tests to be performed during the Phase II analysis will help clarify whether corrosive metals affected the bone. When held to the blue flame of a hand torch a sample fragment of green bone will flare green if copper chloride is present.

The relative proportion of nonstandard animals in Area E was quite elevated, though not as high as in Area A (fig. 219). It should be noted that the remains of deer, elk, gazelle, ibex, and bear were recovered from mixed strata in this area. The vari-

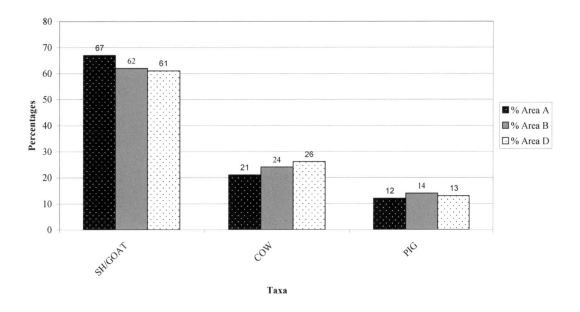

Represents 768 specimens

Fig. 222 Tell Qarqur Iron Age Domesticated Fauna by Area.

ety of nonstandard species represented would indicate procurement of supplemental game resources.

Interpretation of Iron Age IIA Faunal Materials

The types and proportions of domesticated and nonstandard fauna reported in the preliminary summary of Tell Qarqur Iron Age fauna from the 1993, 1994, and 1995 seasons (Arter 1994; 1996) are consistent with those from the 1996, 1997, and 1998 seasons. Domesticated animals account for 78% of the cumulative identifiable fauna. Among these, the relative proportions of caprid, cattle, and pig bones are nearly the same in Areas A, B. and D as shown in fig. 222. Compared to the Early Bronze Age data, cattle and pigs play a much more prominent dietary role during the Iron Age period, accounting for 38% of the domesticated fauna site-wide and from 33% to 39% by area.

Among the most prominent features in Area B were large trash pits. The overwhelming proportion of domesticates from Area B reflect a pattern of consumption to be expected from a residential sector of the site where inhabitants receive meat products in exchange for services. If so, the residents of this area of Tell Qarqur were consuming considerable quantities of beef and pork. The elevated quantities of beef refuse point to a higher standard of living among these inhabitants as cows would tend to be valued more highly for their ability to produce large quantities of milk and for traction in agricultural pursuits than for meat. On the other hand, the elevated number of beef bones indicate that Qarqur's inhabitants probably kept large numbers of these animals, making beef more readily available for consumption.

The consistency with which pigs occur across the site suggests that residents may have raised these animals independently as meat source to supplement the local provisioning system. Pig

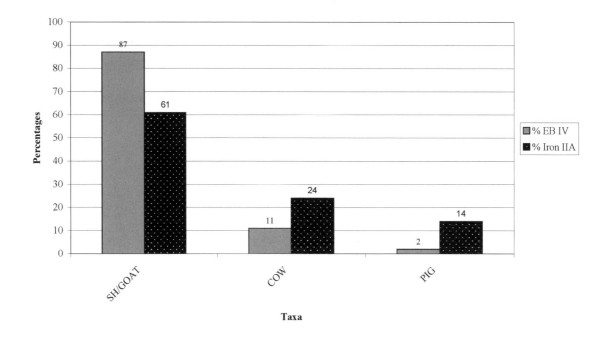

Total number of EB IV specimens = 335
Total number of Iron IIA specimens = 768

Fig. 223. Tell Qarqur Early Bronze Age and Iron Age Domesticated Fauna.

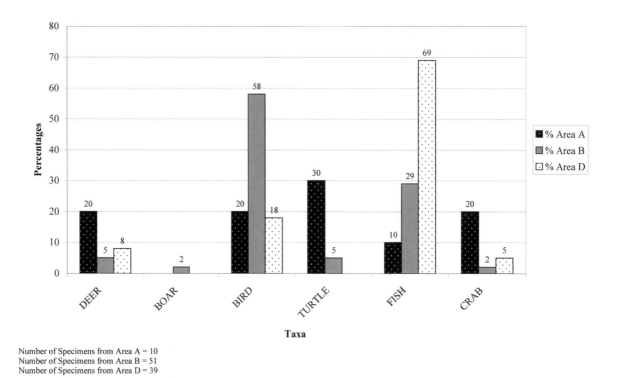

Number of Specimens from Area A = 10
Number of Specimens from Area B = 51
Number of Specimens from Area D = 39

Fig. 224. Tell Qarqur Iron Age Period Nonstandard Fauna from Areas A, B and D.

husbandry in urban archaeological settings has been associated with efforts of independent urban households to supplement urban provisioning systems by raising these prolific meat producers (Zeder 1991). Pigs require minimal space, are easily raised on household refuse, produce significant amounts of meat in a relatively short period of time, and serve as an effective hedge in times of economic downturn. Pigs are consistently represented in all areas of the site.

The exploitation of nonstandard food resources declines to 14% during the Iron IIA period. When examined by area the variety of species remains high, the proportions vary from 17% in Area A to 7% in Area B to 24% in Area D (fig. 224). Bird and fish remains account for majority of game animals represented in Areas B and D indicating a narrow focus on the exploitation of these animals. The exploitation of nonstandard species appears greater in Area A though the sample size is too small to confirm this.

Additional nonstandard specimens were recovered from Area B, but they were unassignable to period. They included the remains of domestic cat, hedgehog, mustelid, wild boar, deer, elk, gazelle, ibex, fox, wolf, and bear. A small fragment of elephant tusk was also recovered from this area. The remains of deer, elk, ibex, and possibly wolf were also recovered from mixed strata in Area D.

CONCLUSIONS BASED ON PALEOZOOLOGICAL ANALYSIS

Faunal remains collected to date indicate that sheep and goats provided the majority of meat consumed by the inhabitants of Tell Qarqur during the Early Bronze Age with an emphasis on the consumption and use of sheep versus goat. Beef (with the exception of Area A) and pork account for a very small percentage of all domesticates recovered from this period.

Based on variations in the proportions of fauna represented in Areas A and E during the Early Bronze Age, it appears that the inhabitants may have had differential access to resources in the two sectors of the site that have been explored. Compared to Area A, there appears to have been limited access to domesticated animal resources in

Area E. The reliance on domesticated sheep and goat with minimal consumption of beef and pork indicates restricted consumer access to available meat products and may indicate regulated control over the distribution of animal resources during this period.

The combined proportion of nonstandard food animals from all Early Bronze Age contexts exceed those of beef and pork remains indicating that supplemental terrestrial and riverine fauna were important and well utilized food resources. A larger sample size is required to reliably assess intrasite variability among nonstandard animals, though preliminary indications suggest some notable shifts in the utilization of these animals between Areas A and E.

A picture of animal-based consumption and economic strategies employed at Tell Qarqur during the Early Bronze Age has begun to emerge. Confirmation of these data must be sought through the recovery of additional bone samples and implementation of stage 2 analytical procedures. More detailed information from a larger corpus of bone will further clarify subsistence strategies and consumption patterns as they relate to the nature and function of the Early Bronze Age.

Dietary refuse from Iron Age deposits reflect more standardized distribution of and access to meat-based food resources with similar proportions of domesticates represented in all three excavations areas. Contrary to the Early Bronze Age fauna, cattle and pigs account for a major portion of all identifiable domesticates signaling a major reliance on these animals for food and in the case of cattle possibly for milk or for traction in agricultural pursuits. Bird and fish are the predominant game animals though overall the number of wild fauna declines in this period.

Increased samples sizes from well provenienced faunal material will confirm emerging patterns of animal utilization at Tell Qarqur. Systematic collection of age and sex data, body part distributions, and butchering information during stage 2 analysis will clarify the nature of animal husbandry strategies, provisioning, procurement, and consumption both within periods and over time at ancient Qarqur.

REFERENCES

Abel, F. M., and Barrois, A.
1928   Fouilles de l'École archéologique française de Jérusalem, effectuées à Neirab du 4 Septembre au 6 Novembre, 1927. *Syria* 9: 187–206, 303–19.

Abou Assaf, A. et al.
1982   *La statue de Tell Fekherye et son inscription bilingue assyro-araméénne.* Paris: Editions Recherche sur les Civilisations.

Adachi, T.
1997   The Fine Carinated Bowl in the Iron Age. *Bulletin of the Ancient Orient Museum* 8: 41–55.

Anderson, W. R
1988   *Sarepta.* Vol. 1: *The Late Bronze and Iron Age of Area II, Y.* Beirut: Librairie Orientaliste.
1990   The Beginnings of Phoenician Pottery: Shape, Style, and Ceramic Technology Early Phases of the Phoenician Iron Age. *Bulletin of the American Schools of Oriental Research* 279: 35–54.

Amiran, R.
1970   *Ancient Pottery of the Holy Land.* New Brunswick: Rutgers University.

Algaze, G. (ed.)
1990   *Town and Country in Southeastern Anatolia. Vol. 2. The Stratigraphic Sequence at Kurban Höyük.* Oriental Institute Publications 10. Chicago, IL: The Oriental Institute of the University of Chicago.

Algaze, G.; Ataman, K.; Ingraham, M.; Marfoe, L.; McDonald, M.; Miller, N.; Snow, C.; Stein, G.; Verharen, B.; Wattenmaker, P.; Wilkinson, T. and Yener, A.
1986   The Chicago Euphrates Archaeological Project 1980–1984: An Interim Report. *Anatolica* 3: 35–148.

Arns, R.; Becker, A.; Kohlmeyer, K.; Ludwig, W.; Schneiders, E.; Selz, G. and Strommenger, E.
1984   Ausgrabungen in Tall Bi'a 1982 and 1983. *Mitteilungen der Deutschen Orient-Gesellschaft* 16: 15–63.

Badre, L.
1980   *Les figurines anthropomorphes en terre cuite à l'âge du bronze en Syrie.* Institut Français d'archéologie du Proche-Orient.

Bibliothèque archéologique et historique 103. Paris: Paul Geuthner.
1982   Les figurines de terre cuite. Pp. 99–107 in *Meskene–Emar: dix ans de travaux 1972–1982.* Paris: Mission archéologique de Meskene - Emar. Editions Recherche sur les Civilisations.
1983   Les peuples de la mer à Ibn Hani. Pp. 203-9 in *Atti del I Congresso Internazionale di Studi Fenici e Punici,* Roma.

Badre, L.; Gubel, E.; Al-Maqdissi, M. and Sader, H.
1990   Tell Kazel, Syria: Excavations of the AUB Museum 1985–1987. *Berytus* 38: 9–124.

Balty, J. C.
1981   *Guide d'Apamée.* Brussels: Musées royaux d'art et d'histoire.

Ben-Tor, A. and Ben-Ami, D.
1998   Hazor and the Archaeology of the Tenth Century B.C.E. *Israel Exploration Journal* 48(1–2): 1–37.

Bikai, R. M.
1978   *The Pottery of Tyre.* Warminster: A Phillips.
1987   *The Phoenician Pottery of Cyprus.* Nicosia: Levantis Foundation.

Birmingham, J.
1963   The Chronology of Some Early and Middle Iron Age Cypriot Sites. *American Journal of Archaeology* 67: 15–42.

Blank, Sharon
1999   Personal Communication. Sharon Blank is a multiple objects conservator in private practice.

Boardman, J.
1959   Greek Potters at Al Mina? *Anatolian Studies* 9: 63–69.
1980   *The Greeks Overseas.* 3rd ed. New York: Thames and Hudson.

Bokonyi, S.
1973   The Fauna from Umm Dabaghiya: A Preliminary Report. *Iraq* 35: 9–11.

Bounni, A.; Lagarce, J. and E.; Saliby, N.; and Badre, L.
1979   Rapport Preliminaire sur la troisième campagne de fouilles (1977) à Ibn Hani (Syrie). *Syria* 56: 217–94.

Bounni, A. and Matthiae, P.
1974   Tell Fray 1973. Pp. 33–41 in *Antiquités de l'Euphrate,* ed. A. Bounni. Aleppo: Directorate General of Antiquities and Museums of Syria.

Braëmer, F.
1986 La céramique à engobe rouge de l'âge du fer à Bassit. *Syria* 63: 221–46.

Braidwood, R. J. and Braidwood, L.
1960 *Excavations in the Plain of Antioch.* Vol. 1. Oriental Institute Publications 61. Chicago, IL: The Oriental Institute of the University of Chicago.

Bridel, P.; Krause, C.; Spycher, H.; Stucky, R.; Suter, P. and Zellweger, S.
1974 *Tell El Hajj in Syrien. Zweiter vorläufiger Bericht Grabungskampagne 1972.* Bern: Archaologischen Seminar der Universitat Bern.

Buchanan, B.
1966 *Catalogue of Ancient Near Eastern Seals in the Ashmolean Museum.* Vol. 1. *Cylinder Seals.* Oxford: Clarendon.

Buhl, M. -L.
1987 Hamath. *The Anchor Bible Dictionary* 3: 33–36.

Bunnens, G., ed.
2000a *Essays on Syria in the Iron Age.* Ancient Near Eastern Studies, Supplement 7. Peeters: Sterling, VA.
2000b Syria in the Iron Age: Problems of Definition. Pp. 3–19 in *Essays on Syria in the Iron Age,* ed. G. Bunnens. Ancient Near Eastern Studies, Supplement 7. Peeters: Sterling, VA.

Chapman, S. V.
1972 A Catalogue of Iron Age Pottery from Cemeteries of Khirbet Silm, Joya, Qraye Qasmieh of South Lebanon. *Berytus* 21: 55–194.

Clason, A.T.
1979 The Animal Remains from Tell es-Sin Compared with Those from Bouqras. *Anatolica* 7: 35–48.

Coldstream, J. N.
1968 *Greek Geometric Pottery.* London: Methuen.
1979 Geometric Skyphoi in Cyprus. *Report of the Department of Antiquities, Cyprus* 1979: 255–69.

Collon, D.
1975 The Seal Impressions from Tell Atchana/Alalakh. *Alter Orient und Altes Testament* 27. Neukirchen-Vluyn: Neukirchener.
1981 The Aleppo Workshop. *Ugarit-Forschungen* 3: 33–40.
1990 *Catalogue of Western Asiatic Seals in the British Museum, Cylinder Seals II: Akkadian – post Akkadian – Ur III Periods.* London: British Museum.

Collon, D.; Otte, M. and Zaqzuq, A.
1975 Sondages au Flanc Sud du Tell de Qal'at El Mudiq. *Fouilles d'Apamée de Syrie.* Miscellanea. Fasc. 1. Brussels: Centre Belge de recherches archéologiques à Apamée de Syrie.

Collon, D. and Zaqzuq, A.
1972 Ceramique des carrés A1 et B1 ouverts au flanc du tell en 1970 et 1971. Pp. 65–78 in *Apamée de Syrie,* eds. J. and J. C. Balty. Fouilles d'Apamée de Syrie. Miscellanea. Fasc. 7. Brussels: Centre Belge de recherches archéologiques a Apamée de Syrie.

Courtois, J.-C.
1962 Sondages 1959: Contribution à L'étude des civilisations du Bronze Ancien à Ras Shamra - Ugarit. Pp. 415–75 in *Ugaritica,* vol. 4, ed. by C. F. A. Schaeffer. Paris: Librairie Orientaliste Paul Geuthner.
1973 Prospection archéologique dans le moyenne vallée de l'Oronte. *Syria* 50: 53–99.

Crowfoot, J. W.; Crowfoot, G. M. and Kenyon, K. M.
1957 *Samaria-Sebeste.* Vol. 3. *The Objects from Samaria.* London: Palestine Exploration Fund.

Culican, W.
1982 The Repertoire of Phoenician Pottery. Pp. 45–82 in *Phönizier im Westen: Die Beiträge des Internationalen Symposium über "Die phönizische Expansion im westlichen Mittelmeer raum" in Köln vom 24. Bis 27. April 1979,* ed H. G. Niemeyer. Madrider Beiträge 8. Mainz: von Zabern.

Desborough, V. R. d'A.
1952 *Protogeometric Pottery.* Oxford: Clarendon.

Dornemann, R. H.
1978 Tell Hadidi: A Bronze Age City on the Euphrates. *Archaeology* 31/6: 20–26.
1979 Tell Hadidi: A Millennium of Bronze City Occupation. Pp. 13–51 in *Excavation Reports from the Tabqa Dam Project-Euphrates Syria,* ed. D.N. Freedman. Annual ofthe American Schools of Oriental Research 44.
1980 *The Archaeology of the Transjordan in the Bronze and Iron Ages.* Milwaukee: Milwaukee Public Museum.
1981 The Late Bronze Age Pottery Tradition at

Tell Hadidi, Syria, *Bulletin of the American Schools of Oriental Research* 241: 29–47, 49.

1981/82   Tall Hadidi. Pp. 219–23 in *Ausgrabungstatigkeit in Syrien*, ed. H. Kühne. *Archiv für Orientforshung* 28.

1984   The Syrian Euphrates as a Bronze Age Cultural Unit Seen from the Point of View of Mari and Tell Hadidi. *Annales Archéologiques Arabes Syriennes* 34.

1985   Salvage Excavations at Tell Hadidi in the Euphrates River Valley. *Biblical Archaeologist* 48: 49–59.

1987   Early Second Millennium Ceramic Parallels Between Tell Hadidi-Azu and Mari. Pp. 77–112 in *Mari at 50: Studies in Honor of the 50th Anniversary of the Discovery of Tell Hariri-Mari*, ed. G.W. Young. Winona Lake, IN: Eisenbrauns.

1988   Tell Hadidi: One Bronze Age Site Among Many in the Tabqa Dam Salvage Area *Bulletin of the American Schools of Oriental Research* 270: 3–42.

1989   Comments on Small Finds and Items of Artistic Significance from Tell Hadidi and Nearby Sites in the Euphrates Valley, Syria. Pp. 59–75 in *Essays in Ancient Civilization Presented to Helene J. Kantor*, ed. A. Leonard, Jr. and B. B. Williams. Studies in Ancient Oriental Civilization 47. Chicago: The Oriental Institute of the University of Chicago.

1990   The Beginning of the Bronze Age in Syria. Pp. 85–100 in *Resurrecting the Past*, eds. P. Matthiae, M. van Loon and H. Weiss. Istanbul: Nederlands Historisch-Archaeologisch Instituut.

1993   Tell Qarqur. *American Schools of Oriental Research Newsletter* 43(3): 5–6.

1994   Report on Tell Qarqur - Proposal to Form consortium. *American Schools of Oriental Research Newsletter* 44(3): 9.

1995   Tell Qarqur. *American Schools of Oriental Research Newsletter* 45 (4): 5.

1996a   Tell Qarqur Update. *American Schools of Oriental Research Newsletter* 46(1): 9–10.

1996b   ASOR Excavations at Tell Qarqur. (6 pp. and 4 illustrations) in ASOR Digs Reports of Affiliated Projects, edited by Paul F. Jacobs, http://www.cobb.msstate.edu/asordigs/qarqur.html

1996c   Amuq. Hama. Til Barsib. Tell Halaf. and Tell Qarqur. Encyclopedia articles in *The Oxford Encyclopedia of Near Eastern Archaeology*, Oxford: New York.

1997   Tell Qarqur. *American Journal of Archaeology* 101: 135.

1998a   Tell Qarqur 1996. *Chronique Archéologique en Syrie* 2: 81–87.

1998b   Tell Qarqur 1997. *Chronique Archéologique en Syrie* 2: 153–59.

1999   Comparisons in the Bronze and Iron Age Inventories Between Orontes Valley Sites, Ugarit and Ebla, from the Point of View of Tell Qarqur. Pp. 37–148 in *Proceedings of the International Colloquium: Aleppo and the Silk Road, Aleppo, Syria, 1994. Annales Archéologiques Arabes Syriennes* 43. Damascus: Direction Générale des Antiquités et des Musées République Arabe Syrienne.

2000   Iron Age Remains at Tell Qarqur in the Orontes Valley. Pp. 459–92 in *Essays on Syria in the Iron Age,* ed. G. Bunnens. Ancient Near Eastern Studies, Supplement 7. Peeters: Sterling, VA.

in press a Renewed Excavations at Tell Qarqur, Syria, the 1993 Season. (8 pp. and 6 illustrations) in *Annales Archélogiques Arabes Syriennes.*

in press b 1994 Excavations at Tell Qarqur, Syria. (8 pp. and 6 illustrations) in *Annales Archélogiques Arabes Syriennes.*

in press c Report on the 1995 Season of Excavations at Tell Qarqur. (16 pp. and 7 illustrations) in *Annales Archélogiques Arabes Syriennes.*

in press d 1996 Excavations at Tell Qarqur, Syria. (8 pp. and 6 illustrations) in *Annales Archéologiques Arabes Syriennes.*

in press e 1997 Excavations at Tell Qarqur, Syria. (8 pp. and 6 illustrations) in *Annales Archélogiques Arabes Syriennes.*

in press f The 1998 Season of Excavations at Tell Qarqur in the Orontes Valley. (15 pp. and 8 illustrations) in *Annales Archéologiques Arabes Syriennes.*

in press g The 1999 Season of Excavations at Tell Qarqur. (5 pp. and 10 illustrations) for *Chronique Archéologique en Syrie.*

in press h The 1999 Season of Excavations at Tell Qarqur. (8 pp. 24 illustrations) for *Annales Archéologiques Arabes Syriennes.*

in press i Early Bronze Age IVB Materials from Tell Qarqur in the Orontes Valley. (20 pp. and 39 illustrations) in Proceedings of the In-

ternational Colloquium: La Syrie moyenne
de la Mer à la Steppe 1999, for *Annales
Archéologiques Arabes Syriennes.*

Dothan, M. and Freedman, D. N..
1967   *Ashdod.* Vol. 1: *The First Season of Exca-
        vations, 1962.* 'Atiqot, 7. Jerusalem.
1971   *Ashdod.* Vol. 2–3: *The Second and Third
        Season of Excavations, 1963, 1965.* 'Atiqot,
        9–10. Jerusalem.

Dothan, M. and Porath, Y.
1982   *Ashdod* Vol. 4: *Excavation of Area M.*
        'Atiqot, 15. Jerusalem.

Dothan, M. and Porath, Y.
1993   *Ashdod.* Vol. 5: *Excavation of Area G. the
        Fourth-sixth Seasons of Excavations.*
        'Atiqot, 23. Jerusalem.

Dothan, Trude, and Moshe Dothan.
1992   *People of the Sea: The Search for the Phi-
        listines.* New York.

du Mesnil de Buisson
1936   *Le site archéologique de Mishrifé-Qatna*
        Paris: Boccard.

Egami, N.
1988   *Tell Mastuma.* Tokyo: Ancient Orient Mu-
        seum.

Egami, N.; Watika, S.; and Gotoh. T.
1984   Tell Mastuma. *Bulletin of the Ancient Ori-
        ent Museum, Tokyo* 6: 106–26.

Eph'al, I.
1984   *The Ancient Arabs. Nomads on the Border
        of the Fertile Crescent 9th–5th Centuries
        B.C.* 2nd rev. reprint. Jerusalem: Magnes.

Fielden, K.
1981   A Late Uruk Pottery Group from Tell Braq,
        1978. *Iraq* 43: 57–66.

Forrer, E. O.
1920   *Die Provinzeinteilung des assyrischen
        Reiches.* Leipzig: Hinrichs.

Friedrich, J.; Meyer, G. R.; Ungnad, A.; and Weidner,
E. F.
1940   *Die Inschriften vom Tell Halaf.* Archiv für
        Orientforschung, Beiheft 6. Berlin: Im
        selbstverlage des herausgebers.

Fugmann, E.
1958   *Hama, Fouilles et Recherches de la Foun-
        dation Carlsberg 1931–1938.* Vol.2:1.
        *L'architecture des periodes pre-
        Hellenistiques II.1.* Copenhagen: National
        Museum.

Gasch, H.; Armstrong, J. A.; Cole, S. W. and
Gurzadyan, V. G.
1998   *Dating the Fall of Babylon: A Reappraisal

of Second Millennium Chronology.*
Mesopotamian History and Environment 2,
Memoirs 4. Ghent and Chicago: University
of Ghent and University of Chicago.

Gilboa, A.
1995   The Typology and Chronology of the Iron
        Age Pottery and the Chronology of Iron Age
        Assemblages. Pp. 1-49 in *Excavations at
        Dor, Final Report.* Vol. B. *Areas A and C.-
        The Finds.* ed. E. Stern. Qedem Reports 2.
        Jerusalem: Institute of Archaeology, He-
        brew University of Jerusalem.

Gitin, S.
1998   Philistia in Transition: The Tenth Century
        BCE and Beyond. Pp. 62–83 in *Mediterra-
        nean Peoples in Transition. Thirteenth to
        Early Tenth Centuries BCE, in Honor of
        Trude Dothan,* eds. S. Gitin, A. Mazar, and
        E. Stern. Jerusalem: Israel Exploration So-
        ciety.

Gjerstad, E.
1948   *The Swedish Cyprus Expedition,* Vol. 4: 2:
        *The Cypro-Geometric, Cypro-Archaic
        Cypro-Classical Periods.* Stockholm:
        Swedish Cyprus Expedition.

Goldman, H.
1963   *Excavations at Gözlü Küle, Tarsus.* Vol. 3.
        The Iron Age. Princeton: Princeton Univer-
        sity.

Haines, R. C.
1971   *Excavations in the Plain of Antioch.* Vol. 2:
        The Structural Remains of the Later Phases.
        Oriental Institute Publications 95. Chicago:
        University of Chicago.

Hamilton, R. W.
1966   A Silver Bowl in the Ashmolean Museum.
        Iraq 28: 1-17.

Hanfmann, E.
1963   The Iron Age Pottery of Tarsus. Pp. 18–332
        in *Excavations at Gözlü Küle, Tarsus.* Vol
        3: *The Iron Age,* ed. H. Goldman. 2 vols.
        Princeton: Princeton University.

Hansen, D. P.
1965   Relative Chronology of Mesopotamia. Part
        II. The Pottery Sequence at Nippur from the
        Middle Uruk to the end of the Old
        Babylonian Period (3400–1600 B.C.). Pp.
        201–13 in *Chronologies in Old World Ar-
        chaeology,* ed. R. W. Ehrich. Chicago, IL:
        University of Chicago.

Hawkins, J. D.
1972   Hamath. Pp. 67–70 in *Reallexikon de*

Assyriologie und Vorderasiatischen Archäologie, Vol. 4, eds. E. Ebeling and B. Meissner. New York: de Gruyter.

1982 The Neo-Hittite States in Syria and Anatolia. Pp. 372-441 in *The Cambridge Ancient History,* Vol. 3, Part 1, eds. J. Boardman, I. E. S. Edwards, N. G. L. Hammond, and E. Solberger. 2nd ed. Cambridge: Cambridge University.

Helck, W.

1962 *Die Beziehungen Ägyptens zu Vorderasien in 3. und 2. Jahrtausend V. Chr.* Ägyptologische Abhandlungen 5. Wiesbaden: Otto Harrassowitz.

Hesse, B.;

1978 Evidence for Husbandry from the Early Neolithic of Ganj Dareh in Western Iran. Unpublished Ph.D. Dissertation, Anthropology Department, Columbia University.

Holladay, J. S. Jr.

1990 Red Slip, Burnish, and the Solomonic Gateway at Gezer. *Bulletin of the American Schools of Oriental Research* 277/78: 23–70.

Holland, T.A.

1976 Preliminary Report on Excavations at Tell Es-Sweyhat, Syria 1973–74. *Levant* 8: 36–70.

1977 Preliminary Report on Excavations at Tell Es-Sweyhat, Syria, 1975. *Levant* 9: 36-65.

1980 Incised Pottery from Tell Sweyhat, Syria and its Foreign Connections. *Ktema* 5: 139–57.

Hrouda, B.

1962 *Tell Halaf.* Vol. 4. *Die Kleinfunde aus historischer Zeit.* Berlin: de Gruyter.

Iacovou M.

1988 *The Pictorial Pottery of Eleventh Century B. C. Cyprus.* Studies in Mediterranean Archaeology 78. Göteborg: Paul Aströms Förlag.

Iacovou, M. and Michaelides D.

1999 *Cyprus, the Historicity of the Geometric Horizon: Proceedings of an Archaeological Workshop, University of Cyprus, Nicosia, 1th October 1998.* Nicosia: Ministry of Education and Culture.

James, F.

1966 *Iron Age at Beth Shan: A Study of Levels VI–IV,* Philadelphia: University of Pennsylvania Musuem.

Jamieson, A. S.

1993 Euphrates Valley and Early Bronze Age Ceramic Traditions. *Abr-Nahrain* 31: 36–92.

Kampschulte, I. and Orthmann, W.

1984 *Gräber des 3. Jahrtausends in Syrischen Euphrattal.* Vol. 1. *Ausgrabungen bie Tawi 1975 und 1978.* Saarbrückner Beiträge zur Altertumskunde 38. Bonn: Rudolph Habelt.

Kearsley, R. A.

1989 *The Pendant Semi-Circle Skyphos.* Institute of Classical Studies. Bulletin Supplement 44. London: University of London.

Kelly-Buccellati, M.

1979 The Outer Fertile Crescent. *Ugarit Forschungen* 1: 413–30.

Kelly-Buccellati, M. and Shelby, W. R.

1977 Terqa Preliminary Reports, No. 4:a: Typology of Ceramic Vessels of the Third and Second Millennia from the First Two Seasons. *Syro-Mesopotamian Studies* 1.4. Malibu, CA: Undena Publications.

Kessler, K.

1980 Untersuchungen zur historischen Topographie Nordmesopotamiens nach *keilschriftlichen Quellen des 1. Jahrtausends v. Chr.* Tübinger Atlas des Vorderen Orients. Beiheft 26. Wiesbaden: Reichert

Khalifeh, I. A.

1988 *Sarepta.* Vol. 2: *The Late Bronze and Iron Age Strate from Area II, X.* Beirut: Librairie Orientale.

Klengel, H.

1992 *Syria 3000 to 300 B.C., A Handbook of Political History.* Berlin.

Krause, C.; Schuler, K. and Stucky, R.

1972 *Tell el Hajj in Syrien: Erster vorlaufger Bericht Grabungskampagne 1971.* Bern: Archaologisches Seminar der Universitat von Bern.

Kühne, H.

1976 *Keramik von Tell Chuera.* Vorderasiatische Forschungen Der Max Freiherr von Oppenheim-Stiftung. Berlin: Gebr. Mann.

1984 Tell Sheikh Hamad/Dur katlimmu 1981–1983. *Archiv für Orientforschung* 31: 66–178.

1989 Tell Sheikh Hamad/Dur katlimmu 1985–1987. *Archiv für Orientforschung* 36–37: 316–23.

1997 Sheikh Hamad/Dur katlimmu. *American Journal of Archaeology* 101: 37–40.

Langenegger, F.; Muller, K.; and Naumann, R.

1950 *Tell Halaf.* Vol. 2: *Die Bauwerke.* Berlin: de Gruyter.

Lebeau, M.
 1981   *La céramique du Fer II-III à Tell Abou Danné et ses rapports avec la céramique contemporaine en Syrie du Nord.* Paris: CRA-CNRS.
Lehmann, G.
 1998   Local Pottery Development in Syria and Lebanon. *Bulletin of the American Schools of Oriental Research* 311: 35-54.
Lines, J.
 1954   Late Assyrian Pottery from Nimrud. *Iraq* 6: 64-67.
Lloyd, S.
 1953   Sultantepe. *Anatolian Studies* 3: 27-51.
 1954   Sultantepe: Part 2. *Anatolian Studies* 4: 101–10.
 1984   *The Archaeology of Mesopotamia from the Old Stone Age to the Persian Conquest.* London: Thames and Hudson.
Lundquist, J.
 1983   Tell Qarqur - The 1983 Season. *Annales Archéologique Arabes Syriennes* 33 (2): 273-88.
Machule, D., Karstens, K., Klapproth, H.-H., Mozer, G., Pape, W., Werner, P., Mayer, W., Mayer-Opificius, R., and Mackensen, M.
 1986   Ausgrabung in Tall Munbaqa 1984. *Mitteilungen der Deutschen Orient-Gesellschaft* 118: 67-146.
Machule, D.; Benter, M.; Boessneck, J.; von den Driesch, A.; de Feyter, T. C.; Karstens, K.; Klapproth, H.-H.; Koellin, S.; Kunze, J.; Tezeren, O. and Werner, P.
 1987   Ausgrabungen in Tall Mumbaqa 1985. *Mitteilungen der Deutschen Orient-Gesellschaft* 19: 73–134.
Matthews, R. J.
 1996   Excavations at Tell Braq. *Iraq* 58: 65–78.
Matthiae, M.P.
 1979   Sondages a Tell Afis (Syrie), 1978. *Akkadica* 4: 2–4.
 1980   Two Princely Tombs at Tell Mardikh-Ebla. *Archaeology* 33: 8–17
 1981   *Ebla An Empire Rediscovered.* Garden City: Doubleday.
 1984   New Discoveries at Ebla: The Excavation of the Western Palace and the Royal Necropolis of the Amorite Period. *Biblical Archaeologist* 47: 18–32.
Mazzoni, S.
 1984   L'insediamento persiano-ellenistico di Mardikh. *Studi Eblaiti* 7: 87–132.
 1985   Elements of the Ceramic Culture of the Early Syrian Ebla in Comparison with Syro-Palestinian EBIV. *Bulletin of the American Schools of Oriental Research* 257: 1–18.
 1990a   Tell Afis and the Chronology of [the] Iron Age in Syria. *Annales Archéologiques Arabes Syriennes* 40: 76–92.
 1990b   La periode perse à Tell Mardikh et dans le cadre de l'évolution l'âge du Fer en Syrie. *Transeuphratène* 2: 87–99.
 1990c   Tell Afis e L'età del Ferro. *Seminari di Orientalistica* 2: 157–96.
 1992   *Le Impronte su Giara Eblaite e Siriane nel Bronzo Antico.* Materiali e Stude Archeologici di Ebla 1. Roma: Missione Archeologica Italiana in Syria.
 1994a   Drinking Vessels in Syria: Ebla and the Early Bronze Age. Pp. 245–76 in *Drinking in Ancient Societies. History and Culture of Drinks in the Ancient Near East.* Papers of a *Symposium held in Rome, May 7 – 1 9 , 1990,* ed. L. Milano. Padova: History of the Ancient Near East / Studies 6.
 1994b   Settlement Pattern and New Urbanization in Syria at the Time of the Assyrian Conquest. Pp.181–91 *in Neo-Assyrian Geography,* ed. Mario Liverani. Roma: Università di Roma, Instituto di studi del Vicino oriente.
 1995a   *Tell Afis e L'età del ferro.* Serninari di orientalistica 2. Pisa: Giardini.
 1995b   Settlement Pattern and New Urbanization in Syria at the Time of the Assyrian Conquest. Pp. 81-91 in *Neo-Assyrian Geography,* ed. M. Liverani. Quaderni di Geografia Storica 5. Rome: Univesita di Roma "La Sapienza." Dipartimento di Scierrre storiche, archeologiche e antropologiche dell' Antichita.
 2000   Syria and the Periodization of the Iron Age: A Cross-Cultural Perspective. Pp. 31–59 in *Essays on Syria in the Iron Age,* ed. G. Bunnens. Ancient Near Eastern Studies, Supplement 7. Peeters: Sterling, VA.
Mazzoni, S.; and Cecchini, S. M.
 1995   Tell Afis (Syria) 1994, Rapporto Preliminare. *Egitto e Vincino Oriente* 18: 243–306.
 1998   *Tell Afis (Syria): The 1998–1992 Excavations on the Acropolis.* Ricerche di archeologia del vincino Oriente, 1. Pisa: Edizioni ETS.

McClellan, T. L.
1992   Twelfth Century B.C. Syria: Comments on H. Sader's paper: The12[th] century B. C. in Syria: The problem of the rise of the Aramaeans. Pp. 164–73 in *The Crisis Years: The 12th Century B.C. From Beyond the Danube to the Tigris*, eds. W. A. Ward and M. S. Joukowsky. Dubuque: Kendall/Hunt.

McEwan, C.
1958   *Sounding at Tell Fakhariyah*. Oriental Institute Publications 70. Chicago: University of Chicago.

McGovern, P. E.
1986   *The Late Bronze and Early Iron Ages of Central Transjordan. The Baq 'ah Valley Project, 1977–1981*. Philadelphia: University of Pennsylvania Museum.

Moorey, R. R. S.
1980   *Cemeteries of the First Millennium B. C. at Deve Hüyük, near Carchemish, Salvaged by T. E. Lawrence and C. L. Woolley in 1913*. BAR International Series 87. Oxford: British Archaeological Reports.

Moortgat, A.
1955   *Tell Halaf*. Vol. 3: *Die Bildewerke*. Berlin: Walter de Gruyter.

Oates, J.
1959   Late Assyrian Pottery from Fort Shalmaneser. *Iraq* 21: 30–46
1982   Some Late Early Dynastic III Pottery from Tell Brak. *Iraq* 44: 205–19.
1985   Tell Brak: Uruk Pottery from the 1984 Season. *Iraq* 47: 75–186.

Ohtsu, T. J.
1991   Late Assyrian "Palace Ware." *Bulletin of the Middle Eastern Culture Center in Japan* 4: 131–53.

Orthmann, W.
1971   *Untersuchungen zur späthethitischen Kunst*. Bonn: Saarbrücker Beiträge zur Altertumskunde 8
1976   Mumbaqat 1974, Vorlaufiger Bericht über die von der Deutschen Orient-Gesellschaft mit Mitteln der Stiftung Volkswagenwerk unternommenen Ausgrabungen. *Mitteilungen der Deutschen Orient- Gesellschaft* 108: 25–44.
1981   *Halawa 1977–1979*. Saarbrückner Beiträge zur Altertumskunde 31. Bonn: Rudolph Habelt.
1984   Tall Halawa. Pp. 142–46 in Ausgrabungs-

tätigkeit in Syrien, ed. H. Kühne. *Archiv für Orientforshung* 31.

Orthmann, W.; and Kühne, II.
1974   Mumbaqat 1973, Vorlaufiger Bericht über die von der Deutschen Orient Gesellschaft mit Mitteln der Stiftung Volkswagenwerk unternommenen Augrabungen. *Mitteilungen der Deutschen Orient Gesellschaft* 106: 53–97.

Palmieri, A.
1981   Excavations at Arslantepe (Malatya). *Anatolian Studies* 31: 101–19.

Pezard, M.
1931   *Qadesh mission archéologique de Tell Nebi Mend 1921–1922*. Bibliothèque archéologique et historique du Service des antiquitèes du Haut Commissariat Français dans les Pays du Levant 5. Paris: Geuthner.

Philip, G.
1989   *Metal Weapons of the Early and Middle Bronze Ages in Syria and Palestine*. Oxford: B. A. R. International Series 526.

Ploug, G.
1973   *Sukas*. Vol. 2: *The Aegean, Corinthian and East, Greek Pottery and Terracottas*. Publications of the Carlsberg Expedition to Phoenicia 2. Copenhagen: Munksgaard.

Poppa, R.
1977   *Kamid el-Loz*. Vol. 2: *Der eisenzeitliche Friedhof: Befunde und Funde*. Saarbrücker Beiträge zur Altertumskunde 8. Bonn: Habelt.

Postgate, J. N.
1974   Some Remarks on Conditions in the Assyrian Countryside. *Journal of the Economic and Social History of the Orient* 7: 225–43.

Prag, K.
1970   The 1969 Deep Sounding at Harran in Turkey. *Levant* 2: 63–94.

Pritchard, J. B.
1955   *Ancient Near Eastern Texts Relating to the Old Testament*. 2nd. ed. Princeton: Princeton University.
1975   *Sarepta. A Preliminary Report on the Iron Age*. Philadelphia.
1988   *Sarepta*. Vol. 4. *The Objects from Area II, X*. Beirut: Librairie Orientale.

Puglisi, S., Meriggi, P.
1964   *Malatya*. Vol. 1. *Rapporto preliminare della campagne 1961 e 1962*. Orientis Antitui Collectio 3.

Rast, W. E.
1978   *Taanach*. Vol. 1. *Studies in the Iron Age Pottery*. Cambridge: American Schools of Oriental Research.

Redding, R.
1981   *Decision making in Subsistence Herding of Sheep and Goats in the Middle East*. Doctoral Dissertation, The University of Michigan, Ann Arbor.

Rice, P. M.
1987   *Pottery Analysis: A Source Book*. Chicago: University of Chicago Press.

Riis, P. J.
1948   *Hama, Fouilles et Recherches 1931-1938*. Vol. 2: 3. *Les cimetières à crémation. Fouilles et Recherches de la Fondation Carlsberg*. Copenhagen.

Riis, P. J., and Buhl, M. -L.
1983   *Sukas*. Vol. 7: *The Near Eastern Pottery and Objects of Other Materials from the Upper Strata*. Publications of the Carlsberg Expedition to Phoenicia 9. Copenhagen: Munksgaard.

1987   *Hama, Fouilles et Recherches 1931-1938*. Vol. 2: 2: *Les objects de la periode cite syro-hittite (Age du Fer)*. Copenhagen: Nationalmuseet.

Sader, H.
1992   The 12th century B. C. in Syria: The problem of the rise of the Aramaeans. Pp. 57–163 in *The Crisis Years: The 12th Century B.C. From Beyond the Danube to the Tigris*, eds. W. A. Ward and M. S. Joukowsky. Dubuque: Kendall/Hunt

Saidah, R. É
1971   Objets grecs d'époque géométrique découverts récemment sur le littoral libanais (à Khalde près de Beyrouth). *Annales Archéologiques Arabes Syriennes* 21: 193-98.

Schaeffer, C. F. A.
1948   *Stratigraphie comparée et chronologie de l'Asie occidentale*. London: Oxford University.

1962   Les fondement prehistorique d'Ugarit. Pp. 51-250 in *Ugaritica*, Vol. 4, ed. C. F. A. Schaeffer. Paris: Geuthner.

Schaub, R. T. and Rast, W. E.
1984   Preliminary Report of the 1981 Expedition to the Dead Sea Plain, Jordan. *Bulletin of the American Schools of Oriental Research* 254: 35-60.

Schaub, R. T. and Rast, W. E., eds.
1981   The Southeastern Dead Sea Plain Expedition: An Interim Report of the 1977 Season. *Annual of the American Schools of Oriental Research* 46. Cambridge, MA: American Schools of Oriental Research.

Schwartz, G. M.
1982   *From Prehistory to History on the Habur Plains: The Operation Sounding at Tell Leilan*. Ph.D. Dissertation, Yale University.

1989   The Origins of the Arameans in Syria and Northern Mesopotamia: Research Problems and Potential Strategies. Pp. 275-91 in *To the Euphrates and Beyond. Archaeological Studies in Honor of Maurits N. Van Loon*, eds. O. C. Haex, H. H. Curvers, and P. M. M. G. Akkermans. Rotterdam: A. Balkema

Sease, C.
1994   A *Conservation Manual for the Field Archaeologist*. Third Edition. Archaeological Research Tools, Vol. 4. The Institute of Archaeology, University of California, Los Angeles.

Seton Williams, M. V.
1961   Preliminary Report on the Excavations at Tell Rifa'at. *Iraq* 23: 68–87.

1967   Second Preliminary Report on the Excavations at Tell Rifa'at. *Iraq* 29: 16–23.

Stern, E.
1982   *Material Culture of the Land of the Bible in the Persian Period 538-332 B.C.* London: Warminster.

Strommenger, E., Schneiders, E., Rittig, D., Kara, H.-C. and Domrose, C.
1986   Ausgrabung in Tall Bi'a 1984. *Mitteilungen der Deutschen Orient-Gesellschaft* 18: 7–44.

Surenhagen, D.
1978   *Keramik produktion in Habuba Kabira-Sud*. Berlin: Bruno Hessling.

Swift, G. F.
1958   *The Pottery of the 'Amuq Phases K to 0, and its Historical Relations*. Chicago: Doctoral Dissertation, University of Chicago.

Taylor, J. du Plat
1959   The Cypriot and Syrian Pottery from Syria. *Iraq* 21: 62–92.

Taylor, M. B.
1984   *The Pottery from the Iron Age Gate at Tell Qarqur*. Masters Thesis, Brigham Young University.

Teffnin, R.
1980   Deux campagnes de fouilles au Tell Abou
        Danné (1975-1976). Pp. 179–201 in *Le
        Moyen Euphrate: Zone de contacts et
        d'échanges*, ed. J. Margueron. Travaux du
        Centre de Recherche sur le Proche-Orient
        et la Gréce Antiques 5. Strasbourg:
        Université de Sciences Humaines.
Teissier, B.
1984   *Ancient Near East Cylinder Seals from the
        Marcopoli Collection.* Berkley and Los
        Angeles, CA: University of California.
Thalmann, J.-P.
1978   Tell 'Arqa (Liban nord): Campagnes I-III
        (1972-1974): chantier I: rapport
        préliminaire. *Syria* 55: 1–151.
1990   Tell 'Arqa de la conquête assyrienne à
        l'époque perse. *Transeuphratène* 2: 51–57.
Thissen, L. C.
1985   The Late Chalcolithic and Early Bronze Age
        Pottery from Hajaz Hoyuk. *Anatolica* 12:
        75–130.
Thureau-Dangin, F.
1933   La stèle d'Asharné. *Revue d'assyriologie et
        d'archéologie orientale* 30/2: 53–56.
Thureau-Dangin, F., and Dunand, M.
1936   *Til-Barsip.* Institut d'archéologie de
        Beyrouth. Bibliothèque archéologique et
        historique 23. Paris: Geuthner.
Todd, I. A.
1973   Anatolia and the Khirbet Kerak Problem.
        Altes Orient und Altes Testament 22: 81–
        206.
Uerpmann, Hans-Peter
1973   Animal Bone Finds and Economic Archae-
        ology: A Critical Study of the 'Osteo-
        Archaeological' Method. *World Archaeol-
        ogy* 4: 307–22.
1982   Faunal Remains from Shams ed-Din
        Tannira, A Halafian Site in Northern Syria.
        Berytus 30: 3–30.
van Buren, E. D.
1930   *Clay Figurines of Babylonia and Assyria.*
        Yale Oriental Series, Researches 6. New
        Haven, CT.: Yale University.
van Loon, M.
1968   First Results of the 1967 Excavations at Tell
        Selenkahiye. *Annales Archéologiques
        Arabes Syriennes* 8: 21–36.
1973   First Results of the 1972 Excavations at Tell
        Selenkahiye. *Annales Archéologiques
        Arabes Syriennes* 23: 45–59.

1979   1974 and 1975 Preliminary Results of the
        Excavations at Selenkahiye near Meskene,
        Syria. Pp. 97–112 in *Excavation Reports
        from the Tabqa Dam Project—Euphrates
        Valley Syria*, ed. D.N. Freedman. *Annual of
        the American Schools of Oriental Research*
        44.
1982   Hammam et-Turkman on the Balikh: Back-
        ground and First Results of the University
        of Amsterdam's 1981 Excavations.
        Akkadica 27: 30–45.
1983   Hammam et-Turkman on the Balikh: First
        Results of the University of Amsterdam's
1982   Excavations. *Akkadica* 35: 1–23.
1984   Hamman et-Turkman on the Balikh: First
        Results of the University of Amsterdam's
1984   Excavations. *Akkadica* 44: 21–40.
Von Luschan, F.
1911   *Ausgrabungen in Sendschirli.* Vol. 4. Ber-
        lin.
Von Luschan, F., and Andrae, W.
1943   *Ausgrabungen in Sendschirli.* Vol. 5: *Die
        Kleinfunde von Sendschirli.* Deutschen
        Orient-Gesellschaft 5. Berlin: de Gruyter.
von Oppenheim, M. A. S.
1960   *Tell Halaf.* Vol. 4: *Die Kleinfunde aus
        historischer Zeit.* ed. B. Hrouda. Berlin: de
        Gruyter.
van Zeist, W.
1985   Past and Present Environments of the Jor-
        dan Valley. Pp.199–204 in *Studies in the
        History and Archaeology of Jordan, 2*, ed.
        A. Hadidi. London: Routledge and Kegan
        Paul.
1986   Plant Remains from Neolithic el Kowm,
        Central Syria. Pp. 65–68 in *A Neolithic Vil-
        lage at Tell el Kowm in the Syrian Desert*,
        by R. H. Dornemann.Studies in Ancient
        Oriental Civilizations 43. Chicago, IL: Th
        eOriental Institute of the University of Chi-
        cago.
1988   Archaeobotanical Studies in the Levant, 4.
        Bronze Age Sites on the North Syrian
        Euphrates. *Palaeohistoria* 27: 247–316.
Waldbaum, J.
1994   Early Greek Contacts with the Southern
        Lavant, ca. 1000–600 B.C.: The Eastern Per-
        spective. *Bulletin of the American Schools
        of Oriental Research* 293: 53–66.
Wakita, Sh.; Asano, I.; Wada, H.; Tsuneki, A.; and
Nakamura, T.
1994   Tell Mastuma - A Preliminary Report of the

Excavations in Idlib, Syria, 1993. *Bulletin of the Ancient Orient Museum* 5: 51–76.

Wakita, S., Asano, I., Wada, H., Adachi, T., Nishiyama, S., Okada, Y. and Ikeda, Y.

1995   Tell Mastuma: A Preliminary Report of the Excavations at Idlib, Syria, in 1994 and 1995. *Bulletin of the Ancient Orient Museum* 6: 1–73.

Weiss, H.

1981/82 Tall Leilan. Pp. 226–29 in Ausgrabungstätigkeit in Syrien, ed. H. Kühne. *Archiv für Orientforshung* 28.

1983   Excavations at Leilan and the Origins of North Mesopotamian Cities in the Third Millennium BC. *Paleorient* 9/2: 39–52.

1985   *Ebla to Damascus.* Washington, D.C. Smithsonian Institution.

1985   Tell Leilan on the Habur Plains of Syria. *Biblical Archaeologist* 48: 5–32.

1986   The Origins of Tell Leilan. In *The Origins of Cities in Dry-Farming Syria and Mesopotamia in the Third Millennium BC*, ed. H. Weiss. Winona Lake, IN: American Schools of Oriental Research.

Woolley, L.

1955   *Alalakh.* Oxford: Oxford University.

Woolley, L. and Hogarth, D. G.

1937   Excavations at Al Mina, Sueida I, II: The Archaeological Report. *Journal of Hellenic Studies* 58: 33–70.

1958   *Charchemish. Report on the Excavations at Jerablus on Behalf of the British Museum, Part 3: The Inner Town.* Oxford: Oxford University.

Wright, G. E.

1961   The Archaeology of Palestine. Pp. 73–112 in *The Bible and the Ancient Near East,* ed. G. E. Wright. Garden City, NY: Doubleday.

Yadin, Y.; Aharoni, Y.; Amiran, R.; Dothan, T.; Dunayevsky, I.; and Perrot, J.

1958   *Hazor.* Vol.: *An Account of the First Season of Excavations 1955.* Jerusalem: Magnes.

1960   *Hazor.* Vol. 2: *An Account of the Second Season of Excavations, 1956.* Jerusalem: Magnes.

Yadin, Y., Aharoni, Y., Amiran, R., Dothan, T., Dothan, M., Dunayevsky, I., and Perrot, J

1961   *Hazor.* Vols. 3–4: *The Third and Fourth Seasons 1957–1958.* Jerusalem: Magnes.

A GAZETTEER OF IRON I SITES IN THE NORTH-CENTRAL HIGHLANDS OF PALESTINE

Robert D. Miller, II

INTRODUCTION

This gazetteer provides a comprehensive listing of all known Iron I sites in the "highlands" north of Jerusalem (cf. limited lists such as Neef 1995: 28–93; Fritz 1996: 75–92). In the Iron I period, these constituted a distinct material culture (Alt 1929; Reviv 1989: 78–79; Redford 1992: 295; A. Mazar 1994c: 39–57). The area south of Jerusalem was sparsely inhabited, largely by seasonal sites, compared with the densely-populated north-central hill country (Finkelstein 1993a: 124). This north-central region was bounded on the north by a line of municipal principalities running from Dor to Beth Shean (Dor, Ein Haggit, Yoqneam, Megiddo, Taanach, Ibleam, Afula, Beth Shean), and on the south by a similar line from Gezer to Jerusalem (Alt 1925: 100–107; Herrmann 1985: 49; Donner 1995: 139–40), which exhibit material cultures distinct from the highland unit until the late 11th century (Gal 1994: 45). A similar line can be drawn on the western edge, from Socho to Aphek to Jaffa (Herrmann 1985: 49; Astour 1995: 1416). On the eastern edge, while it is assumed that the Jordan river was a sufficient boundary on topographic bases (for the effect of a water boundary on lines of trade, see Hodder and Orton 1976: 59–60, 78–80), there is also a similar line part of the way down the river from Beth Shean to Rehov to Hamath to Tell es-Saidiyeh to Deir Allah. All of these lines are of sites whose material culture is totally unlike that of the highlands;

for example, lowland sites, most much larger than those of the highlands (e.g., Tel Miqne/*Ekron* VIIIa–VII of the twelvth century, a 20 ha site with fortifications more than three meters thick; T. Dothan 1989: 9; 1990: 27; T. Dothan and Gitin 1993: 1053; Gitin and T. Dothan 1987: 199), have large amounts of Cypriot-made Mycenaean IIIc pottery (e.g., Afula twelvth century Level IIIB; M. Dothan 1955: 46), cuneiform tablets (e.g., the Iron I tablet TT433 from Taanach written in Northwest Semitic, a receipt for a grain shipment; Glock 1993: 1432), hieroglyphic door lintels, locally-made Egyptian-style bowls (the latter two found in twelvth century Stratum S3 at Beth Shean Area S; Nava Panitz-Cohen [Area Supervisor for Area S], personal communication), large numbers of incense stands, unique pottery form such as "beerjugs" (the latter two also found at Beth Shean Iron I Level VI, Areas N, Q, and S; Nava Panitz-Cohen and Ann Killebrew [Area Supervisor for Area N], personal communications)—the differences from the highlands are quite clear. For an excellent treatment of these issues see Killebrew (1998).

The first systematic surveys of the West Bank in its entirety were undertaken between 1968 and 1972. The published results of this survey are Kochavi (1972), supplemented by Porath (n.d.). Many sociological and historical studies have used the data from these surveys, up to the present day, including Stager (1985), Dorsey (1989), Jamieson-Drake (1991: 56), Neef (1995: 28–62,

68–93), Otto (1997: 24), Frick (1985: 143), and Flanagan (1988: 151)—the latter two actually having relied on Stager's (1985) listing from Kochavi (1972). But in recent years, several other archaeological surveys have reexamined these regions, particularly that half of the West Bank north of Jerusalem: Finkelstein (1983a), Zertal (1984), Finkelstein (1986), Finkelstein (1988a), Zertal (1988), Zertal (1992), Finkelstein and Magen (1993), Zertal (1996), and Finkelstein, Lederman, and Bunimovitz (1997). These surveys not only reexamined all the sites visited in the 1968–72 survey (plus identifying several new ones), but also reexamined the pottery collected in the 1968–72 survey. Often, it was found that the earlier dating of pottery was in error (Finkelstein 1990b: 681).

For the Iron I period, in attempting to identify every Iron I occupation in the northern half of the West Bank, one can rely securely on these surveys undertaken since 1980. Clearly, for the few areas not covered by these surveys, however, Kochavi (1972) cannot be relied upon. In many cases sites identified in Kochavi (1972) as Iron I cannot be considered so now, because reevaluation of the supposed Iron I pottery shows it to be not actually Iron I (usually it turns out to have been EB or Iron II).[1] Therefore, those sites identified as Iron I by Kochavi (1972) or other early surveys (usually Jordanian, pre-1967) and not surveyed again since 1980 had to be re-surveyed. For this purpose a survey was undertaken in 1996 by the present author with permission of the Palestinian Department of Antiquities.[2] With these results, it can be said that with the other surveys of the mid-1970s and later, a useable database of Iron I sites in the West Bank north of the latitude of Jerusalem according to all information available as of 1997 has been created.[3] For areas outside the West Bank, again, pre-1970 surveys have not been considered valid unless they have either been reconfirmed more recently, or been cases where multiple pre-1980 surveys at different times all yielded Iron I results.

The surveys used for the map of the highland settlement in Iron I, then, include Biran (Bergmann) and Brandstetter (1941); Aharoni, T. Dothan, and Frumstein (1950); Glueck (1951);

Zori (1954, 1962, 1971, 1977)[4]; Bach (1958); Mellaart (1962); News from the Survey (1963); de Contenson (1964); Biran (1964); Campbell (1967; 1991); Bull and Campbell (1968); Sapin (1968–69); Survey of the Region of Shechem (1968); Porath (n.d.; 1986); Biran, et al. (1968); Dare (1969); Mittmann (1970); Kochavi, ed. (1972); Ilan (1973); Stager (1974); Lod (1975); Jaro and Deckert (1977); Peterson (1977); Otto (1978); Ben-Tor (1980); Olami (1981); Finkelstein (1981; 1983a; 1986; 1988a; 1988–89; 1993a; 1996); Raban (1982; 1991); Porath, Paley, and Stieglitz (1982); Zertal (1983a; 1984; 1988; 1992; 1996); Porath, Dar, and Applebaum (1985); Dar (1986); Dinur (1987a); Ben-Tor, et al. (1987); Maitlis (1989); Ne'eman (1990); Gal (1991a; 1991b; 1994); M. Marcus (1991–1992); Et-Taiyiba (1991); Finkelstein and Magen (1993); Ofer (1993); Spanier (1994); Kochavi and Beit-Arieh (1994); A. Mazar (1994b); S. Gibson (1995); Finkelstein, Lederman, and Bunimovitz (1997); and Gophna and Beit-Arieh (1997). To this are added various soundings and single-site surveys; such soundings include the following: Albright (1923); Cooke (1925); Abel (1928; 1937); Blair (1936); Bergmann (Biran) (1936a; 1983); B. Mazar (1954); Muilenberg (1955); Kuschke (1958); Wallis (1961); Schunck (1963); Nandrasky (1964); Burgeta (1966); Zobel (1966); Kappus (1968); Wachter (1968); Callaway (1969b); Elliger (1970); Muhaffar (1971); Zori (1975); Vriezen (1975; 1977); Schmitt (1980); Qala' (1981); A. Mazar (1982b); Dinur (1985; 1987b); Porath, Ne'eman, and Boshnino (1989); Shavit (1993); Yannai (1995); examination of various unpublished sherds in the archives of the W. F. Albright Institute of Archaeological Research; and personal communications from excavators (G. Byers; B. Brandl; S. Gibson and E. Lass; H. Salim; R. Mullins; and S. Wolff).

Sites are arranged alphabetically by their primary name, with alternate names provided in parentheses. Alphabetization is not based on geological nouns or prefixes such as "Khirbet," "Tell," "Wadi," "Jebel," or "Har," or the definite article "el-" or "ha-," although the terms "Abu," "Beit," "Izbet," "Jelamet," and "Sheikh" are used for alphabetization. The primary site name given in this gazetteer for a West Bank site is the Arabic name, and for a site in Israel proper the Hebrew name, except in cases where the Arabic name is better known in the published literature (e.g., Izbet Sartah). Site names have not been standardized in the field of Syro-Palestinian archaeology. On paper, the Israel Antiquities Authority has standardized names for all sites in Israel and the West Bank, and one ought to adjust reports from British Mandate or Jordanian period accordingly. Even within the IAA's own files, however, inconsistencies abound, as the site variously known as Keren Zeitim, Abu Faraj, and Tirat Zvi has been multiply filed under each of these names, in files which do not duplicate contents. In the case of many of the sites of the West Bank that have now passed into the jurisdiction of the Palestinian Department of Antiquities, the IAA standardized names no longer have any canonicity. In general, however, cross-references have been given from secondary names to the main entry. Arabic site names have been transliterated according to their spoken, not written, form, e.g., Tell es-Sultan not Tell el-Sultan. Unnamed sites have been placed at the end of the listing, ordered by map reference. Ancient or biblical names for the sites, regardless of their level of certainty, have not been included. The Palestinian Grid Map Reference is given for every site, following the site name. This is followed by the site's modern size, its location, the modern soil type, and nearest source of water. It is likely that soil depletion in Palestine since antiquity renders mapping of modern soil zones useless (Hopkins 1983: 188–91; Dar 1992). For sites that have only been surveyed, the percentage of recovered pottery that was dated to Iron I is provided next. It is the author's opinion that this particular data is, in fact, irrelevant. The percentage of pottery from a given period is proportionate to many more conditions than simply the amount of occupation from that period. A site occupied in the Early Bronze, Late Bronze, and then terminally as a one-hectare village in Iron I will have a much higher percentage of Iron I pottery on the surface than a one-hectare Iron I village re-occupied in Iron II, Hellenistic, and Crusader periods. But lest one think that by somehow incorporating into the calculations of modern size and percent from the desired

period a factor of the number of subsequent occupations (or years), as suggested by Portugali (1982: 171), studies have shown that the decrease of early sherds on the top of a site is less proportionate to the number of later occupations than to the height of the site-top itself, and that earlier levels will not leave sherds at all if buried more than five meters deep (A. Rosen 1986: 246; Finkelstein, Lederman, and Bunimovitz 1997: 14). Nevertheless, as some researchers may find this information useful, it is here provided. In the case of such survey-only sites, this entry also notes whether there was occupation in the Late Bronze or Iron II periods, in order to show which sites were founded in Iron I and which abandoned in Iron I. Other periods of occupation are not mentioned. A bibliography is then provided.

Lengthy discussions of major excavations are not provided. Where publications of site excavations are adequate (e.g., Izbet Sartah), bibliographic entries refer the reader to the publications. In some cases (e.g., Khirbet Seilun), sites were excavated by different people over long periods of time, but no attempt has been made here to combine or integrate all. For sites that have only preliminary reports published (e.g., Tell Balatah), these are referred to, and it is up to the researcher to make the decisions. There are exceptions to this, where extensive research has been done here, more than anyone else at present, and in these cases (e.g., Beitin), the initial information is followed by extensive summary of the Iron I remains, organized by area, field, square, or whatever is used in the terminology of the excavation. Iron I finds are then listed, according to the pottery typologies used by the excavators.

Finally, no conclusions are drawn from this collected information. Certainly there are a wealth of data here from which many observations could be made and that are in need of interpretation, and some preliminary remarks are made in R. Miller (1997, 1998a, 1998b, 1998c, 1999, 2000a, 2000b, in press a, in press b). But the intention here is to present the gazetteer for the use of future researchers.

R. Miller

NOTES

1. There is a separate issue that has emerged regarding conflicting dating of sites explored since 1980. In a 1998 article in *Palestine Exploration Quarterly* entitled "Two Notes on Northern Samaria," Israel Finkelstein has argued that Einun ware should be redated to the MB II period. This might play havoc with many of the sites identified as Iron I herein. Amihai Mazar has responded with "The Bull Site and Einun Pottery Reconsidered" in 1999 *Palestine Exploration Quarterly*, defending the traditional dating. As both of these articles appeared subsequent to the production of this present study, and as the conversation is ongoing, the (post-1980) surveyors' own conclusions regarding pottery dating are accepted throughout.

2. Nineteen sites were surveyed, including one which was discovered in the field and was not previously identified. The survey was undertaken between May and December of 1996. The field surveying was assisted by students of the Palestinian Institute of Archaeology of Birzeit University: Firas Aqel, Salah Tawasheh, and Abdullah Zeid, and W. F. Albright Institute fellows Justin Lev-Tov, Benjamin Porter, and Mark Ziese. Laboratory analysis of pottery was assisted by Gus Van Beek (Smithsonian Institute), and Albright Institute faculty and fellows Seymour Gitin, Jeffrey Blakely, Aaron Brody, Barbara Johnson, Ann Killebrew, Benjamin Porter, Todd Sanders, and Mark Ziese, although all final dating of pottery is that of the present author. Analysis of stone objects was assisted by Fa'ida Abu Ghazzaleh (Birzeit University) and James Philips

(Albright Institute), of glass by Alysia Fischer (Albright Institute), and of bones by Muhammad Al-Zawahra (Birzeit University). The responsibility for any errors in analysis or conclusions of the data is the author's own. The procedure for field surveying was to treat an entire site as a single zone. This was done because artificial transacts, unless determined statistically, are misleading and meaningless, and transacts dictated by topography falsely presume that erosion has not greatly effected the landscape since site deposition (see A. Rosen 1986). The entire surface of the sites was walked. All diagnostic sherds (rims, handles, bases, painted or glazed body sherds) and all metal objects were collected. Additionally, all sherds were collected from cisterns, tombs, walls, wells, and springs. Additionally, site descriptions were taken, and immovable features recorded.

3. There are two known exceptions. Tell ed-Deir [1992.1994] (Mittmann 1970: 132) could not be relocated, and Khirbet es-Sakut [2017.1968] (Kochavi 1972: 214) could not be surveyed as it is now covered with land mines!

4. The use of the early surveys of Zori is an exception to the above stated rule. This is because recent survey of many of Zori's sites by Aren Maier has found that Zori's pottery readings are unanimously reconfirmed (A. Maier, personal communication). It will be assumed that Zori's findings were thus correct in other cases, as well.

ABBREVIATIONS

AASOR	Annual of the American Schools of Oriental Research		Vorderen Orients
ADAJ	*Annual of the Department of Antiquities of Jordan*	BZAW	Beihefte zur *ZAW*
		cm	centimeter(s)
		EI	*Eretz Israel*
ASOR	American Schools of Oriental Research	*ESI*	*Excavations and Surveys in Israel*
		E.T.	English translation
BA	*Biblical Archaeologist*	ha.	hectares
BAR	*Biblical Archaeology Review*	*HA*	*Hadashot Arkaologot*
BAReader	*Biblical Archaeologist Reader*	*HTR*	*Harvard Theological Review*
BARInt	British Archaeological Reports, International Series	*HUCA*	*Hebrew Union College Annual*, Cincinnati
BASOR	Bulletin of the American Schools of Oriental Research	*IEJ*	*Israel Exploration Journal*, Jerusalem
BASORSup	*BASOR* Supplement	*JAOS*	*Journal of the American Oriental Society*, New Haven
BTAVO	Beihefte zum Tübinger Atlas des		

JNES	Journal of Near Eastern Studies, Chicago	PEQ	Palestine Exploration Quarterly, London
JPOS	Journal of the Palestine Oriental Society, Jerusalem	PTS	Pittsburgh Theological Seminary
		RB	Revue biblique, Paris
JSOTSup	Journal for the Study of the Old Testament Supplement Series	TA	Tel Aviv, Tel Aviv
		VT	Vetus Testamentum, Leiden
km	kilometer(s)	ZAW	Zeitschrift für die alttestamentliche Wissenschaft, Berlin
m	meter(s)		
n.d.	no date	ZDPV	Zeitschrift des deutschen Palästina-Vereins
OBO	Orbis biblicus et orientalis		
PEFQSt	Palestine Exploration Fund Quarterly Statement		

ACKNOWLEDGMENTS

This gazetteer catalogues 360 Iron I sites in the north-central highlands of Palestine. There are many individuals and organizations to thank for aid in the pursuit of this project, in areas of funding, access to unpublished field data, and comments.

This study would not have been possible without the opportunity to reside in Jerusalem for two and a half years. The first portion of this stay was funded by a Junior Scholarship-in-Residence from the Tantur Ecumenical Institute for Advanced Theological Study, the latter portion by the Samuel H. Kress Foundation's fellowship administered through the W. F. Albright Institute of Archaeological Research, and the W. F. Albright Institute's James A. Montgomery Fellowship. Special thanks go to Dr. Hamdan Taha, Director of the Palestinian Department of Antiquities, for a permit to survey in the West Bank. Other individuals who helped in that survey are listed below. This survey was funded by the Catholic Biblical Association's Archaeological Research Stipend.

Many people were helpful in gaining access to unpublished archaeological data and the permission to use the material. These are: Israel Finkelstein, Chair of the Nadler Institute of Archaeology of Tel Aviv University for access to the unpublished version of his *Highlands of Many Cultures* survey (Finkelstein, Lederman, and Bunimovitz 1997); David Livingston of Associates for Biblical Research, Inc. and Baruch Brandl for unpublished information on Khirbet Nisya; Bryant Wood and Gary Byers of Associates for Biblical Research, Inc. for unpublished information on the ongoing excavations at Khirbet Mukhatir; Moshe Kochavi of Tel Aviv University for permission to see Israel Antiquities Authority files on Izbet Sartah; Zvi Gal of the Israel Antiquities Authority for permission to see Israel Antiquities Authority files on Keren Zeitim (Tirat Zvi); Nancy Lapp for permission and assistance in seeing materials from Paul Lapp's work at Tell el-Ful and James L. Kelso's at Beitin housed at the Pittsburgh Theological Seminary Kelso Bible Lands Museum (where she is the curator), the Rockefeller Museum, and Birzeit University's Palestinian Institute of Archaeology; Edward F. Campbell of McCormick Theological Seminary for permission to see materials from Tell Balatah housed at the Rockefeller Museum and Albright Institute; Roger Boraas for information on the Tell Balatah pottery he was then responsible for publishing; the late James B. Pritchard for permission to examine materials from el-Jib housed at the Albright Institute, Birzeit University, Rockefeller Museum, and Jordanian Department of Antiquities; Alain Chambon for permission to examine materials from Tell el-Farah North housed at the École Biblique et Archéologique Française, and his assistance with those materials; Robert Cooley and Gary Pratico of Gordon-Conwell Theological Seminary for permission to examine materials from Joseph Free's excavations of Tell Dothan housed at the Rockefeller Museum, St. George's

College Benshoof Cistern Museum, and Jordanian Department of Antiquities; Museum Director Alon Goldberg for access to materials from Tel Amal at the Museum of Regional and Mediterranean Archaeology, Gan HaShlosha; Aren Maier of Hebrew University for access to materials from his survey of the Beth Shean valley; Sam Wolff for access to materials from his excavations of Ein Haggit; and Joel Drinkard of the Southern Baptist Theological Seminary for permission and access to materials from the J. A. Callaway excavations of et-Tell and Khirbet Raddanah housed at the Southern Baptist Theological Seminary Nicol Museum of Biblical Archaeology. All records of the Rockefeller Museum and Israel Antiquities Authority were examined with the assistance of Arieh Rochman-Halperin, Head of the Archives Branch of the Antiquities Authority. Objects housed at the Rockefeller/IAA were examined with permission of Acting Chief Curator Hava Katz and assistance of Joe Zias. Records housed with the Jordanian Department of Antiquities were examined with permission of Ghazi Bisheh, Director of Antiquities, Fawzi Zayadine, Assistant Director, and Muhammad Najjar of the Department, and with the assistance of Mr. M. Zayyat, Curator of the Jordan Archaeological Museum. Materials from Tell Dothan housed at St. George's College, Jerusalem, were examined with the assistance of then-curator of the Benshoof Museum Dorothy Porter. Records and objects housed at Birzeit University were examined with permission of Khaled Nashef, Director of the Palestinian Institute of Archaeology. Records and objects kept at the Albright Institute were used with permission of the Dorot Director Seymour Gitin.

Substantial preliminary assistance in this project came from Dr. Gus Van Beek, curator of Old World archaeology at the Smithsonian Institute Museum of Natural History. Through an Academic Internship in 1995, Gus spent two weeks intensively preparing me for handling the idiosyncracies of material from excavations that are now nearly half a century old.

This project comprised a portion of my doctoral dissertation in Near Eastern Studies for the University of Michigan, and the members of my dissertation committee, Brian Schmidt, Peter Machinist, Charles Krahmalkov, and Henry Wright, deserve a great deal of thanks.

Robert D. Miller II
Emmitsburg, Maryland, August 2000

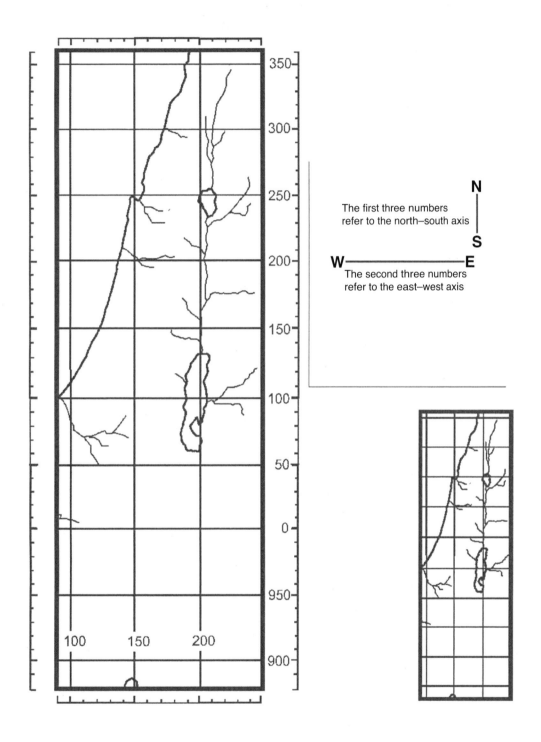

The first three numbers refer to the north–south axis

The second three numbers refer to the east–west axis

Map Reference Grid

A GAZETEER OF IRON I SITES

'ABD EL-'AL, WADI   M.R. 1960.1783

0.1 ha. site, ten meters up the side of a valley. Eroded soil. Three kilometers to nearest water at Wadi Farah. thirty-one percent of sherds found in survey were Iron I, with no LB or Iron II (Zertal 1996: 486–87).

'ABEIDEH, TELL EL-   M.R. 1641.2058

4.5 ha. site on hill eighty meters above the terrain. Rendzina soil. Well four kilometers away. Two percent of sherds found were Iron I, also Iron II (Zertal 1988: 102).

ABU AMIR, KH. — see IBN AMR, KH.

ABU FARAJ — see KEREN ZEITIM

ABU FARAJ, TELL — see KFAR QARAYIM, TEL

ABU GHANNAM, KH.   M.R. 1801.2057

0.2 ha. site on level of terrain. Terra Rosa soil. Ten percent of sherds Iron I, no LB or Iron II (A. Mazar 1982b: 142; Zertal 1988: 105; 155).

ABU KAHUT, KH.   M.R. 1734.2072

3.5 ha. site ten meters above the Dothan Valley. Terra Rosa soil. Four wells. Twenty percent Iron I sherds, also Iron II (Zertal 1988: 98; 1992: 83–84).

ABU MU'AMMAR, KH. (Kh. Badd Abu Mu'ammar; Kh. el-'Uneiziyya; Kh. el-'Anaziyya)   M.R. 1645.15030

0.24 ha. site on hill. Two percent Iron I sherds, also Iron II (Finkelstein and Magen 1993: 29*, 145–46).

ABU MUSARRAH (Ein Fara; Tel Fara)   M.R. 17730.13730

1 ha. site on hilltop. Iron I and II remains (Dinur 1987a: 44; Finkelstein and Magen 1993: 390–91).

ABU NAR, WADI — see QUREIN, JEBEL

ABU RISH   M.R. 1598.1997

Single-period Iron I site of 0.3 hectares. Thirty meter-high hill. Terra Rosa soil. Nearest water at Bir es-Sama' (Bir Abu Rish) two kilometers away (Zertal 1988: 116).

ABU RUJMAN, KH. (Kh. el-'Aqqaba)   M.R. 1578.2059

Iron I and II occupation in three caves hewn in the Middle Bronze Age. On rocky hilltop. Iron I finds include six juglets with stovepipe-neck rims (Ne'eman 1990: 37*–38*, 52).

ABU SHUQEIR, KH.   M.R. 1554.2201

0.55 ha. Iron I site, also LB and Iron II occupation. Spring on site (Olami 1981: 96).

ABU SIDRA, TELL   M.R. 203.178

Iron I site, as well as Iron II, in the Zor Abu Sidra, below the Qattarah hills between the *zor* and *ghor* of the Jordan River Valley (Glueck 1951: 419–20; Kochavi 1972: 419–20).

ABU SIDRA, WADI   M.R. 2002.1769

0.1 ha. site forty meters above Jordan Valley. Nearest water is the Jordan River, three kilometers away. Desert Alluvium soil. Thirty percent Iron I sherds, also Iron II. Iron I sherds include cooking pots with sharp, triangular slanted rims, cooking pots having sharp, triangular rims that are flattened and unaccentuated, and triangular-rimmed cooking pots with an upper lip that has been folded inward, and large bowls with thickened, folded, and inverted rims (Zertal 1996: 574–75).

ABU SIFRY, TELL — see HILU, KH. TELL EL-

ABU ES-SUS, TELL   M.R. 2030.1978

30×100 m site fifty meters from the Jordan River. The site consists of two tells on a rock table one hundred meters above the Jordan, commanding two natural fords. Iron I remains, including storejars with molded rim and ridge at the bottom of the rim that has merged with the rim itself; no LB or Iron II (de Contenson 1964: 41–42; Zobel 1966: 99–100; Zori 1977: 38–39).

ABU EZ-ZARAD — see SHEIKH ABU ZARAD'AISH, TELL
(Kh. el-'Ayash)   M.R. 1978.1508

50 m diameter site. Much Iron I, also Iron II (Glueck 1951: 412–23; Ilan 1973: 264).

'AJJE   M.R. 1685.1965

4 ha. on edge of hill, forty-two meters above the plain of er-Rameh (Wadi en-Nazrani). Two kilometers to nearest water at a spring. Five percent Iron I sherds, also Iron II (Zertal 1984: 131; 1992: 239).

'AJRAM, JEBEL   M.R. 1719.1836

Small ruin, 0.16 hectares, on eighty-five meter high hilltop. One kilometer to spring. Ninety percent of sherds Iron I, no LB or Iron II. Rendzina soil (Zertal 1988: 165; 1992: 380).

ALI, KH.   M.R. 15325.16095

1 ha. site on ridge. Nearest water 3.8 km. One percent Iron I, on the lower south slope. Also Iron II (Finkelstein, Lederman, and Bunimovitz 1997: 89).

'ALMIT, KH.   M.R. 1760.1369

Hilltop site with many caves, both natural and manmade. Wadi Farah is at foot of tell. Iron I and II finds, including collared-rimmed pithoi (Peterson 1977: 429–30; Maitlis 1989: 18; A. Mazar 1994b: 74; unpublished soundings also carried out by G. Lipowitz).

ALYATA, KH.   M.R. 17270.15935

0.7 ha. site on hilltop. 800m to nearest water. Two percent of sherds Iron I, also Iron II. Iron I includes collared-rimmed and hole-mouthed pithoi (Finkelstein 1983a: 143; 1988a: 180; Finkelstein et al. 1985: 173; Finkelstein, Lederman, and Bunimovitz 1997: 343).

AMAL, TEL (Tell el-'Asi)   M.R. 1927.2123

0.3 ha. site. Level 4 was founded in the 11th century on a sterile layer (Feig 1983: 264; Levy 1962: 147). It has been argued, however, that Level 4 must be Iron II, contemporary with Megiddo V–IVb (McClellan 1975: 216, 220), because it has dipper juglet #53.127, everted saucer-rim lamp #60.175, hippo jar #23.157, shallow cooker #20.227, and bowl #02.52.

Locus 34 in Squares M-L.5–6 (northeast part of tell) is a big three-room house (Rooms #33–36). It has two installations in it, a brick semicircle 1.2 cm diameter with a basalt plate over it (Levy and Edelstein 1972: 331), and a round clay hearth with traces of burning and pieces of pottery and alabaster cuttings. Near the latter is a plastered dressed brick bench, at which was found a little jar with the outside surface showing traces of a corrosive liquid (Levy and Edelstein 1972: 331). Finds from the house include: loom in situ with forty-five ovoid clunky white chalk or gypsum loom weights with holes off-center, nearby weaving bowl with two loops for twisting the double threads for warp, stone utensils, an incense burner with an ornate basin decorated with white circles.

Locus 29 in Squares M-L.9–10 (northwest part of tell) is a similar house (Levy and Edelstein 1972: 332). Its finds include: two basalt plates, stone tools, carbonized wood, an animal's horn, animal bone. Iron I remains also in Loci 26–27 in the southwest in Squares K-J.9, and a tunnel 1.5 m high cut into rock for a length of 45 m for water supply (Levy and Edelstein 1972: 333).

Finds (Museum of Mediterranean Archaeology collection; Levy and Edelstein 1972: 335–38): dipper juglets (#50.114), also juglets with lip-shoulder handles; shoulder-handled jars #16.208 and #16.206, hole-mouth jars, small jars with red and brown paint and burnishing (Levy and Edelstein 1972: 336), and ovoid-down jar #24.213; flared chalices with stepped base (southern-style); lamps; jugs with painted stripes, including long-necked piriform jugs and decanters with splayed rims; handleless krater, vertical-rimmed with oval section; red-slipped bowls that are hemispherical but have a long neck; Philistine "Beerjugs" with painted bands (Levy and Edelstein 1972: 337). From Sector A: dark red slip with black painted bands, also carinated bowls (Levy 1962: 147).

The site was destroyed by fire after less than twenty years (Levy 1962: 147; Levy and Edelstein 1972: 330).

AMIR, KH. — see IBN 'AMR, KH.

'ANAHUM, KH.
(Kh. en-Nahm)   **M.R. 1799.2009**

0.8–1.0 ha. site on slope. Terra Rosa soil. Five kilometers to nearest water at well of Bir el-Khaphireh. Ten percent of sherds Iron I, also LB and Iron II. Iron I includes collared-rimmed pithoi with short, thick everted rims, cooking pots having sharp triangular slanted rim with ridge on bottom edge of rim, and punctured jar handles (Zertal 1996: 115; survey by the author on 31 August 1996).

'ANATA   **M.R. 17490.13560**

Modern village on a ridge. No springs or wells nearby. Few Iron I remains, also Iron II (Finkelstein and Magen 1993: 359–60), although E. P. Blair (1936) had found no Iron I. There is no Iron I at Ras el-Kharrubeh, at 1748.1351, 17451.13500, or at 17460.13500 (Finkelstein and Magen 1993: 358; Dinur 1985: 22; Biran 1936a; Biran 1983: 38–39; Peterson 1977: 422)—although Albright believed one of Biran's 1936 cooking pots was Iron I (Albright 1936: 26).

'ANAZIYYA, KH. EL- — see ABU MU'AMMAR, KH.

'AQABE, KH. EL-   **M.R. 1732.1829**

0.2 ha. site five meters up Mt. Ebal. Terra Rosa soil. One kilometer to nearest spring. Twenty percent of sherds Iron I, also Iron II (Zertal 1988: 167; 1992: 486).

'AQQABA, KH. EL- — see ABU RUJMAN, KH.

ARD EL-MAFJIR (TELL 2) — see EL-MEFJIR SITE

'ARURA   **M.R. 16625.16100**

1.4 ha. site on ridge. 1.4% Iron I, on northwest side of site. Water 600 m away. Also Iron II (Finkelstein, Lederman, and Bunimovitz 1997: 262).

'ASAS, WADI EL-
(Qurnat Shahtura)   **M.R. 1776.1469**

Iron I sherds (and no others) were found in stone-lined cisterns in the Wadi el-'Asas about one hundred meters northeast of Khirbet Khudriyya (Schmitt 1980: 57; Callaway 1969b: 4; 1969c: 2).

ASAWIR, TELL EL- — see ESUR, TEL

'ASI, TELL EL- — see AMAL, TEL ASIRA ESH-SHAMALIYYA

SITE A
(et-Hatab Asyret; Azirat el-Hatab)
                                   M.R. 17535.18395

6 ha. site. Sixty-five meters up in hills of Mt. Ebal. Terra Rosa soil. Thirty percent Iron I sherds, also Iron II. Five kilometers to spring (Zertal 1992: 485).

SITE B: **M.R. 1758.1838**

Iron I sherd scatter of 0.1 ha. on slope. Terra Rosa soil. Five kilometers to the spring (Zertal 1992: 485).

ASKAR, KH. TELL EL-   **M.R. 17675.14305**

1.2 ha. site on peak of hill. Fifty-four percent Iron I sherds, also Iron II. Iron I sherds include cooking pots of types outcurving lipped-rim, triangular-rimmed with molded lower edge, and triangular-rimmed with an upper lip that has been folded inward, and jars with simple rims (Finkelstein and Magen 1993: 37*, 187–88).

'ATARA   **M.R. 16990.15680**

2 ha. site on east and west sides of ridge. 100 m to nearest water. 4.8%–6% Iron I sherds, concentrated east and west of the oldest part of this modern Arab village. No LB or early Iron II. Iron I sherds include collared-rimmed pithoi (Finkelstein 1988a: 170, 181; Finkelstein, Lederman, and Bunimovitz 1997: 235).

ATARUD, KH. (et-Tarud)   **M.R. 1729.1713**

1.2–1.5 ha. site on hilltop above Makhaneh Valley. 1.65 km to nearest water. Both 6.3% and 20% reported as Iron I portion of survey pottery. Also Iron II. Iron I sherds include cooking pots with sharp, triangular slanted rims, and some having sharp, triangular rims that are flattened and unaccentuated, collared-rimmed and hole-mouth pithoi, and punctured jar handles (Finkelstein 1986: 136–37; 1988a: 179; Finkelstein, Lederman, and Bunimovitz 1997: 447).

ATTIL   **M.R. 1570.1973**

5 ha. site twenty meters up a slope. Terra Rosa soil. Three kilometers to closest water at Bir Zeita. Ten percent Iron I, also Iron II (Zertal 1988: 121).

'AUJA EL-FOQA, KH.
(Tell et-Truni; Tell Trunet el-'Auja)
                          M.R. 18792.15046

This is not to be confused with the Chalcolithic site called Kh. 'Auja el-Foqa by Glueck (1951: 411), which is also called Kh. Umm Adhbeh, nor with the Kh. 'Auja el-Foqa also named Tell et-Truni about one kilometer to the east of this one. The site in question here is a hilltop, with occupation in Iron I and II (Glueck 1951: 408–11; Spanier 1994: 79).

AZIRAT EL-HATAB — see ASIRA ESH-SHAMALIYYA

BAB ED-DAIYQ   **M.R. 1935.1760**

The site is 0.3ha, fifty meters above the Wadi Farah, which is 300 meters away. Terra Rosa soil. Twenty percent Iron I, also Iron II (Zertal 1988: 172; cf. QASR EL-ASBAH).

BADD ABU MU'AMMAR, KH. — see ABU MU'AMMAR, KH.

BALATAH, TELL   **M.R. 1755.1805**

Large site at the eastern end of the pass between Mts. Gerizim and Ebal. Terra rosa soil, water at Ein Balatah on southern edge of site. Also LB occupation, but no early Iron II. The excavations of the site, both the German and American expeditions, have not yet been adequately published. Nevertheless, extensive preliminary reports exist, as well as important interpretive studies, to which the reader should refer. These include Böhl (1960?), Boraas (1986), Bull (1960; 1998), Bull and Campbell (1968), Campbell (1960; 1967; 1969; 1983; 1991; 1993), Campbell and G. E. Wright (1965), Currid (1989), Dever (1973), Fowler (1983), Harrelson (1978), Horn (1960?; 1962; 1964; 1966; 1968; 1973), Horn and Moulds (1969), Jaroš (1976), Le Du (1996), B. Mazar (1973), Moulds (1967), Müller (1987), Shechem (1968a; 1972; 1973), Na'aman (1986b), Nielsen (1954), Peterson (1977), Ross (1971), Ross and

Toombs (1961; 1962; 1976), Seger (1970; 1972; 1997), Sellin (1914; 1922; 1960?), Sellin and Steckeweh (1941), Soggin (1967), Stager (1998), Toombs (1963; 1972; 1976; 1979; 1992), Toombs, Campbell, and Ross (1971), Toombs and Kee (1957), Toombs and G. E. Wright (1961; 1962; 1963), Welter (1932a; 1932b), Wilhelm (1970), G. E. Wright (1957; 1965; 1967; 1973), and G. R. H. Wright (1967; 1968; 1970; 1971; 1985; 1992a; 1992b; 1993–94; 1994).

BANAT BARR, KH.   M.R. 15535.16225

0.55 ha. site on slope. 1.9 km to Nahal Shiloh. 4.7% Iron I sherds, no LB or early Iron II. Sherds included collared-rimmed pithoi (Finkelstein 1988a: 167, 181; Marcus 1991–92: 1.157; Finkelstein, Lederman, and Bunimovitz 1997: 98).

BANI FADIL, KH.   M.R. 18595.16545

0.3–0.5 ha. site on slope of Wadi Fasil. 1.2 km to nearest water at Ein Jahin spring. Minimal Iron I pottery, no LB or Iron II. Iron I includes collared-rimmed pithoi (Herrmann 1964: 63; Ilan 1973: 294; Finkelstein 1988a: 143; Marcus 1991–92, 2: 118–19).

BARTA'A, KH.
(esh-Sheikh Barta'a)   M.R. 15995.20885

0.89 ha. site on hilltop ninety meters above the surrounding terrain. Terra Rosa soil. Twenty percent Iron I, also Iron II (Zertal 1988: 95; Ne'eman 1990: 31*, 35).

BATIN, JEBEL EL-
(Horvat Maaleh Levonah)   M.R. 17345.16255

1 ha. site on saddle of mountain. 1.2 km to nearest water. 10%–20.9% Iron I sherds, also Iron II. Iron I finds include cooking pots with outcurving lipped-rim, triangular-rimmed cooking pots with molded lower edge, and cooking pots having sharp triangular slanted rim with ridge on bottom edge of rim, collared-rimmed pithoi, bell-shaped *cyma* bowls, and punctured jar handles (Finkelstein

1986: 141; 1988a: 155, 179; Finkelstein, Lederman, and Bunimovitz 1997: 398).

BATN ES-SAMA   M.R. 1724.2093

5 ha. site on hilltop eighty meters above the surrounding terrain. Terra Rosa soil. 500 m to well of Bir es-Saba. Ten percent Iron I, also Iron II (Zertal 1988: 94).

BATN UMM NARI
(Bir es-Safa)   M.R. 1668.1992

3.5 ha. site on summit of hill fifty meters above the surrounding terrain. Rendzina soil. Well of Bir es-Safa is in the site. Twenty-three percent Iron I, also LB (Zertal 1988: 117).

BEIT FARR, KH. (A)   M.R. 1848.1831

0.65 ha. tell fifteen meters high in Wadi Farah valley. Terra Rosa soil. 500 m to nearest water at Ein Farr. Ten percent Iron I, also Iron II. Iron I includes curved-rimmed storejars, platters, cooking pots with ridge just below the lip and with plain rims, and "man's face" punctured jar handles (Finkelstein 1986: 167; Zertal 1996: 404–6).

BEIT IWEIS   M.R. 15870.15190

0.8 ha. site on slope. 1.3 km to nearest water. 8.5% Iron I, no LB or early Iron II (Finkelstein, Lederman, and Bunimovitz 1997: 64).

BEIT QAD   M.R. 1837.2084

Iron I and II sherds found in the modern village, which is situated on a small hill (Biran, Mazar, et al. 1968: 12; Zori 1977: 42–43).

BEIT RIMA   M.R. 15995.1600

3 ha. site on level terrain on summit of ridge. Wells 900 m to the west. 6.7% Iron I sherds, the rest Iron II. Iron I includes collared-rimmed pithoi (Finkelstein 1986: 151; 1988a: 181).

BEIT 'UR EL-FOQA   M.R. 1609.1437

0.6 ha. site on hill. 500 m to nearest water. 2.6% Iron I, also LB and Iron II. Iron I includes everted-rimmed and simple-rimmed storejars (Peterson 1977: 287, 289; Finkelstein, Lederman, and Bunimovitz 1997: 132).

BEIT 'UR ET-TAHTA   M.R. 15820.14465

The site itself is a 2.8 ha. hill. Nearest water is 2.8 km away. 0.7% Iron I sherds, also LB and Iron II—Iron I consisting of a single collared-rimmed pithos (Finkelstein 1988a: 177, 181; Finkelstein, Lederman, and Bunimovitz 1997: 23–24). In 1971, a salvage excavation by Muhammed Ali Nasir and I. Damati cleared an Iron I tomb, finding lamps and juglets (Report to the Israel Antiquities Authority "7 & 12.9.71").

BEITIN   M.R. 172.148

Situated seventeen km north of Jerusalem, the site's nearest spring is just north of Deir Dibwan. Late Bronze and Iron II remains are also present. The excavations of the site have not been published adequately. The following synthesis of the Iron I remains is that of the present author.

Phase 1: Founded 1240 on LB destruction layer (Kelso 1934: 417; 1961a: 16), or in 1225 (Kelso 1962: 15). Includes Areas (by their 1934 names) Sub32–Sub46 and Sub145–Sub148 and Sub152–Sub158 (Fieldbook "Beitin 1934"). MB IIB walls were repaired in the west of Area I (by 1934 numbering; it is 1960's Area A or M or N, at the north end of site; "1960 Report to Department of Antiquities"; Kelso 1934: 416), although it is not clear when (or if) the breaches made in it during the LB destruction were fixed—in the south, a house appears to straddle the wall (Lemche 1985: 399 n.60). In Area I (by 1934 numbering), LB Walls were reused (Kelso 1958: 8), and pithoi were found, such as one from Locus 5, 1 m from top.

The first house built was #310/312 (by 1954 Season numbering). The style is piered masonry stonework (Albright and Kelso 1968: 32), thin walls (H. Weippert 1988: 357), with crude masonry on a different plan than LB (Albright 1934:

9). Actually, masonry at Beitin gets worse each phase through Phase 3 (Albright 1934: 11) in both (by 1934 numbering) Areas I and II (Albright 1934: 12; Area II, in the center of the site, is called Area B in 1960). Another house is House #35 (Albright and Kelso 1968: 32; it is the same as Room #3 of the 1934 season): a three-room house 5 by at least 6 m (Braemer 1982: 201), but difficult to interpret (Braemer 1982: 201). Other houses include 1957 Room 5: Wall 6 (eastern wall) along Room 2, Pier 1; and Room 2: shares a wall with Room 5 and one with Room 3 ("1957 Room Cards and Daybook"). The LB Palace foundation walls were made into sub-dwellings. In the LB Palace court, houses were added (Kelso 1934: 417), as they were also on the collapsed LB walls (Kelso 1955: 6).

Finds (Albright and Kelso 1968: 63–65): cooking pots with plain rims; collared-rim pithoi with long collars and thick folded rims; coarse, thick, unornamented bowls; chalices; juglets with slightly thickened button-base, some burnished; pitchers spherical; jugs similar to Philistine beer jugs but with no metope designs; paste scarab of cobra, bent lines, and hawk (#442 at Rockefeller Museum; Albright and Kelso 1968: 84) and other scarabs; two bronze knives (Albright 1934: 13); pilgrim flasks LB-like in form but thicker; krater; pyxides with small horizontal loop handles; large lamp with rounded base. Finds specifically in House 310/312: paste scarab #1012; pithoi, one of which has a seal on the handle (Albright and Kelso 1968: 118). Room 310 (once called Room 20) from 8.30 to 8.27 (but including no floors) produced bowl #1123 with burnish, hemispherical bowl with simple, rounded rims bowl #1120, bone spatula #1083, copper ring #1091, iron arrowhead #1079, and two fragments of bitumen #1081. Room 312 (originally "22") produced plate with flaring sides #1121, southern-style chalice #1104, limestone cylinder #1098, sling stone #1102, stone bead #1100, and whetstone #1102. In Sub145: brown painted LBish jar neck (#806); in Sub153: stone spindle whorl (#634 = Pittsburgh Theological Seminary 2.0–091); in Sub154: dark red painted LBish sherd (#805). In House 35: Cypriote painted jar handle (#329 = PTS 2-206). From Sub36:

bronze pin ("Beitin 1934"). From Sub38: bone inlay (#446; "Beitin 1934")—a spatula with two holes at one end. From Sub41: marble bead (#451), quartz weight (#281 = PTS 2.0–056; "Beitin 1934"), copper sheet (#452). From Sub146: flint sickle (#603 = PTS 2.0–038). From Sub147: bone needle (#610). Room 308 (originally "18"): poor pavement 8.36, two lamps, bone pendant with many holes #1051, figurine of a horse's bust #1054, yellow bead #1070, carnelian bead #1076, redstone scarab #1073.

This phase was destroyed, as seen in the fire in Sub 32 and 50 (Albright and Kelso 1968: 33), and (by 1954 names) 308, 310, 301, 302 (Albright and Kelso 1968: 33).

Phase 2 (1175–1100) exhibits new building patterns, but cruder: no foundations, mixed stones and bricks. Houses are three/four-room houses standardized 15×12 m (for example, House 38, of a type consisting of a rectangular space bordered with rooms on side and end with walls, creating four rooms; Braemer 1982: 66, 202; H. Weippert 1988: 399). There is a crude wall low on hillside, north of the spring (Kelso 1961b: 2). Finds, of which all pottery is poorly thrown and thick (Albright and Kelso 1968: 32, 34): collared-rim pithoi (Albright 1934: 12; examples from [by 1934 names] Loci 207A, 50, 42 in Albright Institute collection); bronze socketed spearheads (#613, Albright and Kelso 1968: 85—actually this was found in the wall between rooms 146 and 148); bowls in Locus 50 along with pithoi. Locus 207A also has cooking pots and incised jar handle (#315). Locus 42 is quite rich with pithoi, cooking pots, bowls, limestone tools, stone pendant (#326). Other finds: human head on a jar handle (#638, Albright 1934: 13—this not "man's face" puncturing, but is really an elaborate cartoon face with some sort of headband, drawn on the handle); paste scaraboid with boat full of lotus (#445, Albright and Kelso 1968: 84); punctured jar handles (#324, 386, and 388); iron point (#338 = PTS 2.0–187).

This phase ended in a very severe fire in Sub32 (Kelso 1934: 417; 1956: 40).

Phase 3 (1100–1030): even cruder pottery, although some new hand-burnished pithoi (Albright

and Kelso 1968: 34), and cruder masonry (no foundations, mixed sizes of stones, bricks). Room 403 at 150 cm: Wall 10–11+7 (east wall), very poor, irregular mix, with two pavements at 9.200 and 9.000. It contained a carinated bowl with burnish inside and everted rim—a southern form, bone spatula (#2028b–c), bone awl (#2028a), and stone bead (#2034 = PTS 2.2–031).

Finds in Area 32, which may be Phase 2 or 3, include bowl, limestone potters' wheel or grinder (#304), bronze pin (#298), bone pendant with incising (#245), copper sheet (Albright and Kelso 1968: 118), pottery jar stopper shaped like a cork with a loop on top (#277 = PTS 2–11), bronze slug (#285 = PTS 2.0–185), lamp (#438).

Phase 3 produced some Philistine pottery (Kelso 1934: 417). It was also burned (Albright and Kelso 1968: 35), although early reports indicated no destruction (Kelso 1934: 417).

Phase 4a (1050–): Room 4: wall on north side along Room 7, Piers 31, 32, and 30; Pavement 28 at 9.320; two piers are dressed, indicating the improvement in masonry techniques. There is improvement in pottery as well: burnished and other new pottery. No more Philistine pottery found (Kelso 1955: 7). Finds include: long-collared collared-rim pithoi (Albright and Kelso 1968: 34, 63); pyxide (#3095 = PTS 2–13) from Pit 5 (in 1960's Area P, the East Garden); basalt seal of a lion attacking antelope (Albright 1934: 13); frit scarab (#1012, Albright and Kelso 1968: 88); figurine of a bust of a horse with bulging eyes (#1112). This stratum continues into early Iron II.

Much Iron I material cannot be assigned to phase. Such finds include (from "1954 Daybooks 1–2"; "1954 Object Cards"; "1954 Record Book"; "1957 Room Cards"; "1957 Daybooks"; "1957 Artifact Books 1–2"): seals; beads of carnelian and steatite; bone tools (spatula #3071 = PTS 2.3–048); bronze jewelry; sling stones, iron, bronze, copper, and flint arrowheads (for flint, #3065a = PTS 2.3–012 from 1960 SW Room Pit 5 in Area P East Garden); iron and flint javelin heads; flint knives (#3066 = PTS 2.3–049 from 1960 Pit 5); flint scraper (#3073 from Pit 5); four flint sickles (including #3068 = PTS 2.3–025 from Pit 5, #3074 = PTS 2.3–013, and #3080 = PTS 2.3–014); iron hammer; copper wire; Baal figurine (#328 from Locus 44); Astarte/Anat/Athirath/Asherah plaque (#104 from Sub6, found with carnelian bead #116 = PTS 2.0–019); ovens; querns, pestles, and grinders (Albright and Kelso 1968: 113); seven-wick lamp (Kelso 1956: 40); flint drill; stone pendant (#3064a = PTS 2.3–024 from Pit 5); hemispherical bowls with simple, rounded rims bowls (#3120 and #3136 from the West Garden), hemispherical bowl with flat, rectangular rims bowls (#3137) from Pit 5, and globular bowl with handles emphasizing the inturning of the rim to make the bowl seem more spherical #3131 from Pit 5. From 1957 "Madafeh Room" (1960's "Area H", southern end of site) at 2.3–5 m, Upper, West Wall: Vertical-rimmed, oval section krater (#2280), iron arrowhead (#2225 = PTS 2.2–089), whetstone #2224. From Room 401, at Walls 34 (the north one), 16–17 (east), and the southern one, but including no floors: flint awl (#1296 = PTS 2.2–027). From Room 402 at Walls 29(N), 16–17(W), 12+21(S), and 14. From Room 404: sickle teeth (#2033). From Room 407 at Walls 59(W), 20(E), 44(N), and 45(S), and 17 and Door-jamb 51: sherd of Philistine bichrome (#116), pithos #2272, and inside that pithos, a juglet (#2289 = PTS 2–211). From Room 408 at Pavements 9.180 and 9.130: southern-form chalice (#2245 = PTS 2–28); at Walls 58(S) and 48–49(W): bone spatula (#2082 = PTS 2.2–044), carnelian bead (#2091 = PTS 2.2–048). From Room 409 at 130 cm at Door-jamb 52, Piers 2–3, Wall 34, and Doorway 57: pithos base #2274, southern-type chalice (#2241 = PTS 2–56), iron arrowhead (#2134), bone awl (#2129), and pottery stamp (#2119 = PTS 2–2091). From Room 16: four astragal bones (#2035) used for gaming (Gilmour 1997a: 171), or possibly for ritual use (Gilmour 1997a: 172–73). From Room 307(originally #17) above the *huwwar* floors, 60 cm below the door to Room 305 (old #15) at the upper courses of N wall: flints at 8.795, large bowl with thickened, folded, and inverted rim #1036, copper wire #1044, iron arrowhead #1058, quartz spindle whorl #1048, lamps, bone awl made from a sheep's bone #1114. Room 304(old 14) has two Iron I phases, one above and one below the stone pavement—but which phases these are relative to

the site's phasing is unclear; from the 2nd phase of this room at E wall: low trumpet foot of a chalice. From Room 313(old 24 [sic]): juglet #1077 with lip-shoulder handle, copper bracelet #1086 in the NW, limestone dagger pommel #1090 in the NW, ceramic bullroarer or loom weight #1088, carnelian beads #1082 and 1087, piece of pumice #1089. From Room 305(old15): southern-type bowl #1038, pithos #1151 with a simple rim and high neck, astragal bones #1056 (see above), spindle whorl #1061, carnelian bead #1046. From Room 306(old16): copper bracelet #1045, copper ring #1050, sling stone #1042, *Zebar* refuse from pressing olive oil #1053. From Room 303(old13): pestle #1049. From Room 315: jar with seal on handle #1150. From "Area 6": carinated southern-type bowls #1003 and #1039.

BIR EL-HADAB (Tzur Natan) M.R. 1524.1831

A single-period Iron I isolated four-roomed house or lodge. The house is 15.4×19.8 m, with rubble walls 1.5 m-thick, indicative of a second story. There was likely a hedge or wooden fence around the yard. The well of Bir el-Hadab is less than a meter from the structure (Dar 1986: 77).

BIR EL-HAMAM, KH.   M.R. 17155.1413

0.4 ha. site with Iron I and no LB or Iron II (Dinur 1987a: 43).

BIR EL-HILU (Kh. Hamida) M.R. 1492.1372

The site was 1.4 ha. in Iron I (and in LB), and also inhabited in Iron II. Iron I finds include simple-rimmed storejars, cooking pots with sharp, triangular slanted rims, outflaring-necked non-carinated cooking pots, cooking pots with plain rims, kraters with everted rims and no handles, and painted Philistine bowls with out-flaring rims and two handles (Aharoni 1969: esp. 140; Finkelstein 1996: 237).

BIR EL-KHARAYIB   M.R. 1706.1665

0.5 ha. site. 1.25 km to nearest water. Iron I and II remains, the Iron I including collared-rimmed and hole-mouth pithoi (Finkelstein et al. 1985: 173; Finkelstein 1988a: 181).

BIR ES-SAFA — see BATN UMM NARI

BIR ESH-SHUWEIHA — see SHUWEIHA, KH.

BIR ET-TELL   M.R. 16335.16600

0.3 ha. site on hilltop. 400 m to nearest water. Eight percent Iron I sherds, including collared-rimmed and hole-mouth pithoi (Finkelstein 1983a: 140; 1988a: 165–66, 181).

EL-BIRD (Ras Hamoud)   M.R. 1943.1923

1.85 ha. site in valley sixty meters below surrounding terrain. Mediterranean Brown Forest soil and Colluvial soil. Spring of Ein el-Mitah is on-site. Ten percent Iron I sherds, of which half are "Einun" jars (having flared rims with 2–3 steps on the neck). The other half includes collared-rimmed pithoi with short, thick everted rims, and rim puncturing and "man's face" puncturing on handles (Zertal 1996: 273–76).

BIRZEIT, KH.   M.R. 16825.15250

Hilltop site of four hectares. Site survey conducted in 1996 by Hamid Salim, along with the first season of excavations of the site by the Birzeit University Palestinian Institute of Archaeology under Khaled Nashef, for which the present author was pottery manager, revealed occupation from LB (one sherd from the survey, sherd KB96–34 from excavations), Iron I (from excavations, sherds KB96–60, KB96–77, KB96–155, and KB96–159; confirming earlier work by Abel 1937: 224; and Finkelstein 1983a: 144), and Iron II (KB96–511, KB96–587, KB96–595, KB96–617, KB96–709, KB96–716, KB96–761). There is an emptied Iron I tomb on the south slope (Abel 1928: 50; 1996 survey and excavations).

BULL SITE — see DHAHRAT ET-TAWILEH

BURAK, KH. EL-   M.R. 16085.1681

0.5 ha. site. 2.9 km to nearest water source. Less than two percent Iron I, all from the southwestern slope. Also Iron II. Iron I finds include collared-rimmed and hole-mouth pithoi (Finkelstein 1986: 147; 1988a: 164, 180). Unpublished examination of the site was undertaken by S. Dar, E. Kindler, A. Zigelman, and E. Cohen on behalf of the Eretz Israel Museum, Tel Aviv.

BURGETA, TEL — see SHITRAI, TELL or BURJ, KH. EL-

EL-BURJ   M.R. 15210.14550

Site, which in Iron I was 0.5ha, situated on a hill. Also inhabited in Iron II (Shavit 1992: 89–90).

BURJ, KH. EL-   M.R. 16787.13675

3 ha. site on hill. Terra Rosa soil. Few Iron I sherds, also Iron II (Finkelstein and Magen 1993: 46*, 231–33).

BURJ EL-HUBIS — see TITTORAH, HORVAT

EL-BURNAT SITTI SALAAMIYYA (Mt. Ebal)   M.R. 1773.1829

The site is on the north spur of Mt. Ebal (Jebel et-Tur), 150 m below the peak and 25 m up from the base (Zertal 1983b: 72). Terra Rosa soil (Liphschitz 1986/87: 190). 1.5 km to spring (Zertal 1992: 490). Stratum II is an LB village/campsite, which was not destroyed, but is remodeled as Stratum IB: 1200–1140. This stratum shows no domestic architecture (Gilmour 1995: 114). The controversial nature of the results of this site's excavation merit a full discussion here.

Its prominent feature is what Zertal calls the "Altar": in Area A, it is a square structure of unhewn stones 9×14 m with walls 1.45 m thick (Zertal

1983b: 22; 1985: 30; 1986–87: 113). No floor or entrance (Zertal 1985: 31). Possibly filled deliberately with four layers of bones of male bulls, caprovids, and fallow deer, Iron I pottery including a whole collared-rim pithos, and ash of Kermesian oak (Zertal 1986–87: 113). It is possible, however, that the filling is from the LB Stratum II (Gilmour 1995). Corners of the structure are oriented N–S (Zertal 1985: 32). Two walls come partway in to the center but do not meet (1985: 32). On the outside walls, 1.2 m down is a little ledge (Zertal 1985: 38). On SE side is a ramp, 1.2 m wide, 7 m long, with 22 degree rise to full 2 m height at its NW end (Zertal 1985: 32), and on the sides of that are two paved courtyards totaling 27×7 m (Zertal 1983: 22), the southern one 6×8 m. One has three stone installations and the other four. Some of these installations are chalked, all of them are either filled with bones and ash (#53, 63, 64) or with jars, jugs, juglets, and pyxides (42, 51, 249), but never mixed both bones/ash and pottery (Zertal 1985).

Surrounding this is a figure-eight shaped thin enclosure wall (W29–W75). It encloses 3500 m³, is 1 m high, 110 m long. In Area B there is a gate (Locus 220, built over earlier domestic rooms), 7 m wide with 3 steps, and a paved courtyard platform (Zertal 1985: 34; 1986/87: 119–20). Inside the enclosure there are more installations similar to those in the courtyards—hundreds of them. But, contra to Zertal (1986/87: 111, 148), it seems these were sealed before LB Stratum II (Gilmour 1995: 109). Beyond the thin wall, 7 m to the west and down-slope, is a retaining wall 250 m long and 1.7–2.5 m wide (Zertal 1986/87: 108)

Stratum IB finds: Overall, too few cooking pots and too many jugs and jars for a simply domestic occupation (Gilmour 1995: 111). From the enclosure installations (Zertal 1986/87: 139–40): pithoi (some collared-rimmed, some with simple rim and low neck), bowls (see below), jugs (globular body, ring base), juglets (small, one-handled, pointed base), no bones. Scarab: Rameses II issue of Thutmose III commemorative, dated 1250–1200 (Zertal 1986: 52). Overall, bowls are large bowls with thickened, folded, and inverted rims or bell-shaped bowls (Zertal 1986/87: 125; cf. Gilmour

1995: 114, who maintains the bell-shaped bowls are from LB Stratum II). 69 kraters (straight walls, curved rims; Zertal 1986/87: 139). 51 cooking pots—with plain rims or with ridge just below the lip (81%; Bunimovitz and Finkelstein 1993: 157; Zertal 1986/87: 130, 140). 49 jars, some with punctured handles, 250 pithoi (84% collared-rimmed; Bunimovitz and Finkelstein 1993: 158), 142 jugs, many with man's face decoration, one Biconical (Zertal 1986/87: 140), 47 juglets, no sickle blades (Zertal 1986/87: 148), bronze loop earring, bronze ingot (Gilmour 1995), iron nail (Zertal 1986/87: 150), 32 sandstone basins (Zertal 1986/87: 148).

Floral remains: ash of terebinth and Kermesian oak, also rare olive and almond. Faunal remains: No equids, pigs, or carnivores. Fallow Deer: 10% overall, which is high; 63% of them in "altar" (Horwitz 1986/87: 175). All are two years old or more, indicating they were hunted. Half the bones are cranial bones, meaning antlers were likely sought. Some butchered at joints (Horwitz 1986/87: 180). Caprovids: 65% overall (Horwitz 1986/87: 174). They constitute 81% of all the burnt bones (4% of all bones), 44% of which are in the altar. Burnt in open flame at 285–525$_8$C (Horwitz 1986/87: 179), that is, roasted. Cattle: 21% overall. Most adult males, meaning plough animals. They constitute almost half of the joint-cut animals (3% of all bones; this is unit-butchering), almost half of which are in the altar (Horwitz 1986/87: 177, 179). Also Mottled Polecat (*Vormella peregusna*, a local species), Red-Billed Chukar partridge (*Alectoris cypriotes*, a local game-bird), Arabian rock pigeon (*Columba livia*), falcon, fish (in the altar), and Cardium shell of Mediterranean *Glycymerys violacescens* (Horwitz 1986/87: 173; this is used for jewelry, as at Tell Taanach where it is a moon symbol). None of these are burned (Horwitz 1986/87: 180).

Stratum IA: around 1140 there was a (deliberate?) covering of stones in Areas A and B (Zertal 1986/87: 123).

BURQIN   M.R. 1748.2069

Not to be confused with Khirbet Burqin, the modern town is itself a 3.5 ha. site. It is 38 m above the

Dothan Valley. Terra Rosa soil. Nearest spring is 35 m away. Ten percent Iron I sherds, also LB and Iron II (Zertal 1988: 101; 1992: 98).

BURRA'ISH, KH.   M.R. 15280.16160

0.8 ha. site on a ridge. 4.1 km to nearest water source. 2.2%–5% Iron I sherds, including collared-rimmed pithoi. Also Iron II (Finkelstein 1988a: 176, 181; Finkelstein, Lederman, and Bunimovitz 1997: 85).

EL-BUSEILIYYA — see MARAH EL-INAB, KH.

DAWARA   M.R. 17865.17000

0.8 ha. site on a hill. 1.3 km to water. 86.4% Iron I sherds, mostly on the southwest side, and the rest of the habitation is from Iron II. Iron I finds include cooking pots with erect or slanted rims , other cooking pots, forty collared-rimmed pithoi, one with reed impressions, two punctured jar handles, and four kraters (Finkelstein 1986: 137; 1988a: 151, 179).

DAWWARA, KH. ED-   M.R. 17775.14150

This excavated site is well-documented and discussed in Braemer (1982), Bunimovitz and Finkelstein (1993), Finkelstein (1985b; 1987; 1988; 1990a), and Fritz (1995).

ED-DEIR   M.R. 1796.1969

Entirely Iron I sherd scatter of 0.04 ha. on slope fifteen meters above surrounding terrain. Terra Rosa soil. Five kilometers to nearest spring at Ein Jerba. Pottery includes rolled pithos rim, bowl rim, jar base (Finkelstein 1986: 125; Zertal 1996: 143).

DEIR, KH. ED- — see DUWEIR, KH. ED-

DEIR, KH. ED-, EAST
(Kh. Siniyya)   M.R. 1865.1906

0.6–1.0 ha. site covering entire five-meter tall hill

in Tubas Valley. Eroded and alluvial soil. Thirty percent Iron I sherds, no LB or Iron II. Iron I wares include the so-called "Einun" storejars, outcurving, lipped-rim cooking pots, and jugs, some with trumpet bases (the so-called "Einun" jugs). Iron I stone tools were also found (Finkelstein 1986: 148; Zertal 1996: 207–8).

DEIR 'AMMAR   M.R. 15985.15270

0.55 ha. site on hilltop. 300 m to water. 1.5% Iron I sherds, including cooking pots with erect or slanted rims cooking pot, also Iron II (Finkelstein 1988a: 172, 181; Finkelstein, Lederman, and Bunimovitz 1997: 15).

DEIR EL-'AZER
(Deir el-Azhar)   M.R. 1595.1345

Not to be confused with the site on the south slope now called Tel Kiryat Yearim, this site lies underneath the "Our Lady Ark of the Covenant" church of the Sisters of St. Joseph of the Apparition. Iron I remains include a "jar-krater" found 15 March 1997, now in the Albright Institute collection (see also Ahituv 1984: 126). Also, at the foot of the east slope, three Iron I bench tombs were excavated by Cooke (1925: esp. 115).

DEIR EL-AZHAR — see DEIR EL-'AZER

DEIR DAQLA, KH.   M.R. 1521.16215

0.8 ha. site on ridge. 600 m to nearest water. 6%–7.5% Iron I, also Iron II. Iron I includes collared-rimmed pithoi (Finkelstein 1988a: 175, 179; Finkelstein, Lederman, and Bunimovitz 1997: 87).

DEIR GHASSANA   M.R. 15935.16150

4.2 ha. site on plateau. 900 m to nearest water. 12.5% Iron I sherds, also Iron II. Collared-rimmed pithoi represented (Finkelstein 1988a: 168, 181; Finkelstein, Lederman, and Bunimovitz 1997: 116).

DEIR EL-MIR
(Kh. el-Emir)   M.R. 15385.16290

2.5 ha. site on hilltop and slope. 1.2 km to nearest water. 2.5% Iron I sherds, also Iron II. Collared-rimmed pithoi and punctured jar handles represented (Finkelstein 1983a: 156; 1988a: 175, 181; Finkelstein, Lederman, and Bunimovitz 1997: 91; Otto 1997: 11).

DEIR EL-QASSIS, KH.
(Kh. Jami 'Umar Bin Khattab) M.R. 1532.1667

0.6 ha. site on southwest side of hilltop. 3.9 km to nearest water. 1.4% Iron I sherds, including collared-rimmed pithoi (Finkelstein 1983a: 156; 1988a: 174; Finkelstein, Lederman, and Bunimovitz 1997: 92).

DEIR YASSIN — see MISPE HAR NOF

DHAHRAT ES-SENOBAR   M.R. 1719.1862

0.12 ha. site on ridge 180 m above the surrounding terrain in mountainous area. Rendzina soil. Nearest spring two kilometers. Thirty percent Iron I (Zertal 1992: 436–37).

DHAHRAT ET-TAWILEH (Bull Site)
M.R. 18065.2016

A hilltop site on ridge 75 m above surrounding terrain. Terra Rosa soil. 5 km to nearest spring. Survey found only five percent of sherds Iron I (Zertal 1992: 169), yet the excavator (A. Mazar 1982a; 1982c) describes it as a single-period Iron I site. The nature of the excavation of this site justifies its thorough discussion.

The site is a 20.5×23 m elliptical enclosure made of large stones, up to 1.2 m long each (Wenning and Zenger 1986: 75). There is an opening in the east (H. Weippert 1988: 407). On the east side is a stone ca. 1 m long, a little under 1 m high, and ca. 10 cm thick (A. Mazar 1982a: 36). The bedrock in front of this stone had been leveled and paved (A. Mazar 1982a: 36). In the southern half of the enclosure was a small stone installation and a rectangular dressed stone laying on its side—some sort of monolith, table, or fallen pillar (A. Mazar and Rosen 1982; Coogan 1987: 1). The excavator states that in Iron I a tree stood in the center of the enclosure (A. Mazar 1997: 384).

Finds: The most notable find was made on the site not by archaeologists, but as a chance discovery by a soldier (Ahlström 1993: 363). This is a bronze bull, possibly hump-backed Zebu bull (although this may be merely a feature of its construction; Edelman 1996: 51). It is 17.5 cm long, 12.4 m high made by lost-wax technique (A. Mazar 1982a: 27; Ahlström 1990: 78–79). Its eyes were likely glass or gems (A. Mazar 1982a: 27; 1983: 37). Analogous figurines are from LB Ugarit or Hazor (A. Mazar 1982a: 29), an identical statue in the Ashmolean Museum from North Syria/Lebanon from the 8th century B.C. (Moorey 1971: 91), similar ones from Urartu (Moorey 1971: 90), and one from Tell Halaf ca. 900 B.C. (Moorey 1971: 90).

Other finds: No ash, few bones (A. Mazar 1982a: 33); bronze Egyptian-style mirror (A. Mazar 1982a: 36, fig.11); pottery incense burner (if analogous to ones from Megiddo and Beth Shean) or model of a shrine (if analogous to one at Tell el-Farah North; A. Mazar 1982a: 36–37, fig. 10; cf. Coogan 1987: 1); domestic flint tools, including 3 perforator-awls, 5 scrapers, 1 sickle 4.6×2.4×.8 cm, 9 notches and denticulates, 1 nosed scraper, 1 notched borer-drill, 1 thumbnail scraper—all made on-site except one of the scrapers (A. Mazar 1982a: 41; this is the assemblage of a leather hide-working industry); pottery includes (A. Mazar and Rosen 1982: 140; Coogan 1987: 1), cooking pots having sharp, triangular rims that are flattened and unaccentuated, cooking pots that are triangular-rimmed with molded lower edge, and triangular-rimmed cooking pots with an upper lip that has been folded inward (A. Mazar 1982c: 140–41), large bowls with thickened, folded, and inverted rims, and hemispherical bowls with beveled rims whose upper surface slopes outward diagonally (A. Mazar 1982c).

DHAHRAT EZ-ZABAN, JEBEL
M.R. 17365.15845

0.1 ha. site on plain. 700 m to nearest water. 84.6% Iron I, also Iron II. Iron I includes collared-rimmed and hole-mouth pithoi (Finkelstein 1986: 151; Finkelstein, Lederman, and Bunimovitz 1997: 352).

DHIYAB, KH. (Kh. Ibn Nasr;
Ras Juleijil)   M.R. 17920.17835

0.2–0.3 ha. site on summit of a hill on the north peak of the Ras Muhammed ridge. 2.4 km to nearest water. Terra Rosa soil. 90%–95.5% Iron I sherds, no LB or early Iron II. Iron I pottery includes cooking pots having sharp, triangular rims that are flattened and unaccentuated, collared-rimmed store jars, punctured jar handles (such as Albright Institute collection #S19.14), hemispherical bowls with simple, rounded rims (such as #S19.2, 11), kraters, and jugs (Campbell 1984: 69; 1991: 6, 44; Finkelstein 1986: 133; 1988a: 179; Finkelstein, Lederman, and Bunimovitz 1997: 485; pottery in Albright Institute collection).

DHUQ, KH. EDH-
(Kh. el-Fukhar)   M.R. 1851.1813

Unpublished survey by E. F. Campbell on 4 July 1960 found Iron I and II pottery, which is stored in the Albright Institute collection.

DOTHAN, TELL   M.R. 1727.2021

Tell site 42 m above the terrain on Terra Rosa soil. Spring on south side of tell. Settled area ten hectares (Cooley 1983: 50). Also LB and Iron II remains. Although the excavations of the site are rather poorly published, research on the site continues, as does its publication. Relevant published discussions to which the reader should refer include Abercrombie (1979), Cockerham (1995), Cooley (1980; 1983; 1998), Cooley and Pratico (1994; 1995), Free (1954; 1955; 1956a; 1956b; 1957; 1958; 1959; 1960; 1962), Molin (1954–56), Dothan II (1980), Negbi (1991: 231), Ribar (1973: 45–76), and Schmidt (1994: 28, 197).

DUWEIR, KH. ED-
(Kh. ed-Deir)   M.R. 1649.1845

Hilltop site of 0.2 ha. Nearest water is Wadi el-Ban, 1.75 km away. Site surveyed by the author on 31 December 1996. Iron I and II sherds found. Iron I includes large jugs with rim-shoulder handles and ridge-necked jugs.

DUWWAR, KH. ED-   M.R. 15275.16015

0.7 ha. site on slope. 4.2 km to nearest water. 8.4%–10% Iron I sherds, the remainder are Iron II. Iron I include cooking pots with erect or slanted rims and cooking pots with sharp, triangular slanted rims and collared-rimmed pithoi (Finkelstein 1983a: 157; 1988a: 176, 181; Finkelstein, Lederman, and Bunimovitz 1997: 446).

EBAL, MT. — see EL-BURNAT

EIN ABUS — see EINABUS

EIN BEIT FARR — see BEIT FARR, KH.

EIN FANDAQUMIYYA — see EL-MUSTAH

EIN FARA — see ABU MUSARRAH, KH.

EIN FARR, KH.   M.R. 1855.1829

1.8 ha. site in valley slope and declivity seventy meters above the surrounding terrain. Rendzina soil. Spring of Ein Farr is in the site. Twenty percent Iron I, no LB or Iron II. Iron I pottery includes cooking pots having sharp triangular slanted rim with ridge on bottom edge of rim, cooking pots with plain rims, and hemispherical bowls with pointed or simple, rounded rims (Zertal 1996: 409–11).

EIN EL-MEIYITA — see EN JEZREEL

EIN MISKA — see MISKI, TELL

EIN ES-SAMIYYA — see MARJAMA, TELL

EINABUS (Ein Abus)   M.R. 1733.1726

1.1 ha. site, being the south slope of the modern Arab village. One kilometer to nearest water. 25.6%–32% of sherds found were Iron I, also LB and Iron II. Iron I ceramics include collared-rimmed pithoi and punctured jar handles (Finkelstein 1988a: 149, 179; Finkelstein, Lederman, and Bunimovitz 1997: 450).

EINUN, KH.   M.R. 1875.1898

3.2 ha. site on hilltop thirty meters high. Terra Rosa soil. Five kilometers to nearest water at Ein el-Farah. The site was fortified in Iron I (Zertal 1983a: 44; 1996: 213–24). Seventy percent of sherds found were Iron I, also Iron II. Iron I ceramics include punctured and "man's face" punctured jar and jug handles, storejars with thickened rim and ridge on neck, storejars with thickened rim and ridge at the bottom of the rim that has merged with the rim itself, the so-called "Einun" jars, large bowls with thickened, folded, and inverted rims, cooking pots with outcurving, lipped-rim and cooking pots having sharp triangular slanted rim with ridge on bottom edge of rim or just below the lip, and flared-neck, metope-painted jugs (Ilan 1973: 362; Zertal 1983a: 44; 1996: 213–14).

'ELEQ, HORVAT — see UMM EL-'ALAQ, KH.

EMIR, KH. EL- — see DEIR EL-MIR

**EN JEZREEL
(Ein el-Meiyita)   M.R. 1819.2182**

LB and Iron I site. Iron I remains include large bowls with thickened, folded, and inverted rims (Zori 1977: 19).

**ESUR, TEL (Tell el-Asawir;
Kh. es-Sumrah)   M.R. 1521.2098**

200 m to spring at En Arubboth (En Esur). Contrary to M. Dothan (*EAEHL*, 100), there are Iron I remains on the northern mound of the tell (Ne'eman 1990: 25*, 23). Also LB, no Iron II.

FAKHAKHIR, KH. EL — see HAMAD, KH.

FARA, TEL — see ABU MUSARRAH, KH.

FARAH, TELL EL- (NORTH) M.R. 1823.1882

Ten-hectare site (Joffe 1997: 304). 160 m to spring of Ein Farah. LB and Iron II occupation also. The definitive publication for the Iron I remains from this excavated site is Chambon (1984). Other relevant publications are Braemer (1982: 71), Joffe (1997), de Vaux (1951a; 1951b; 1952; 1955a; 1955b; 1956; 1957; 1967), and de Vaux and Steve (1947).

FARISIYYA, KH. EL-   M.R. 1652.1932

0.5 ha. site thirty meters above the plain of er-Rameh. Rendzina soil. Spring 2.5 m away. Five percent Iron I sherds, also Iron II (Zertal 1992: 253–54).

FARIA EL-JIFTLIK — see EL-JIFTLIK

FARKHA   M.R. 16410.16405

2.2 ha. Arab village on hilltop at edge of ridge. 800 m to nearest water. Ancient pottery from terraces on north slope: 2.8% Iron I, including collared-rimmed pithoi, and Iron II (Finkelstein 1988a: 167–68; 181; Finkelstein, Lederman, and Bunimovitz 1997: 255).

FARRIYYA, KH. EL- — see PARUS, TEL

EL-FARSHE — see MARAH EL-INAB, KH.

FASSA, KH.   M.R. 16240.15870

3 ha. site on a hill. 400 m to water. 0.7% Iron I, also Iron II (Finkelstein, Lederman, and Bunimovitz 1997: 199).

FENDAKUMIE — see EL-MUSTAH

FIRR, TELL EL- — see SHALWIM, TEL

FUKHAR, KH. EL- — see DHUQ, KH. EDH-

FUL, TELL EL-   M.R. 172.137

150×90 m site atop thirty-meter high hill. No water source in the immediate vicinity of the site. Also Iron II remains. N. Lapp (1981) provides a full publication of the site. See also Albright (1924b; 1924c; 1933; 1934), Birch (1911), Brug (1985: 96), Gibson (1996), Kurinsky (1991: 119), N. Lapp (1997), P. Lapp (1965; 1975), J. M. Miller (1975), Masterman (1913), A. Mazar (1994: 76–78), Sinclair (1960), Stager (1968: 9), H. Weippert (1988), and G. R. H. Wright (1985).

FUQAHA, KH.
(Kh. es-Sumra)   M.R. 1850.1933

6 ha. tell site sixty meters above the Tubas Valley. Terra Rosa soil. Seven kilometers to spring at Ein el-Farah. Fortified in Iron I. Five percent of sherds Iron I, also Iron II. Iron I pottery includes cooking pots having sharp triangular slanted rim with ridge on bottom edge of rim, and collared-rimmed pithoi with short, thick everted rims (Finkelstein 1986: 134; Zertal 1983a: 44; 1996: 196–97).

FUREIR, KH. — see PARUS, TEL

GHANNAM, KH.   M.R. 18335.17385

0.7 ha. site in Wadi Fusil, 700 m to the water. Five percent of sherds Iron I, the rest Iron II. Iron I sherds include cooking pots with sharp, triangular slanted rims and other cooking pots, collared-rimmed and hole-mouth pithoi (Finkelstein 1986: 135; 1988a: 179).

GHURABA, KH.   M.R. 17290.16115

0.7-1.0 ha. site. 550 m to nearest water. Some Iron I sherds on southeastern slope, also Iron II. Iron I includes collared-rimmed pithoi (Finkelstein 1983a: 142-43; 1988a: 180; Finkelstein, Lederman, and Bunimovitz 1997: 393).

GHUREITIS, KH.   M.R. 17220.15075

0.2 ha. site. 100 m to nearest water. 2.5% Iron I sherds, from the south edge of the site, no LB or Iron II. Iron I includes collared-rimmed pithoi (Finkelstein 1988a: 160, 180; Finkelstein, Lederman, and Bunimovitz 1997: 339).

GIMZO (Jimzu)   M.R. 145.1485

Iron I village (Finkelstein 1996: 237–38).

GIVAT JONATHAN
(Kh. Kermat; el-Kurum)   M.R. 1847.2164

3.5 ha. site with LB, Iron I, and Iron II occupation (Zori 1977: 8–10).

GIVIT, HORVAT — see JIBIT, KH.

HADERA, NAHAL — see QUREIN, JEBEL

HADID, TELL
(el-Haditha)   M.R. 14540.15250

0.2–0.5 ha. site with LB, Iron I, and Iron II remains, located to the northwest of the larger tell. Iron I includes collared-rimmed pithoi, cooking pots triangular-rimmed with molded lower edge, and cooking pots having sharp triangular slanted rim with ridge on bottom edge of rim (Menorah 1975: 45; Dagan 1996: 122; Finkelstein 1996: 238; Gophna and Beit-Arieh 1997: 77–78, 62*–63*).

HAFI, KH. EL-   **M.R. 16335.14550**

0.3 ha. site on hilltop on ridge. 400 m to nearest water. Seven percent Iron I sherds, also Iron II. Iron I includes cooking pots with erect or slanted rims and collared-rimmed and hole-mouth storejars (Finkelstein 1988a: 174, 181).

HAMAD, KH.
(Kh. el-Fakhakhir)   **M.R. 15965.16605**

0.6 ha. site on ridge. 4.3% of pottery from survey was Iron I, also Iron II. Excavations revealed an Iron I enclosure 31×75 m (2300 m²) on the top and extending down the east slope, and a threshing floor on the northern edge (Dar 1986: 38–42; Finkelstein, Lederman, and Bunimovitz 1997: 118).

HAMAMAT, KH.   **M.R. 1962.1895**

0.4 ha. site on cliff fifty meters above the surrounding terrain. Three kilometers to nearest water at Ein Hilu spring. Rendzina soil. Thirty percent Iron I, also LB. Iron I pottery includes collared-rimmed pithoi with short, thick everted rims and the so-called "Einun Jars" (Zertal 1996: 314-16).

HAMID, TEL — see RAS ABU HAMID

HAMIDA, KH. — see BIR EL-HILU

HAMMAM, WADI EL-   **M.R. 17185.15410**

0.2 ha. site on ridge. 400 meters to water. 14.3% of sherds Iron I, no LB or Iron II (Finkelstein, Lederman, and Bunimovitz 1997: 336).

HAMME, TELL EL-   **M.R. 19735.1977**

0.5 ha. hilltop site, equaling 90×120 m occupation surface in a 500×500 m area (Zori 1977: 37). Thirty meters above Beth Shean valley. Occupation from LB, Iron I, and Iron II (de Contenson 1964: 41). There are three Iron I phases (Cahill et al. 1989b: 38), in the Area K and J terraces (Cahill et al. 1988: 193). Earliest Phase: Beaten earth floor

in J6-7, 1.384. Rectangular building 6.5 m long in K8-J6-7. Finds: 5 pithoi, flint pounders, basalt grinders, unbaked clay loom weights. Destroyed. Middle Phase: mudbrick building on stone foundation. Last Phase: stone and mudbrick buildings, beaten earth floor in K6. Also Iron I sherds found in Trench I6.

HANNUN   **M.R. 17530.17550**

0.05 ha. site on slope. 800 m to water. 85.7% of sherds Iron I, also Iron II (Finkelstein, Lederman, and Bunimovitz 1997: 462).

HARA EL-FOQA, KH. EL-M.R. 17630.14240

4 ha. site. Twelve percent Iron I sherds, also Iron II. Iron I sherds include collared-rimmed and simple-rimmed pithoi (Finkelstein and Magen 1993: 36*, 185).

EL-HATAB ASYRET — see ASIRA ESH-SHAMALIYYA

HAUSH, KH. EL- — see KHAUSH, KH. EL-

HILU, KH. TELL EL- (Tell Abu Sifry;
Tell Sheikh Sifry)   **M.R. 19775.1926**

0.2-0.32 ha. site on hill forty meters above valley floor. Spring of Ein Hilu is on-site. Mediterranean Brown Forest soil. Ten percent Iron I, also LB and Iron II. Iron I includes cooking pots with outcurving, lipped-rim and cooking pots having sharp triangular slanted rim with ridge on bottom edge of rim (Mittmann 1970: 129; Ilan 1973: 347; Finkelstein 1986: 141; Zertal 1996: 283–85).

EL-HISH   **M.R. 1647.1934**

Iron I (100%) site of 0.04 ha. on ten meter high rise in mountainous area. Three kilometers to nearest water. Rendzina soil (Zertal 1992: 252).

HIZMA   **M.R. 17535.13815**

Iron I sherds, with no LB or Iron II, have been found in the old center of the modern village (Dinur 1987b: 37; S. Gibson 1995: 428).

HULU, TELL EL- — see HILU, KH. TELL EL-

IBN 'AMR, KH.
(Kh. Abu Amir)   **M.R. 1703.2095**

3 ha. site on hilltop twenty-five meters above terrain. Rendzina soil. Five percent Iron I, also Iron II (Zertal 1988: 92).

IBN NASR, KH. — see DHIYAB, KH.

IJENISINIYYA (Jenesinia)   M.R. 1705.1865

3.2 ha. site with spring on it. Rendzina soil. Five percent Iron I, also Iron II (Zertal 1988: 157; 1992: 433–34).

IKHREIN, KH. EL — see QUREIN, JEBEL

'ILLAN, JEBEL   **M.R. 1658.1909**

0.2 ha. site on an 80 m-high mountain. Rendzina soil. 500 m to nearest spring. Five percent Iron I, no LB or Iron II (Zertal 1988: 146; 1992: 293–94).

IRAQ BURIN   **M.R. 1727.1788**

LB and Iron I tomb (Bull and Campbell 1968: 38; Jaroš and Deckert 1977: 33).

IRAQ EL-HAMRA   **M.R. 1902.1800**

1.5 ha. site on 30 m-high hill. Terra Rosa soil. 700 m to Wadi Farah. Twelve percent Iron I, no LB or Iron II (Zertal 1996: 450–53).

IRAQ MATAR   **M.R. 2002.1765**

0.2 ha. site on ridge/cliff-top forty meters above the Jordan Valley. Soils are Stony Serozems, Stony Light Brown soils, and Brown Desert Skeletal soil. Eighty percent Iron I, no LB or Iron II. Iron I pottery includes cooking pots having sharp triangular slanted rim with ridge on bottom edge of rim, or with ridge just below the lip, or with plain rims (Zertal 1996: 578–79; survey by the present author on 16 May 1996 found no Iron I pottery).

IRAQ RAJJAH   **M.R. 1866.1900**

0.1 ha. entirely Iron I site fifteen meters above the surrounding terrain on valley slope and hill. Eroded soil. Four kilometers to nearest water at Ein el-Farah spring. Site consists of a small building, 4×2 m, atop the hill, and another wall fragment in the north declivity of the hill. On the northeast edge, there is a double press with another stone circle above it. Pottery includes "Einun wares" (both the jars and trumpet-based jugs), hemispherical bowls, some with beveled rims whose upper surface slopes outward diagonally, cooking pots with outcurving, lipped-rims, cooking pots with sharp, triangular slanted rims, cooking pots having sharp triangular slanted rim with ridge on bottom edge of rim, cooking pots with ridge just below the lip, and cooking pots with plain rims (Zertal 1996: 210).

IRAQ ET-TAYYIH   **M.R. 1770.1805**

Several tombs used in LB and Iron I (Campbell 1991: 20).

IRHA, KH.   **M.R. 1724.1394**

Although Finkelstein and Magen (1993: Site #430) found no Iron I, Shimon Gibson has found Iron I and II sherds (Gibson 1995: 428).

IZBET ABU HALIL   **M.R. 16005.1722**

0.2 ha. site on ridge. 400 m to nearest water at Wadi el-Majur. 85.7% Iron I sherds, also Iron II. Iron I pottery includes cooking pots having sharp, triangular rims that are flattened and unaccentuated, and punctured jar handles (Finkelstein 1988a: 162, 180; Finkelstein, Lederman, and Bunimovitz 1997: 277).

IZBET SARTAH   M.R. 1468.1679

Site of 0.4 ha in Iron I, situated on a small hill at the end of a spur overlooking the alluvial coastal plain. Rocky Terra Rosa soil, with adjacent Red Colluvial-Alluvial soil and Grumsol; within one kilometer radius is Brown Grumsol (A. Rosen 1986: 158). Also Iron II remains. This excavated site is published in Finkelstein (1985a). Other important discussions include Braemer (1982: 61, 71), Brug (1985), Bunimovitz and Finkelstein (1993), De Groot and Lehmann (1996), Dever (1991; 1992), Dotan (1981), Finkelstein (1983a; 1992b), Garbini (1978), Garsiel and Finkelstein (1978), Helwig, Sade, and Kishon (1993), Kochavi (1977), Kochavi and Demsky (1978), Daliyat (1978), Naveh (1978), A. Rosen (1986: 158), and Watkins (1997a).

JABA NORTH (Jeba')   M.R. 1712.1923

3 ha. site forty meters above terrain. Spring of Ein el-Gharbiyya is on-site. Twelve percent Iron I sherds, also Iron II (Zertal 1988: 139).

JABA SOUTH   M.R. 17495.14050

2 ha. site on hill. Two percent Iron I sherds, on east and north sides of modern Arab village. Also Iron II. Iron I pottery includes collared-rimmed, hole-mouth, and simple-rimmed pithoi (Finkelstein and Magen 1993: 35*, 177–78).

JALBUN   M.R. 1893.2073

Modern Arab village in valley between Mt. Abinadab and Ma'aleh Gilboa in the Wadi er-Rish and Wadi en-Nisaf. Iron I and II pottery was found under the village school, under the old train depot, on the south edge of the village, at the *weli* of Sheikh Ghashum, and at another weli. The Iron I pottery between the tombs was largely Cypriote (Zori 1977: 14-15).

JAMMA'IN   M.R. 1690.1709

Not to be confused with the Kh. Jamma'in at M.R. 1569.1752, this modern Arab village of 6.6 ha. contains ancient remains on the western slope. 3–4.1 km to nearest water. 3.8% Iron I sherds, no LB or early Iron II. Iron I includes neckless pithoi (Finkelstein 1988a: 163, 180; Finkelstein, Lederman, and Bunimovitz 1997: 293).

JAMI 'UMAR BIN KHATTAB, KH. — see DEIR EL-QASSIS, KH.

JANZAR, KH. (Kh. Janzur; Kh. el-Jinzur; Kh. el-Jinzar)   M.R. 1739.2034

2 ha. site on hillock four meters above the Dothan Valley. Alluvial soil. Nearest water is a well 39 m away. Twenty percent Iron I sherds, fifty percent if only looking at the eastern area. No LB or Iron II. Iron I remains include collared-rimmed pithoi with short, thick everted rims, and pithoi with ridge on neck below molded rim (Zertal 1984: 107; 1992: 134–35).

JARAYISH, KH. EL-   M.R. 18535.17105

0.7 ha. site. 100 m to nearest water. Ten percent Iron I sherds, also Iron II. Iron I pottery includes collared-rimmed pithoi and punctured jar handles (Finkelstein 1986: 132; 1988a: 143, 179; Finkelstein, Lederman, and Bunimovitz 1997: 577).

JELAMET 'AMER   M.R. 1881.1897

Ninety percent Iron I cemetery (rest Iron II) 0.12 ha. in size, ten meters up valley slope. Six kilometers to Ein el-Farah. Iron I finds include large bowls with thickened, folded, and inverted rims and long-necked piriform jugs (Zertal 1996: 215).

JELAMET HAMUL (Jelamet el-Hamula)   M.R. 1922.2018

Entirely Iron I site of 0.03 ha. on slope. Colluvial soil. Two kilometers to water at Ein Qa'un. Site contains a 9×7 m four-roomed house made of large unhewn stones (Zertal 1996: 155–56).

JENESINIA — see IJENISINIYYA

JEZREEL, TEL (Tel Yizreʻel; Zerin)   M.R. 1819.2182

6 ha. site 100 m above Jezreel Valley on ridge. Excavations revealed Iron I pottery in the western fills of Iron II in Area B. Also LB habitation (Porat et al. 1988/89: 191; Ussishkin and Woodhead 1992: 50; 1994: 21; 1997: 68). Iron I pottery includes Philistine bichrome bowls (such as Reg #1850/1) and chalices, and Cypriote red-and-black painted jugs and flasks made of Cypriote clay (Reg. #11817/1 and 11867/1, respectively; Zimhoni 1997: 85).

EL-JIB   M.R. 1676.1397

This is a 375×300 m site, with eight springs in its vicinity. It was occupied in LB only by tombs. In 1200 it was built, the first phase being the Pre-Fortress Period or Period I (Pritchard 1962a: 63; 1964a: 37, 39), a thriving city (Reed 1967). The site also has Iron II. The idiosyncratic publication of the excavations of this site and the unlikelihood that a final publication will ever be produced warrant a complete treatment herein.

The city is walled by the "Inner" Wall (Pritchard 1960a: 8; 1961: 22; 1963: 7; H. Weippert 1988: 403) in Areas 8, 9, and 10 (Pritchard 1962b: 122 1964a: 33), especially visible in 10-L-5, 1.6-3.4 m wide (Pritchard 1960a: 8; 1963: 10). In the area north of the "stairwell" another section is visible (Fieldbook "El-Jib Expedition 3rd Season").

Area 8: 8-G-6 has a fireplace in open court. Finds from that square include: Ledge-rimmed krater with three to four handles (#740; "No.1 Notebook" p.799), six bowls with ring bases, one with disc base and four handles ("No.2 Notebook"), cup ("No.2 Notebook"), glass orange ring bead (#856; "No.2 Notebook" p.1132), lamp, bronze needle (#915; "No.2 Notebook" p.1148), flint sickle blades.

Area 10: 10-L-5 by the wall has a larger-than-average house adjacent to wall, with living Floors 12–14 (Pritchard 1963: 12). It had a wooden roof, supported by hewn pillars in a line in the center.

Two big ovens adjacent to this domicile serve as a kitchen. Finds: double-ridged collared-rim pithoi (#3529 P3450 from Loci 21–23 Floor 14), bowls, cooking pots (from Loci 21–23 Floor 14, #3528 P3449 which is outcurving, lipped-rim or non-carinated; Pritchard 1964a: 35, 104; Fieldbook "El-Jib 1962 vol. 3").

Also in Area 10 is the "House with Pillars" in 10-M/N-3/4, Floors 3–4. Flooring is cobblestone in one place, clay in another (Pritchard 1964a: 36). The house is perpendicular to the city wall. In the house, Floor 4 in the northeast corner of Room 2 has a stone weight with possible ʻ (aleph) inscription (#3691 ST318 "El-Jib 1962 vol. 3"), a sherd with red paint, slip and burnish, and also a highly polished stone (#3690 ST317). Floor 3 has, from Room 2, a 25.3 cm-high hollow flared-top columnar cylinder with a narrowing bore and two broken handles (#3677 M341), a sherd with cream slip and burnish and hatching on the shoulder (#3676 P3500), and a collared-rim pithos (#3703 P3509). From Room 1: store-jar with flat base (#3650 P3478), a burnished rim of bell-shaped cyma bowl (#3646 P3474). From Floor 3 of this house, room uncertain, Cypriote Base-ring ware handle #3340.P3250 ("El-Jib 1962 vol.2")—this cannot be residual because there is no LB at el-Jib; combed sherd (#3341.P3251; ibid); outcurving, lipped-rim cooking pot #3409P3305 and cooking pot with sharp, triangular slanted rim #3410P3306; carinated bowl with cream slip and burnish and ring base (#3412P3308); red painted sherds (#3647P3475; #3679P3502; "El-Jib 1962 vol.3"). Also from Area 10, floor uncertain: 2 ovens, 2 store-jars, including hole-mouth (#3481P3354, #3482P3355, #3483P3356, #3484P3357, #3485P3358), cooking pot, bowls (some hemispherical bowls with beveled rims whose upper surface slopes outward diagonally, some have red paint on shoulder and rim), jugs (large with wide neck, trefoil mouth, and handle drawn from rim to shoulder; Pritchard 1964a: 104; and flared-neck, metope-painted #3487P3360).

Area 15: maybe an Iron I structure in 15-K-18. Area 17: Iron I stone-walled building in the west under Iron II house in 17-F/G-18/19/20 (Pritchard 1964a: 48).

An important feature of el-Jib is the water system. The consensus is that the "pool" was the Iron I system (Hallote 1997: 403; Cox 1974: 40). The "pool" is a cylindrical cut into the bedrock 11.8 m in diameter and 10.8 m deep. There is a spiral staircase along the north and east sides, which at the bottom continues into a tunnel to a spring room 13.6 m below the pool floor. The construction of this pool required the quarrying of some 3000 tons of rock, certainly a matter of conscripted labor. Caution should be exercised here, however, as some have suggested that the only basis for dating this pool to Iron I was the biblical account of the "Pool of Gibeon" in 2 Samuel 2 (A. Mazar 1990: 478–81, 527 n.15). Others, constructing a typology of water systems, date the pool to the 7th century B.C. (Galling 1965: 243; Shiloh 1987: 212). In fact, there is some evidence that the excavators initially saw the stratigraphic relationship between the pool and the nearby 9th-century stepped tunnel such that the pool was the later of the two (Pritchard 1961: 4–8).

This Period was destroyed in Area 8-G-6 and 17-F/G-18/19/20 (Pritchard 1964a: 37, 50–51).

JIBIT, KH. (Horvat Givit)   M.R. 18455.1598

5 ha. site on hilltop. 1.1-1.5 km to nearest water. Iron I and II remains, the Iron I including cooking pots having sharp, triangular rims that are flattened and unaccentuated and collared-rimmed and hole-mouth pithoi (Finkelstein 1986: 132; 1988a: 179; Finkelstein, Lederman, and Bunimovitz 1997: 512; Elon and Demsky 1990: 115).

EL-JIFTLIK   M.R. 197.172

Three Iron I tombs, possibly with LB use also, located above the Chalcolithic site of Jiftlik in the Wadi Farah (Mellaart 1962: 154; Kochavi 1972: 102).

JIMZU — see GIMZO

JINZAR, or JINZUR, KH. EL- — see KH. JANZAR

JORET 'AMER   M.R. 1713.2062

1 ha. site 28 m above the Dothan Valley. Ten percent Iron I, also Iron II (Zertal 1984: 91; 1992: 93–94).

JORET EL-WARD   M.R. 1694.2051

2.0-3.5 ha. site in Dothan Valley. 33 m to nearest well. Alluvial soil. Fifty percent Iron I, no LB or Iron II. Among Iron I ceramics found are triangular-rimmed cooking pots with molded lower edge, simple-rimmed pithoi, and punctured jar rims (Zertal 1984: 96–97; 1992: 123).

JUREISH (Jurish)   M.R. 18065.16765

1.4 ha. site on hilltop. 200 m to nearest water. Ancient pottery on north and east sides of the modern Arab village. 25% Iron I remains, also Iron II. Iron I includes collared-rimmed and hole-mouth pithoi and punctured jar handles (Finkelstein 1983a: 139; 1988a: 153, 179).

KADHIYYA, TELL EL- — see TELL MISKI

KAFIREH, KH. EL
(Tel Kefira)   M.R. 16020.13755

1.5 ha. site with much Iron II construction. Iron I sherds found on west slope outside the big Iron I lower city wall (Vriezen 1975: 142–43; 1977; Finkelstein and Magen 1993: 41*, 209–11).

KAFR DUKK — see FUQHA, KH.

KAFR KUZ   M.R. 1782.1823

350×175 m site on a peak of Mt. Ebal, with spring below. Although Finkelstein (1986: 168) and Zertal (1992: 498) found no Iron I, Iron I sherds were found by Campbell (Bull and Campbell 1968: 23; Jaroš and Deckert 1977: 19, 33), and are kept in the collections of the Albright Institute (three bags in WD5).

KAFR QASIM, TELL   M.R. 14755.16875

1.5 ha. site on hilltop with a minimal amount of
Iron I pottery and also Iron II (Finkelstein 1978:
26; Kochavi and Beit-Arieh 1994: 28*, 33).

KAFR TAS, KH.   M.R. 17195.14195

0.3 ha. site in declivity on hilltop. 33% Iron I
sherds, no LB or Iron II (Finkelstein and Magen
1993: 164).

KALA' — see KLIA

KARAK, KH. EL- — see QARIQ, KH. EL-

KARAWA — see MAZAR, TELL EL-

KAUBAR   M.R. 16515.15535

1.4 ha. site on hill. 300 m to water. 3.2% Iron I,
also Iron II (Finkelstein, Lederman, and
Bunimovitz 1997: 208).

**KAZIYYA ER-RATRUT (Shunet el-Masna'a;
Umm Safa)   M.R. 1948-63.1732-50**

As the name suggests, the "site" is a gas station,
belonging to Mr. Ratrut. The gas station was constructed in the 1950s or '60s, without any regard
to the archaeological site it was being built over.
The fill from the excavation of the station foundations and the tanks for the fuel is still present,
mounded up behind the gas station (covering much
of the area M.R. 1963.1738 to 1948.1750). This
fill was surveyed by the author on 14 December
1996, producing Iron I pottery (and EB), no LB
or Iron II. In addition to ceramics, which included
coarse, thick, unornamented bowls, a flint blade
was found, likely Iron I (it is later than EB and
there are only minimal Byzantine remains). Nearest water is Wadi Farah, 500 m away.

KEBAR, KH. — see KHEIBAR, KH.

EL-KEBARRA   M.R. 1793.1967

3.5 ha. site in the Sanur Valley. Terra Rosa soil.
Ten kilometers to nearest spring. Thirty percent
Iron I, also LB and Iron II (Zertal 1988: 125; 1992:
224–25).

KEFIRA, TEL — see KAFIREH, KH. EL-

**KEREN ZEITIM (Tirat Zvi; Abu Faraj
                        M.R. 1995.2038**

Site one kilometer from nearest water (Jordan
River). No LB or II. Stratum II is Iron I (Gal 1979),
namely 12th century (Menorah 1975: 21). Large
mudbrick complex (Gal 1979: 138), centered in
Squares A1-3, B1-3. Walls usually 0.6 m thick.
Main two-room house (one main room, one
broadroom at end separated by wall) is 8.5 m×6
m. Mudbrick oven #1.29 in Room 2 (the
broadroom), along with domestic granary #1.31.
Floors are beaten-earth. Finds include (Israel Antiquities Authority File A-510[1975]) the following. From Room 2: bowls, lamps, juglet. From
Main Room: 2 lamps, 2 pithoi. From south of the
house: juglet. From SE of house, lamp on floor.
Other finds include bowl, chalices, juglet, lamp,
jugs. All finds are local except shoddy Iron I-ish
chalice #75-382 and shoddy pyxide #75-425 from
broadroom (Gal 1979: 141) with white potters'
mark on base. Bowls are string-cut or disk bases,
red painted bands, some carinated, chalices one
shoddy, mentioned above, and the other painted
red. Jugs have red painted bands, everted rim, ridge
neck, red-slip, one-handle, and ring base, or with
twisted basket handle, saucer spout, and red paint.
Juglet is 1-handled (Gal 1979: 142). Flasks are all
two-handled, one with concentric circles, one with
concentric circles around cross. Lamps are either
LB-ish round-based, or flat-based. Overall, pottery is almost identical to Beth Shean VI–V.

KERMAT, KH. — see GIVAT JONATHAN

EL-KERUM — see GIVAT JONATHAN

KFAR QARAYIM, TEL (Tell Abu Faraj; Tel Menorah)   M.R. 1994.2035

30×40 m site occupied in LB, Iron I, and Iron II. Iron I pottery includes cooking pots having sharp, triangular rims that are flattened and unaccentuated, bowls with ring-rims, and handleless kraters (Bergman and Brandstetter 1941: 89; Zori 1962: 165-66; unpublished survey undertaken in 1990s by Aharon Maier for Hebrew University).

KFAR QASIM   M.R. 14705.16935

1 ha. site just west of modern Kafr Qasim. LB, Iron I and II remains. Iron I pottery includes Philistine pottery and collared-rimmed pithoi (Lod 1975: 15; Kochavi and Beit-Arieh 1994: 24*, 25).

KHARAIYEQ EN-NATSARAH   M.R. 1672.1960

0.45 ha. site 28 m above the plain of er-Rameh. Rendzina soil. Forty percent Iron I sherds, no LB or Iron II (Zertal 1992: 243–44).

KHAUSH, KH. EL- (Kh. el-Haush)   M.R. 16795.17245

1.2 ha. site on hilltop. 2.75 km to nearest water. 16.7%-20% Iron I sherds, also Iron II. Iron I sherds include collared-rimmed pithoi and punctured jar handles (Finkelstein 1986: 146; 1988a: 162, 180; Finkelstein, Lederman, and Bunimovitz 1997: 289).

KHEIBAR, KH. (Tell Kheibar; Kh. Kebar)   M.R. 1764.1954

3.5 ha. site on hilltop 45 m above the Sanur Valley. Terra Rosa soil. Five kilometers to nearest water. Twenty percent Iron I sherds, also LB. Iron I includes collared-rimmed pithoi (Porath 1986: 78; Zertal 1992: 227).

KHEIR-ALLAH   M.R. 1703.1958

1.5 ha. site ten meters above the plain of er-Rameh. Terra Rosa soil. Thirty percent Iron I, also LB and Iron II (Zertal 1988: 127; 1992: 247).

EL-KHIRBEH MAHRUN (Qasr Mahrun)   M.R. 1747.2013

0.8 ha. site in Dothan Valley. 1.5 km to nearest water source. Thirty percent Iron I, also Iron II. Iron I includes collared-rimmed pithoi with short, thick everted rims, and cooking pots having sharp triangular slanted rim with ridge on bottom edge of rim (Ahituv 1984: 137; Zertal 1984: 117–18; 1992: 145).

EL-KHIRBEH RA'Y   M.R. 1641.1969

0.6 ha. site on mountainous height thirty meters above surrounding terrain. Rendzina soil. Four kilometers to nearest water at well of Bir Katab. Thirty percent Iron I, also Iron II (Zertal 1988: 123).

KHOMRAH, KH. EL- — see TERUMOT, TEL

EL-KHRAB   M.R. 1645.10465

1 ha. site thirty meters above surrounding terrain. Terra Rosa soil. Twenty percent Iron I sherds, including collared-rimmed pithoi, also Iron II (Zertal 1984: 101; 1992: 118).

KHREBAT, KH. EL- (A) (Sufi el-Khureibat)   M.R. 1930.1901

0.2 ha. site fifteen meters above the surrounding terrain, consisting of a cliff and declivity. Terra Rosa soil. Four kilometers to water at Ein el-Mitah. Seventy percent Iron I, no LB or Iron II (Ilan 1973: 352; Zertal 1988: 137; 1996: 262–63).

KLIA (Qli'a; Kala')   M.R. 15840.16240

0.65 ha. site on ridge with declivity on the northeast. 450 m to nearest water. Few Iron I sherds, the rest Iron II. Iron I sherds only found in Area A, which is between the two mounds (Area B east of the mounds had only Iron II). Iron I finds include neckless pithoi. Evidence of olive oil and wine production in Iron I (Qala' 1981: 17; Finkelstein 1988a: 168, 181; 1986: 68–69).

KOKAH, TELL EL- — see YALU

KOM EL-GHABY   **M.R. 1668.1929**

1.45 ha. site five meters above the plain of er-Rameh. Alluvial soil. Two kilometers to spring. Forty percent Iron I, also Iron II (Zertal 1988: 138; 1992: 258).

KULILEH, TELL EL- — see SAUL, HAR

KULESAN, KH.
(Kh. Qalasun)   **M.R. 1819.1595**

0.28-0.4 ha. site on ridge. 3.1 km to nearest water. Fifteen percent Iron I sherds, including collared-rimmed pithoi, no LB or Iron II (Finkelstein et al. 1985: 173; Finkelstein 1988a: 180; Finkelstein, Lederman, and Bunimovitz 1997: 508).

KUMA (Kumeh, Qumei, Qumy)
                         M.R. 1707.1832

Site is situated on a small knoll, and is 1.5 ha. with terraces extending out another 200-300 m on all sides. Terra Rosa soil. One kilometer to nearest spring, Ein Zawata. Forty percent of sherds Iron I, on both the summit and west, south, and east terraces, along with LB on both and Iron II on the terraces (Williams and Campbell 1965: 5; Bull and Campbell 1968: 38; Campbell 1991: 84; Zertal 1992: 377–78).

KURKUF, KH. — see QARQAF, KH.

EL-KURRUM (A)   **M.R. 1698.1881**

0.4 ha. site in valley. Rendzina soil. 500 m to spring. Fifty percent Iron I sherds, also Iron II (Zertal 1988: 154; 1992: 405–6).

KURUM (Kh. el-Kurum)   **M.R. 1827.1715**

Site of minimal size occupied in Iron I and II. 1.2 km to water (Finkelstein, Lederman, and Bunimovitz 1997: 569).

KURUS, KH. EL-   **M.R. 16794.13648**

Iron I and II site of minimal size. Iron I finds include neckless pithoi (Maitlis 1989: 16, fig. 4.9).

KUWAIB, KH. EL- — see ER-RAME

LOD (Lydda)   **M.R. 14050.15150**

Among the many remains found in the modern town are LB, Iron I, and Iron II (Gophna and Beit-Arieh 1997: 88-89, 66*–68*). The Iron I was predominately Philistine remains (E. Yannai, personal communication).

MAALEH LEVONAH, HORVAT — see JEBEL EL-BATIN

MAHRUN — see EL-KHIRBEH MAHRUN

MAJDAL, KH. (Horvat Migdal; esh-Sheikh Musharaf)   **M.R. 1519.1832**

Iron I and II site with Iron I tomb containing lamp with closed wick hole (Yannai 1995: 279; Et-Taiyiba 1991: 18–19).

MAKATER, KH. EL- see MUKHATIR, KH. EL-

MAK-HUL, KHALLET   **M.R. 1984.1847**

0.15 ha. site on valley side forty meters up. Eroded soil. Eight kilometers to nearest water, at Ein Hilu spring. Forty percent Iron I, also Iron II. Iron I includes biconical jug, collared-rimmed and hole-mouth pithoi, and outcurving, lipped-rim cooking pots (Zertal 1996: 355–57).

MAKNEH EL-FOQA, KH. — see EN-NEBI

MALAT, TELL EL- — see MALOT, TEL

MALOT, TEL (Tell el-Malat) M.R. 1374.1404

0.7 ha. site. Late Bronze and Iron II occupation as well; Stratum 4 is Iron I. It consists of mudbrick walls. Finds include much Philistine pottery and a zoomorphic figurine (Ahituv 1984: 101; Shavit 1993; Finkelstein 1996: 238).

MALQOKH, TEL (Maqhuz) M.R. 1966.2011

Tell 40×50 m in size. Spring of Ein Maqhuz is on-site. LB, Iron I, and Iron II occupation. Iron I finds include cooking pots having sharp triangular slanted rim with ridge on bottom edge of rim and vertical-rimmed, oval section kraters (Zori 1962: 174; unpublished survey undertaken in 1990s by Aharon Maier for Hebrew University).

EL-MAMALEH M.R. 1746.1931

0.05 ha. entirely Iron I site on an eight-meter rise atop the high summit of Jebel Hureish. Mediterranean Brown Forest soil. Five kilometers to water at well of Bir Fuwwar (Finkelstein 1986: 134).

EL-MAQABAR M.R. 1885.1841

0.4 ha. site in branch of Wadi Farah, fifteen meters up and two kilometers from the wadi. Rendzina soil. Ten percent Iron I, also LB (Finkelstein 1986: 164; Zertal 1996: 401).

MAQATIR, KH. EL- — see MUKHATIR, KH. EL

EL-MAQBARAH M.R. 1879.1841

0.1 ha. site fifteen meters above the Wadi Farah, which is 1.5 km away. Rendzina soil. Ten percent Iron I, also LB and Iron II (Finkelstein 1986: 163; Zertal 1996: 400).

MARAH EL-'INAB, KH. (el-Farshe; el-Buseiliyya; Kh. el-Yaqlum) M.R. 19275.17885

0.4-1.68 ha. tell fifty meters up above Wadi Farah, which is half a kilometer away. Terra Rosa Soil. Twenty percent of sherds Iron I, also Iron II. Iron

I pottery includes cooking pots with outcurving, lipped-rim and cooking pots having sharp, triangular rims that are flattened and unaccentuated, and "man's face" puncturing. Iron I or II stone implements include one flake, one blade, two geometric sickle blades, one broken middle section of a blade, and one serration/dentation on a blank— all indicative of cereal production (Ilan 1973: 34; Finkelstein 1986: 172; Zertal 1996: 455–58).

MAQHUZ — see MALQOKH, TEL

MARAH EL-KHARARIB M.R. 1809.2032

0.4 ha. site eight meters above the surrounding terrain. Four kilometers to nearest spring. Ten percent Iron I, no LB or Iron II (Zertal 1988: 111; 1992: 163-64).

MARAJIM, KH. EL- (Kh. el-Merajem) M.R. 1840.1616

0.42-0.6 ha. site on hilltop. 800 m to nearest water. Five percent Iron I, also Iron II. Iron I sherds include collared-rimmed and hole-mouth pithoi (Herrmann 1964: 69; Finkelstein 1986: 132; 1988a: 179; Finkelstein, Lederman, and Bunimovitz 1997: 537; Marcus 1991–92, 2: 126–27).

MARJAMA, TELL (Tell Merjama; Kh. Marjeme; Kh. el-Merjemeh; Ein Samiyya; Ein es-Samiyya) M.R. 1816.15535

4 ha. site (see below) in a small oasis in a declivity, with a rich spring on the premises. Also LB (Zohar 1980: 220). In Iron I, three hectares of the total four were occupied (Finkelstein 1986: 132; A. Mazar 1982b: 172). Noth found Iron I sherds (1966: 258), as did A. Mazar (1992: 181), and Zohar (1980: 220), scattered over the entire three hectares. But there was no architecture until the 10th or 9th century (Zohar 1980: 220; Dever 1997a: 36).

Tombs: on the route north to Dhar Mirzbaneh, Bakiza Shantur excavated a number of tombs. In one group of 44 tombs, 16 were Roman/Byzantine and 27 LBI, and one is "Iron" and may be Iron I (Ain Samiya 1971: 23). The cemetery covers Kh. Samiya, Dhar el-Mirzbaneh (EB, MB only), and Kh. el-Aqibat (MBI only).

MASALLEH ESH-SHEIKH HATIM — see ESH-SHEIKH HATIM

MASA'OD, KH.   M.R. 1622.2054

Hilltop site of 0.25 ha. Nearest water is Wadi el-Ghamiyya, 500 m. away. Surveyed by the author on 31 August 1996. Iron I and II sherds found. Iron I includes collared-rimmed pithoi with long collars.

MATWI, KH.   M.R. 1618.1651

1.8 ha. site. 700 m to nearest water. Thirty percent Iron I sherds, from the north side of the ruin. Also Iron II. Iron I pottery includes erect-rimmed cooking pots and cooking pots with sharp, triangular slanted rims and collared-rimmed pithoi (Finkelstein 1983a: 149; 1988a: 166, 181).

MAYYASE, KH. (Kh. Maiyaseh)
    M.R. 1798.1860

0.15 ha. site. One kilometer to nearest spring. Terra Rosa soil. Ten percent Iron I sherds, also Iron II (Zertal 1992: 479–80).

EL-MAZAR — see MAZRIM, HORVAT

MAZAR, TELL EL-
(Karawa; Qarawa)   M.R. 19625.1710

The site at these coordinates is not called "Tell es-Simadi" as per Zertal (1996), a name which does not actually belong to any location (Peterson 1977: 267-68; see SAMADI, WAQF ES-). Nelson Glueck knew this place by the correct name (1951: 4.418). It is a site that commands the lower Wadi Farah. Iron I and II occupation. Iron I finds include many red-slipped sherds, cooking pots having sharp triangular slanted rim with ridge on bot-

tom edge of rim, cooking pots with ridge just below the lip, and bowls with spiral burnish inside, vertical walls and rims, and ring-bases or a foot (Peterson 1977: 272-73; Israel Antiquities Authority Records File #138 [=sherds Rockefeller Museum #225 and #441 collections]).

MAZOR, NAHAL   M.R. 14499.16240

0.6 ha. site occupied in LB and Iron I. Iron I pottery includes Cypriote wares (Kochavi and Beit Arieh 1994: 63*, 226).

MAZRIM, HORVAT
(el-Mazar; Nebi Mazar)   M.R. 1841.2147

LB, Iron I, and Iron II site (Zori 1977: 6–7).

MEDHIAB, EL- — see ZE'EVIM, TEL

EL-MEFJIR SITE
(Ard el-Mafjir Tell 2)   M.R. 1936.1436

Two kilometers to nearest water at spring of Ein Ghor Masayid. Most pottery found was Iron II, some Iron I: including outcurving, lipped-rim or outflaring-necked non-carinated cooking pots (Muilenberg 1955: 25, 27).

MEIDAN, KH. EL- — see SHUNA, KH. ESH-

MENNUNIYEH, KH. — see MINUNIYYA, KH. EL-

MENORAH, TEL — see KFAR QARAYIM, TEL

MERAJEM, KH. EL- — see MARAJIM, KH. EL-

MHALLAL, KH.   M.R. 1939.1948

1.5 ha. site on hilltop forty meters above the surrounding terrain. Two kilometers to nearest water

at spring of Ein Malih. The site contains only two strata, MB and Iron I, along with some scattered Iron II sherds. The Iron I makes up 36% of the surface collection of sherds. Iron I ceramic remains include outcurving, lipped-rim cooking pots, neckless, non-carinated cooking pots, and large, cylindrical-necked jugs (Zertal 1996: 245-47).

MIGDAL, HORVAT — see MAJDAL, KH.

MINUNIYYA, KH. EL-
(Kh. Mennuniyeh)   M.R. 1793.1865

0.1 ha. site forty meters above the surrounding terrain in mountainous area. Terra Rosa soil. Two kilometers to nearest spring. Fifty percent Iron I sherds, no LB or Iron II (Zertal 1988: 158; 1992: 477–78).

MISKI, TELL (Tell Misk; Tell el-Kadhiyeh; Qaziyya; Ein Miska; Tell Umm es-Semayeh)
M.R. 18735.18245

1.55 ha. site ten meters above Wadi Farah, on northeast side of the swamp. Terra Rosa soil. Ein Miski is in the site, and Ein Shilbleh is just below. Twenty to thirty percent Iron I, also LB and Iron II. Iron I sherds include one sherd that is Transjordanian and in the Cisjordanian district is rare (Kappus 1968: 81–82), as well as punctured jar handles, hemispherical bowls with pointed rims, simple-rimmed storejars with low necks, and cooking pots having sharp triangular slanted rim with ridge on bottom edge of rim (Finkelstein 1986: 169; Zertal 1996: 412–15; also Glueck 1951: 422; Ilan 1973: 316).

MISPE HAR NOF
(Deir Yassin)   M.R. 16685.13230

Entirely Iron I site on flat ridge. Nearest spring is ca. 250 km to the north. Iron I finds include collared-rimmed pithoi (Harel 1984: 80; Maitlis 1989: 30; A. Mazar 1994b: 73).

MIYAMAS, KH.   M.R. 1695.18585

Site of between 0.5 and 0.9ha, fifty meters above the terrain. Rendzina soil. One kilometer to nearest spring. Forty percent Iron I, also Iron II (Zertal 1988: 161; 1992: 430–31).

MNEITRAH, KH.   M.R. 17160.15200

0.35 ha. site on ridge. 800 m to nearest water. Sixty percent Iron I pottery, mostly from north end, no LB or Iron II. Iron I finds include collared-rimmed pithoi (Finkelstein 1988a: 172, 181).

MUBARAK, TELL — see MEVORAKH, TEL

MUHAFFAR, TELL EL- (Kh. Umm el-Haffeh)
M.R. 1707.20525

The site is variously reported as being 10–12 hectares or 0.4–0.5 ha. The larger figure matches most maps and reports. The site is a tell rising eighteen meters above the Dothan Valley. Rendzina soil. Spring in the wadi along the west edge of the tell, and possibly the whole north edge of the plain has springs. Possible spring on the tell where a saddle connects it to the higher hills to the north. Ten percent of sherds Iron I, also Iron II. Iron I includes cooking pots with sharp, triangular slanted rims and cooking pots having sharp triangular slanted rim with ridge on bottom edge of rim, and collared-rimmed pithoi with short, thick everted rims (Williams and Campbell 1965: 2–3; Muhaffar 1971: 4; Zertal 1988: 103; 1992: 109).

MUKHATIR, KH. EL- (Kh. el-Maqatir; Kh. el-Makater)   M.R. 17375.14690

0.15–0.3 ha. site. One kilometer to nearest water. Surveys found 57% Iron I, also Iron II. 1996 excavations by Bryant Wood have found Iron I pottery in Iron II fills and in one pit, including cooking pots with sharp, triangular slanted rims and collared-rimmed pithoi with long collar and thick folded rims (Bryant Wood, personal communication; Gary Byers, personal communication).

MUKHMAS   M.R. 17670.14220

Modern Arab village in declivity on ridge over the east edge of the Wadi Suweinit. Four percent Iron I sherds, also Iron II (Finkelstein and Magen 1993: 184).

EL-MUNTAR (A)   M.R. 1834.1902

Not to be confused with el-Muntar (B) at M.R. 1855.2107, this site is situated on a hilltop sixty meters above the surrounding terrain. Terra Rosa soil. Two kilometers to nearest spring. Forty percent Iron I (Zertal 1988: 148; 1992: 329–30).

MUNTAR ESH-SHAQQ (Muntar esh-Shukk) M.R. 1978.1944

0.1 ha. entirely Iron I site on hilltop. Rendzina soil. Three Iron I cisterns on-site, 800 m to spring at Ein esh-Shaqq. Site consists of a 10 m-diameter circular casemate wall three meters wide, of which a fifteen meter-long section was exposed. There is a stone heap in its center, and also assorted other wall fragments. Northwest and west of this structure is where most of the pottery was found (Zertal 1996: 257–59).

EL-MUSTAH (Ein Fandaqumiyya; Fendakumie)   M.R. 1685.1921

2 ha. site on a level plain and depression. Rendzina soil. Spring of Ein Fandaqumiyya is on-site. Five percent of sherds Iron I, no LB or Iron II (Zertal 1988: 138).

NAHM, KH. EN- — see ANAHUM, KH.
EN-NAJAMA (WEST)   M.R. 17520.16705

0.5 ha. site on a ridge. 500 m to nearest water. 7.1% Iron I, also Iron II (Finkelstein, Lederman, and Bunimovitz 1997: 416).

EN-NAJAMA (EAST)   M.R. 18315.1510

0.3-0.4 ha. site. 1.6-3.65 km to nearest water (varying reports). Eighty percent Iron I, also Iron II. Iron I includes collared-rimmed pithoi (Finkelstein

1986: 133; 1988a: 179; Edelman 1988: 51; Finkelstein, Lederman, and Bunimovitz 1997: 510).

NAJMAT KHUNEIFIS, KH. M.R. 1803.1620

0.105–0.15 ha. site on hilltop. Ninety percent of sherds Iron I, no LB or Iron II. Iron I includes collared-rimmed pithoi and "man's face" jar handle puncturing (Finkelstein et al. 1985: 173; Finkelstein 1988a: 157, 180).

NAKHLEH, KHALLET EN- M.R. 1899.1901

Single-period Iron I site of 0.2 ha. The site consists of a cliff and hilltop on a summit 200 m above the surrounding terrain. Rendzina soil. Nearest water is 7.5 km away at the spring of Ein el-Farah. Remains consist of crumbled architectural fragments, including one wall of large prepared stones. Ceramic remains include large bowls with thickened, folded, and inverted rims, platters, outcurving, lipped-rim cooking pots, collared-rimmed pithoi with short, thick everted rims, storejars with ridge on neck below thickened rim, large jugs with medium-short neck and rim-shoulder handle, large jugs with high cylindrical necks, and stepped-base chalices (Finkelstein 1986: 152; Zertal 1996: 305–6).

NAMLEH, KH. EN-   M.R. 1723.2028

0.05 ha. site "entirely Iron I" on the north edge of Widyan et-Tuffah, at the foot of the rise of el-Mushatta, five meters up. The site consists of Iron I tombs and a stone circle. One kilometer to nearest water. Iron I pottery includes hemispherical bowls with simple, rounded rims. Although described as single-period Iron I (Zertal 1984: 110; 1992: 140), Zertal mentions an Iron II cooking pot (1992: 140) and other Iron II pottery (1984: 188).

NASBEH, TELL EN-   M.R. 1706.14355

Large site on low plateau. 500 m to spring at Ein Abu Iskander, 1 km to Ein el-Jidi (Zorn 1993: 276). Soils are Colluvial-Alluvial, Terra Rosa, Alluvium, Rendzina, and Mediterranean Brown Forest (Zorn 1993: 205–6). Also Iron II remains. The multi-volume study by Zorn (1993) provides an authoritative analysis of the site. Other references that ought to be consulted include Badè (1927; 1928; 1929; 1936), Braemer (1982: 267), Briese (1985: 14-16), T. Dothan (1982: 44-54), Graham (1981: 33), Gunneweg et al. (1994), Herzog (1992: 231), N. Lapp (1981: 61), Loffreda (1968: 263), McClellan (1985), McCown (1947), McCown and Wampler (1947), Tufnel (1948), G. E. Wright (1947; 1948), and Zorn (1997).

NASRIYYA, KH. EN-
(Horvat Natzor)   M.R. 1535.2074

Site occupied in Iron I and II (Ne'eman 1990: 32*, 36).

NATZOR, HORVAT — see NASRIYYA, KH. EN-

EN-NEBI (Kh. en-Nebi Isma'il;
Kh. Makneh el-Foqa)   M.R. 17545.17575

0.5–1.2 ha. site on slope. 350 m to nearest water at spring of Ein Makneh. 6.2%-7% Iron I sherds, from the east and northwest sides of the site. Also Iron II. Iron I includes cooking pots with sharp, triangular slanted rims, cooking pots having sharp, triangular rims that are flattened and unaccentuated, and collared-rimmed pithoi (Bull and Campbell 1968: 35; Campbell 1984: 68; 1991: 63; Finkelstein 1986: 134; 1988a: 179; Finkelstein, Lederman, and Bunimovitz 1997: 463).

NEBI 'ANNIR, KH. EN-   M.R. 16030.15135

3 ha. site on ridge and saddle between Wadi Nada and Wadi Joz. 275 m to nearest water at spring of Ein Butmah. 5%–8.2% Iron I sherds, no LB or early Iron II. Iron I includes collared-rimmed pithoi (Finkelstein 1988a: 173–74, 181; Marcus 1991–92: 1.111; Finkelstein, Lederman, and Bunimovitz 1997: 179).

NEBI ISMAI'IL, KH. EN- — see EN-NEBI

EN-NEBI NUN   M.R. 18435.1722

Hillock in the Wadi Fasil valley. 1.45 km to nearest water source. Minimal Iron I remains, no LB or early Iron II. Iron I includes collared-rimmed pithoi and "man's face" puncturing on jar handles (Finkelstein 1986: 132; 1988a: 179; Finkelstein, Lederman, and Bunimovitz 1997: 574).

EN-NEBI MAZAR — see MAZRIM, HORVAT

EN-NEBI UZEIR — see RAS, TELL ER-

NIB, KH.   M.R. 1748.1857

1.8 ha. site on high hill forty meters above surrounding terrain. Terra Rosa soil. Six kilometers to nearest spring. Fifty percent Iron I, also Iron II (Zertal 1988: 173; 1992: 453–54).

NISYA, KH.   M.R. 17175.14495

1.5 ha. site on slope. Four percent of survey pottery was Iron I, also Iron II. 75 m to Ein Yunus spring (Finkelstein and Magen 1993: 166–67; Blizzard 1973/74: 225). More Iron I was found in fills by Livingston excavations beginning in 1979. The Iron I and II tell was leveled in the Hellenistic period to obtain soil for new agricultural terraces, and later periods also obliterated earlier buildings down to bedrock (Livingston 1990: 3).

Iron I finds (from fill): hole-mouth jar rim from Area E/G (Livingston 1990: 11, 14), jar ring-base from Square 78 of Area E/G (Livingston 1990: 11, 15), 11th-century bowl or krater straight rim from Square 78 (Livingston 1990: 11, 14–15), cooking pot rim with sharp, triangular slanted rim (Livingston 1990: 11, 15) from Square 78.

Off the site, an undisturbed cave tomb of fifty individuals was found (Byers 1994): two-chambered tomb #65, on the southeast edge near spring (Byers 1995). Its contents were: three skulls; 792 teeth—fifty people ages 50–60, standard distribution, all had equal wear on teeth, that of grain-eaters; 18 early Iron I crude jugs and jars; 50–57 car-

nelian beads; cut cowry shells; 2 lotus-seedpod-
type pendants; 2 elongated-stone-type pendants
made of limestone plated with metal; 6 bronze
rings; 1 iron ring; 12 bronze bracelets, well-made;
9 iron bracelets of high-carbon steel from
Transjordanian source; 2 Hyksos scarabs, one with
cross and curl, and the other one from MB IIC
which belongs to earlier use of the cave (Baruch
Brandl, personal communication); 6–8 bronze
toggle pins; conoidal seal with man with arms up
and two squiggles at his sides; limestone half-dag-
ger pommel (also from the MBIIC period; Baruch
Brandl, personal communication); basalt loop;
spindle whorl; an unidentifiable ivory object. Al-
together, fifty metal items for fifty people, in ratio
of 18 iron to 33 bronze.

NURIS (Nurit)   M.R. 1845.2158

Site occupied in Iron I and II (Zori 1977: 6).

PARUS, TEL (Kh. Fureir; Kh. el-Farriyya)   M.R. 1599.2266

1 ha. site occupied in Iron I and II (Olami 1981:
39–40).

QA‘ADAT ES-SEIYAD   M.R. 1741.1913

0.6 ha. site in forty-meter deep ravine. Terra Rosa
soil. Four kilometers to nearest spring at Ein esh-
Sharqiyya. 25% Iron I, also Iron II (Zertal 1988:
143).

QABALAN   M.R. 17740.16790

1.05 ha. site on southwest slope of modern Arab
village, above valley. 600 m to nearest water. 33%
Iron I sherds, including collared-rimmed pithoi,
the rest of the pottery is Iron II (Finkelstein 1983a:
138–39; 1988a: 179; Finkelstein, Lederman, and
Bunimovitz 1997: 433).

QAFQAF, KH. — see QARQAF, KH.

QALASUN, KH. — see KULESAN, KH.

QALAT TANTURA — see TITTORAH, HORVAT

QARAWA — see MAZAR, TELL EL-

QARIQ, KH. EL- (Kh. el-Karak)   M.R. 18015.16535

0.56 ha. site on hillside. Iron I and II occupation
(Finkelstein 1983a: 131; Finkelstein et al. 1985:
173).

QARQAF, KH. (Kh. Kurkuf; Kh. Qafqaf)   M.R. 1643.1859

2 ha. site seventy meters above terrain. 800 m to
nearest water. Forty percent Iron I pottery, also
Iron II. Iron I includes short-necked collared-
rimmed pithoi (Bach 1958: 50; Zertal 1992: 357–
58).

QARQAFA, KH.   M.R. 18025.16675

0.21–0.3 ha. site on hilltop. One kilometer to nearest water. 35% Iron I sherds, the rest Iron II. Iron I
includes cooking pots with erect or slanted rims
and cooking pots with sharp, triangular slanted
rims, collared-rimmed pithoi, and punctured jar
handles (Finkelstein 1988a: 179; Finkelstein et al.
1985: 173).

QASR EL-ASBAH   M.R. 1936.1759

The author's survey of this region established that
this site is what Zertal (1996: 466–67) has called
"Bab ed-Daiyq," and that he in fact missed the real
site of Bab ed-Daiyq. His confusion apparently
originated between the first and second survey
expeditions to this region, as the 1988 publication
identified a different site as "Bab ed-Daiyq" (the
correct one). Using the 1996 data for "Bab ed-
Daiyq," which matches Porath's (n.d. #110) data
for Qasr el-Asbah, the following obtains: 0.3 ha.
site on big hill with cliff on one side, fifty meters
above the Wadi Farah. Terra Rosa soil. Forty percent Iron I pottery, of which half is Einun wares
(storejars and Trumpet-based jugs). Other Iron I

pottery includes cooking pots having sharp, triangular rims that are flattened and unaccentuated.

QASR FARA (Ras Tuwanik) M.R. 1851.1745

The site, of which it is unclear what proportion is Iron I, consists of three areas. Area I is a pentagonal acropolis 50.8×27.1×44.6×42.5×20.5 m, with pits. This area, particularly its northern portion, produced the most pottery. Area II is the first terrace, and Area III is the second terrace. Iron I pottery includes pithoi with simple rims and low necks and handled-kraters with rope decoration (Otto 1978: 114–16).

QASR MAHRUN — see EL-KHIRBE MAHRUN

EL-QAUQA'A — see YALU

QAZIYYA — see MISKI, TELL

QEBUBEH, KH. EL-   M.R. 16555.1856

0.68 ha. site on 45 m-high hilltop above the Wadi Shair, which is 300 m away. Terra Rosa soil. 25% Iron I sherds, also Iron II (Bach 1958: 50; Zertal 1988: 161; 1992: 361–62).

QLI'A — see KLIA

QUBBE, KH. EL-   M.R. 17730.14130

0.5 ha. site. Nine percent Iron I sherds, no LB or Iron II. Iron I sherds include collared-rimmed pithoi with short, thick everted rims, and simple-rimmed pithoi (Finkelstein and Magen 1993: 38*, 194).

QUMY — see KUMA

QUREIN, JEBEL (Kh. el-Ikhrein; Nahal Hadera; Wadi Abu Nar)   M.R. 1594.2026

0.14 ha. site on copse 25 m above Wadi Abu Nar. Five kilometers to nearest well. Rendzina soil. Sixty percent Iron I, no LB or Iron II (Zertal 1988: 111; Ne'eman 1990: 43*, 62).

EL-QUREINAT   M.R. 1665.2025

Twenty percent Iron I sherds, also Iron II (Zertal 1984: 109).

QURNAT HARAMIYYA   M.R. 14625.16650

4 ha. site with Iron I and II occupation (Kochavi and Beit-Arieh 1994: 38*, 52–53).

QURNAT SHAHTURA — see 'ASAS, WADI EL-

QUSIN, TELL EL-   M.R. 1673.1928

Not to be confused with Kh. Qusin es-Sahal (M.R. 1658.1867), this is a site on a mountaintop, with nearest water in the wadi below. Sherds found on south, southwest, and southeast sides. Iron I and II sherds found; Iron I including punctured jar handles (Peterson 1977: 225).

RADDANAH, KH.   M.R. 1694.1467

1.2 ha. built-up area (Cooley 1975: 13). Springs are found on the north and south sides of the site. No final publication of the site's excavations has come forth or seems imminent. The following discussion is based on the author's own extensive research. Phase 2 was founded in 1225 as a fresh site (Callaway 1984: 54; there was some EBI). The cisterns (bell-shaped) were built before, not with, the houses: they are under floors and under roof supports (Cooley 1975: 9). Site has a 1 m-thick wall, maybe casemate, on the E side (Callaway and Cooley 1971: 12)—really houses lined along the edges and spaces filled with limestone rubble curtain wall (G. R. H. Wright 1985: 1.75).

Site R (east side of tell): Five or six compounds of two or three houses each around courtyards with cisterns (Callaway 1984: 54; Stager 1985: 18; Cooley 1975: 8). Groups of houses on the three sides of a little square exterior work space are isolated from the rest. Also pits. Finds: pithoi, pestles, mortars, stone grinding tools (Callaway and Cooley 1971: 14).

Site S (north side): houses larger than in Sites T (west side) and R. Central hewn-pillared 3-room pier-house 16×5 m, EW orientation, *huwwar*-roofed (Callaway 1970c: 231), with 4 square chiseled pillars 0.5 m-thick (Cooley 1975: 8), of a type of rectangular space bordered on side and end with rooms where end is set off by a wall and side by pillars (Braemer 1982: 60)—taller, bigger, with more storage and more workshops than Sites R and T. Even in large houses, roofs are at 1.85 m from floor (Cooley 1975: 8). Houses 13–14 make a cluster. But one must be careful, with two pen-strokes one of these Site S houses can be redrawn as a 3-room house with typical non-communicating side room that was cut by later construction, rather than as an irregular courtyard (Routledge 1996). Finds: collared-rimmed and hole-mouth pithoi; cooking pots with sharp, triangular slanted rims; juglet (round base, trefoil rim); large lamp with rounded base; jug; black steatite conical seal with pierce at apex for hanging, depicting a cow, suckling calf, the hind of another animal, and an ibex—similar to #3009 from Tell el-Farah North Iron I and to one from Tell en-Nasbeh Tomb 32; bronze battle axe; bronze section of armor (Callaway 1970c: 231–32).

Site T: Two offering stands. One is three-footed, globular, 26 cm high, with no handles, possibly similar to ones at Megiddo (Allen 1980: 8, 46). The other is ridge-rimmed, everted opening with two triangular ridges below, no handles, 25 cm high, with fenestration near the base (Allen 1980: 9–10).

There is no Philistine pottery on the site (Bunimovitz and Finkelstein 1993: 160). Other finds with no site provenance include a krater with flattened, thickened rim, saddles and querns, stone mortars and pestles, rubbing stones, and sickle blades (Cooley 1975).

The site was terraced for cereal production (Cooley 1975: 9), but every house has caprovid bones. There is a trace of pig bones, but that may be Byzantine (Hesse 1990: 216, 225n.5).

In 1150/1125 begins Phase 3. It is characterized by overcrowding, poor houses, some silos covered over (Cooley 1975: 10). Pits are filled, abandoned, some rooms filled with trash and junk (Callaway and Cooley 1971: 11).

Finds: from Site R, Area R.III in a room with unique mudbrick-paved floor, was found a 20-handled (from the rim) wheeled kernos krater. It has a channel running along the upper wall, leading to inward-pointing spouts shaped like the heads of bulls on the inner wall (Cooley 1975: 12; Callaway 1974: 92; Callaway and Cooley). This unusual vessel is unique in Syria-Palestine, and has analogies only in Anatolia: at Inankik and Eskyaper (Allen 1980: 64). There is a similar vessel from Gezer with channel rim and zoomorphic spout (Allen 1980: 49), but it is a jar and not a krater, and most interesting is that the Gezer vessel is itself identical to one at Alaca Huyuk in Anatolia ("Denyer 1976" report in the Nicol Museum).

Also in same room, a jar handle was found inscribed with the letters *'HL* or *'HR* (Cross and Freedman 1971: 20). If the former reading is correct, it may be a diminutive of the personal name "Ahilud," "Ahilah." It could also be "Ahlay" (Cross and Freedman 1971: 22), perhaps a diminutive of "Ahiram," which happens to be the name of a Benjaminite clan in Numbers 26: 38 (Aharoni 1971: 130–31). Stratigraphically, the inscription comes from Phase 3 (Callaway 1973), but epigraphically it has been dated to the 13th or 12th centuries (Aharoni 1971: 132; Cross and Freedman 1971: 20–22). In this case, since there is no 13th century occupation at Khirbet Raddanah, it would have been manufactured in Phase 2 (Cooley 1975: 12; Callaway and Cooley 1971: 15).

Other finds include pithoi, only hole-mouth (Callaway 1974: 11); an iron digging-iron/horizontal pick-axe (Kurinsky 1991: 118); bronze slag-encrusted copper-making crucibles (Callaway 1974: 12; there is no smoke on the crucibles, so the ingots were smelted elsewhere and traded in, then put in crucibles; Cooley 1975: 11); an iron knife, iron rod (Waldbaum 1978: 25); bronze knives, points, coats of mail, daggers (one of which is in Philistine style and has writing on it; Cooley 1975: 12), needles, spear and javelin points, and bellows nozzle (Cooley 1975). In Site S there is a furnace, made from an altered pithos-core (Cooley 1975: 11).

In 1050 most of the site was destroyed (Cooley 1997b: 402), and the rest abandoned.

In both periods, most pottery is petrographically from the local Motza-Aminadav group (Glass, et al. 1993: 272). There are no burnished wares (Callaway and Cooley 1971: 12). From Site R in one of these phases, Area R.VIII, Locus 700.1, came a ram's head bowl handle 5 cm in length similar to ones at Megiddo and Ashdod ("Denyer 1976" Report in Nicol Museum).

RADGHA, TELL — see SHALEM, TEL

ER-RAFID (Kh. er-Rafid)   M.R. 17670.16180

0.3–0.7 ha. site on summit of hill. 1.5 km to nearest water. Minimal Iron I sherds (collared-rimmed pithoi), also Iron II (Finkelstein 1983a: 143; 1988a: 179; Finkelstein, Lederman, and Bunimovitz 1997: 420; Otto 1997: 11).

RAHAYA, KH. ER-   M.R. 1850.1616

0.21–0.3 ha. site. 400 m to nearest water. Ten percent Iron I sherds, no LB or Iron II. Iron I includes cooking pots having sharp, triangular rims that are flattened and unaccentuated, collared-rimmed pithoi, and punctured jar handles (Finkelstein 1988a: 144, 179; Finkelstein, Lederman, and Bunimovitz 1997: 544).

ER-RAM   M.R. 17210.14020

3 ha. site covered by modern town. Nearest water is a well 2 km to the south. One percent Iron I, also Iron II (Schunck 1963: 21; B. Mazar 1975: 80; Finkelstein and Magen 1993: 33*, 168–69).

RAMA, KH. ER- — see ER-RAME

ER-RAME (Kh. er-Rama; Kh. el-Kuwaib)   M.R. 1676.1955

Hilltop site of 1.6 ha. in the middle of the plain of er-Rame (Sahal er-Rama). Nearest water is Wadi en-Nasrini, 100 m away. Surveyed by the author on 12 December, 1996. Pottery found was LB, Iron I, and Iron II (along with others). Iron I finds included hemispherical bowls with beveled rims whose upper surface slopes outward diagonally, jugs with painted metope design, jugs with ridged necks, and collared-rimmed pithoi, both short- and long-collared.

RAMMUN (Kh. Umm er-Rammin)   M.R. 17850.14840

22%–25% Iron I sherds found on the west slope of the hilltop of this Arab village. No LB or Iron II. 1.7 km to nearest water. Iron I remains include cooking pots with erect or slanted rims, collared-rimmed and hole-mouth pithoi (Schmitt 1980: 57; Ben-Yosef 1983: 18; Finkelstein 1983a: 145; 1988a: 180; Finkelstein and Magen 1993: 23*, 89; Finkelstein, Lederman, and Bunimovitz 1997: 324).

ER-RAS NORTH   M.R. 1659.1956

0.03 ha. Iron I sherd scatter 45 m above the surrounding terrain on a mountainous peak. No pottery from the summit itself, only from slightly below. Terra Rosa soil. One Iron I cistern, spring is five kilometers away at Kheir Allah (Finkelstein 1986: 126).

ER-RAS WEST   M.R. 15075.14890

2.5 ha. site on hill. One kilometer to nearest water. 1.4% Iron I remains, no early Iron II. Iron I remains include collared-rimmed pithoi (Finkelstein 1988a: 181; Finkelstein and Magen 1993: 13*, 30; Finkelstein, Lederman, and Bunimovitz 1997: 1).

RAS, TELL ER- (en-Nebi 'Uzeir)
M.R. 17675.17405

2.5 ha. site on hilltop. 600 m to nearest water. 1.1%–7% Iron I sherds, also LB and Iron II. Iron I sherds include collared-rimmed pithoi (Finkelstein 1988a: 147–48, 179; Finkelstein, Lederman, and Bunimovitz 1997: 467).

RAS ABU HAMID (Tel Hamid)
M.R. 1397.1455

2 ha. site on coastal plain. Wadi at the site. LB, Iron I, and Iron II occupation (B. Mazar 1975: 108). Although 1996 excavations by S. Wolff on behalf of the Israel Antiquities Authority found no Iron I strata, Iron I pottery was plentiful (S. Wolff, personal communication), as had been indicated by a letter from J. Kaplan to the Israel Department of Antiquities dated 22 December 1950 (Aharoni, et al. 1950: 48). The 1996 excavations found collared-rimmed pithoi, but no Philistine pottery. Nor was any Philistine pottery found by J. Naveh in 1962 (letter to Israel Department of Antiquities dated 3 October 1962, kept in Israel Antiquities Records File). A Philistine krater was found, however, with grey slip and a bichrome painted swan, by B. Mazar in the 1950s (B. Mazar 1954: 234–55).

RAS EL-'AIN   M.R. 1695.1899

0.2 ha. site thirty meters above surrounding terrain. Rendzina soil. Spring on-site. Seventy percent Iron I, also LB (Zertal 1988: 150; 1992: 393–94).

RAS EL-AWAR, KH. (Kh. Ras Abu el-Awar)   M.R. 1668.1888

0.25 ha. site on twenty-meter high hillock. Rendzina soil. Nearest spring one kilometer away. Eighty percent Iron I sherds, also Iron II (Bach 1958: 48; Zertal 1988: 153; 1992: 399–400).

RAS EL-BURJ   M.R. 1586.1829

0.3 ha. site, on hilltop. Nearest water is Wadi en-Naml, one kilometer away. Site was surveyed by the author on 23 November 1996. LB, Iron I, and Iron II pottery was found (as well as others). Iron I pottery includes cooking pots with ridge just below the lip, neckless, non-carinated cooking pots, and a ledge-rimmed krater.

RAS DHUKEIR   M.R. 17435.13785

Site on hill. Few Iron I sherds, no LB or Iron II (Sapin 1968–69: 28, 59; Finkelstein and Magen 1993: 60*, 360–61; S. Gibson 1995: 428; unpublished soundings were also undertaken by E. Kamiski, E. Ben-Yishai, and D. Ben-Tor).

RAS ED-DIYAR   M.R. 18515.17825

Iron I remains are from the north and west slopes east of the village of Beit Dajan (Bull and Campbell 1968: 29; Campbell 1991: 33; Jaroš and Deckert 1977: 33).

RAS HAMOUD — see EL-BIRD

RAS JADIR   M.R. 1891.1908

Single-period Iron I sherd scatter of 0.05 ha. Site is on five-meter high hillock atop a mountain. Terra Rosa soil. Seven kilometers to nearest water at Ein el-Farah spring. Finds include collared-rimmed pithoi with short, thick everted rims, outcurving, lipped-rim cooking pots, and punctured jar handles (Zertal 1996: 297).

RAS JULEIJIL — see DHIYAB, KH.

RAS EL-KHARUBEH (6)   M.R. 1979.1736

0.5 ha. site 75 m above the surrounding terrain. Mediterranean Brown Forest soil. Seven percent Iron I sherds, no LB or Iron II. Iron I includes holemouth storejars and large bowls with thickened, folded, and inverted rims (Zertal 1996: 583–87).

RAS EL-KHARUBEH (7)   M.R. 1971.1728

0.4 ha. site ten meters above the surrounding terrain. Mediterranean Brown Forest soil. 25% Iron I sherds, no LB or Iron II (Zertal 1996: 583–88).

RAS EL-KHARUBEH, KH.   M.R. 1966.1766

0.5 ha. sherd scatter in thirty-meter deep declivity. Mediterranean Brown Forest soil. Three kilometers to Wadi Farah. Eleven percent Iron I sherds, also Iron II (Zertal 1996: 501–2).

RAS EL-KHARUBEH EL-MARAH, WADI
                             M.R. 1956.1757

0.2 ha. site fifty meters down into a depression (the Wadi Ras el-Kharubeh el-Marah). Nearest water, however, is really Wadi Farah, 1.5 km away. Eroded soil. Ten percent Iron I sherds, also Iron II. Iron I includes cooking pots with ridge just below the lip and triangular-rimmed cooking pots with an upper lip that has been folded inward (Zertal 1996: 508–9).

RAS MARAH EL-WAWIYAT
                             M.R. 1921.1902

0.1 ha. sherd scatter on hill ten meters above the surrounding terrain. Three kilometers to spring at Ein el-Mitah. Terra Rosa soil. 58% Iron I, also Iron II (Zertal 1996: 299–300).

RAS QURRA, KH.   M.R. 1689.1673

0.35–0.5 ha. site on hilltop. 1.6 km to nearest water. Eight percent Iron I sherds, also Iron II. Iron I ceramics include cooking pots with erect or slanted rims, collared-rimmed and hole-mouth pithoi (Finkelstein 1986: 147; 1988a: 180; Finkelstein et al. 1985: 173).

RAS ES-SALMEH   M.R. 1864.1981

0.6 ha. site on high summit 180 m above the terrain. Terra Rosa soil. 11 km to water at Ein el-Mitah. Fifty percent Iron I (all late 11th-century, supposedly), also Iron II (Finkelstein 1986: 121; Zertal 1996: 182).

RAS ET-TAHUNEH   M.R. 17017.1464

0.5 ha. hilltop site in the middle of modern El-Bireh city. 800 m to nearest water. Scattered Iron I sherds, no LB or early Iron II. Iron I sherds include cooking pots with sharp, triangular slanted rims (Finkelstein 1983a: 145; 1988a: 180; Finkelstein, Lederman, and Bunimovitz 1997: 296).

RAS TAMMIM (Ras Tumeim)
                             M.R. 1754.13317

0.5 ha. hilltop site. Iron I, no LB or Iron II (Dinur 1987: 44; Maitlis 1989: 28; S. Gibson 1995: 428).

RAS ET-TURFINEH — see TARAFEIN, KH.

RAS ET-TAWIL, KH.   M.R. 1735.1376

Iron I remains from the south slopes, at the Iron II tombs and Roman columbaria (Ofer 1993: 32*; S. Gibson 1995: 285, 428). In August 1997, the site, along with the Iron II tombs and Roman columbaria, was completely demolished during the night by construction workers building an extension to Highway 1.

RAS TUMEIM — see RAS TAMMIM

RAS TUWANIK — see QASR FARA

RAS ZEID, KH.   M.R. 17415.17125

0.8 ha. site on hilltop at bottom of descent to Wadi Einabus. One kilometer to nearest water. 57.1%–85% Iron I sherds, the rest Iron II. Iron I ceramics include cooking pots with sharp, triangular slanted rims, cooking pots having sharp, triangular rims that are flattened and unaccentuated, collared-rimmed pithoi, punctured jar handles, and bell-shaped *cyma* bowls (Finkelstein 1986: 137; 1988a: 179; Finkelstein, Lederman, and Bunimovitz 1997: 452).

ER-REQUQ   **M.R. 1606.1945**

1 ha. site on level terrain in highlands. Terra Rosa soil. Three kilometers to nearest water. 25% Iron I sherds, also LB and Iron II (Zertal 1988: 130).

ER-RUJAM — see RUJJAM, KH.

RUJAM, KH. — see RUJAN, KH.

RUJAN, KH. (Kh. Rujam) M.R. 17950.17190

0.8 ha. site on hilltop. 600 m to nearest water. 2.4% Iron I sherds, including collared-rimmed pithoi. Also Iron II (Finkelstein 1988a: 150, 179; Finkelstein, Lederman, and Bunimovitz 1997: 481).

RUJEIB   **M.R. 17795.1774**

Scant Iron I sherds found on the upper southern slopes of the modern village. Also LB (Bull and Campbell 1968: 31; stored in Albright Institute).

RUJJAM, KH. (er-Rujam) M.R. 1662.20475

1.5 ha. site ten meters above the Dothan Valley. Alluvial soil. 32 m to nearest well. Twenty to thirty percent Iron I sherds, also LB and Iron II. Iron I pottery includes collared-rimmed pithoi, cooking pots having sharp, triangular rims that are flattened and unaccentuated, triangular-rimmed cooking pots with an upper lip that has been folded inward, neckless, non-carinated cooking pots, bowls with red painted lines, and other bowls with painted circles (Zertal 1984: 102, 179; 1992: 120–21).

SABATTAH, KH. (Kh. Sabata; Kh. Sebata)
       M.R. 1745.1913

0.9 ha. site in declivity fifty meters deep. Terra Rosa soil. Four kilometers to spring at Ein esh-Sharqiyya. Fifteen percent Iron I, also Iron II (Zertal 1988: 144).

SABEN, KH.   **M.R. 1812.2046**

0.82 ha. site eight meters above valley floor. Mediterranean Brown Forest soil. Ten percent Iron I, no LB or Iron II (Zertal 1992: 156–57).

SAFIRIYYA, KH. — see SHEIKH SAFIRIYYAN, KH. ESH-

ES-SALAH   **M.R. 1671.1993**

0.1 ha. site on level terrain. Rendzina soil. 500 m to well of Bir es-Safa. Ten percent Iron I, also Iron II (Zertal 1988: 117).

SALHAB, KH.   **M.R. 18535.1956**

0.3–1.5 ha. site on hillock ten meters above valley. Eroded soil. Ten kilometers to nearest water at Ein el-Farah spring. Three percent Iron I, also Iron II. Iron I sherds include "Einun" storejars, "man's face" puncturing, and other punctured jar handles (Ilan 1973: 370; Zertal 1988: 129; 1996: 148–50).

SALIH, KH. ES- (Kh. esh-Sheikh Salih)
       M.R. 2021.1791

0.4–1.0 ha. site on edge of the Jordan River *ghor*. Spring on-site (Bergman and Brandsteter 1941: 88–89; Glueck 1951: 420; Kochavi 1972: 226).

SALIM — see ESH-SHEIKH NASRALLAH

SAMADI, WAQF ES-   **M.R. 1958.1718**

This site is sometimes called "Tell es-Simadi," but in reality no site bears that name (Peterson 1977: 268). The site is a tell of ten hectares, of which only 0.88 ha. has been surveyed in recent decades, as it is a closed military area. The site is fifteen meters above the terrain of the Wadi Farah, which is 104 m away. Alluvial soil. Ten percent of the sherds of the surveyed area were Iron I, along with LB and Iron II (Finkelstein 1986: 173).

SANHEDRIA   **M.R. 1709.1340**

From the area known as the "Tombs of the Sanhedrin" or, less accurately, "Tombs of the Judges," came at an unknown date a single small Iron I lamp with flat base. It is in the collection of the Albright Institute (#28.2[6300]), currently #13 in the main display case.

SANUR   **M.R. 1735.1957**

6 ha. site on hilltop guarding a pass to the east. Terra Rosa soil. Two kilometers to nearest spring. Ten percent Iron I, also Iron II (Zertal 1988: 128; 1992: 225–26).

SANUR EL-KHIRBEH   **M.R. 1728.1953**

0.9 ha. site eight meters above the terrain. Two kilometers to nearest spring. Ten percent Iron I, no LB or Iron II (Zertal 1988: 128; 1992: 195).

SARSARA, KH.   **M.R. 1524.1629**

0.6 ha. site on ridge. 250 m to nearest water. 52.8% Iron I sherds, also Iron II. Iron I ceramics include cooking pots with erect or slanted rims, outcurving, lipped-rim cooking pots, collared-rimmed and hole-mouth pithoi, punctured jar handles and "man's face" punctured jar handles (Finkelstein 1983a: 156; 1988a: 181; Finkelstein, Lederman, and Bunimovitz 1997; Otto 1997: 11).

SAUL, HAR (Tell el-Kulileh) M.R. 1853.2158

Site in the Gilboa hills, consisting of three stone buildings, one 0.8×1.7 m, one 30×8 m, and the other 32×25 m. Iron I and II occupation. Iron I remains consist of bowls, some with red slip (Zori 1977: 6–8).

SEBASTIYYA   **M.R. 168.187**

Large site, predominantly Iron II, on 91 m high hill. Recent work by Stager (1990) and Tappy (1992) has dated Pottery Period I=Building Phase 0 to the Iron I period, whereas Kenyon had dated this to the 9th century (Stager 1990: 101). The studies of Stager and especially Tappy are quite thorough and should be consulted. The original publications of the excavations (Crowfoot, Kenyon, and Sukenik 1942; Crowfoot, Crowfoot, and Kenyon 1957; Reisner, Fisher, and Lyon 1924) should also be consulted.

SEBATA, KH. — see SABATTAH, KH.

SEIF, KHALLET   **M.R. 1721.2071**

0.95 ha. site forty meters above the Dothan Valley. One kilometer to nearest well. Sixty percent of sherds Iron I, no LB or Iron II (Zertal 1988: 97; 1992: 81).

SEILUN, KH.   **M.R. 1775.1626**

1.2 ha. site on hillside in broad valley. Nearest water is Ein Seilun, 900 m away. Also LB occupation. The most recent excavations of the site are published in Finkelstein, Bunimovitz, and Lederman (1993), along with correlation with earlier excavations on the site. Other relevant publications include Buhl and Holm-Nielsen (1969), Eran (1994), Finkelstein (1983b; 1985a; 1992c), Finkelstein et al. (1985), Gilmour (1997b: 26), Haran (1961), Kaufman (1988), Kjaer (1930; 1931), Shiloh (1965; 1983), Schley (1988), Shiloh (1973), Weinfeld (1993), and Wood (1983).

SHAJARA, KH. ESH-   **M.R. 16755.16690**

1 ha. site. Ten percent Iron I sherds, mostly from the east side of the site, the rest Iron II. Iron I sherds include collared-rimmed pithoi and punctured jar handles (Finkelstein 1988a: 164, 180).

SHALEM, TEL
(Tell Radgha)   **M.R. 1998.2006**

80×100 m tell. Alluvial soil. Iron I sherds include painted (monochrome) stripes and metope designs (Zori 1962: 163–64).

SHALWIM, TEL
(Tell el-Firr)   M.R. 1885.2161

LB, Iron I, and Iron II site. Iron I finds include cooking pots and a bichrome krater (Zori 1977: 83).

SHARDE, KHALLET ESH-   M.R. 1939.1889

0.5 ha. site on hill 35 m above the surrounding terrain. Six kilometers to springs at Einun Hilu. Sherds Iron I and II. There are also five assemblages of Iron I or II presses. Assemblage I consists of two simple oil presses and two cups. Assemblage II consists of a conical cup and a conical crater with a water-storage hole. Assemblage III consists of a big basin and concavity with a cup and concave crater. Assemblage IV consists of five elliptical basins and a simple oil press. Assemblage VI (V is Roman), which is east of III, contains three conical cups and a shallow flat cup. Assemblage VII cannot be dated even generally(Zertal 1996: 308–9, 721–23).

SHEIKH ABU ZARAD
(Tell Abu ez-Zarad)   M.R. 17195.16805

1.2–2.8 ha. site on hilltop. Nearest water is a well 275 m to the northeast. Ten percent Iron I, also LB and Iron II. Iron I pottery includes cooking pots with sharp, triangular slanted rims, cooking pots having sharp, triangular rims that are flattened and unaccentuated, collared-rimmed and hole-mouth pithoi, punctured jar handles, and "man's face" punctured jar handles (Jaroš and Deckert 1977: 23; Kallai 1986b: 152; Finkelstein 1983a: 138; 1988a: 179; Finkelstein, Lederman, and Bunimovitz 1997: 389).

ESH-SHEIKH 'AKRALLAH
                        M.R. 17205.14295

1.3 ha. site on slope. Ten percent Iron I, no LB or Iron II. Iron I pottery includes outcurving, lipped-rim cooking pots and simple-rimmed and "Einun" storejars (Finkelstein and Magen 1993: 33*, 169).

ESH-SHEIKH BARTA'A — see BARTA'A, KH.

ESH-SHEIKH BILAL   ca. M.R. 1831.1785

Zertal (1996: 109) describes a site of this name containing Iron I sherds somewhere on Jebel Kebir, but does not provide specific information or location. Nothing matching this name could be located on any maps or on the ground.

SHEIKH HASAN, TELL ESH-
(Tel Yosef HaYashnah)   M.R. 18815.21515

110 m×60 m site. 500 m to nearest water at Nahal HaZoram. LB, Iron I, and Iron II occupation. Iron I pottery includes cooking pots with sharp, triangular slanted rims and "man's face" puncturing on jar handles. Other Iron I finds include bronze axes, lances, and saws, and a clay figurine, although the latter may be LB (Zori 1971: 18; 1977: 26–27).

ESH-SHEIKH HATIM (Masalleh
esh-Sheikh Hatim)   M.R. 17990.16815

0.7–1.0 ha. site on plateau. 100 m to water. Ten percent Iron I sherds, including cooking pots and collared-rimmed pithoi; also Iron II (Finkelstein 1983a: 138; Finkelstein et al. 1985: 173; Finkelstein, Lederman, and Bunimovitz 1997: 443).

ESH-SHEIKH 'ISSA   M.R. 16355.15010

1.1 ha. site on hill. 300 m to water. 1.6% Iron I, also Iron II (Finkelstein, Lederman, and Bunimovitz 1997: 200).

ESH-SHEIKH MAZAR   M.R. 18505.16485

Not to be confused with the esh-Sheikh Mazar at M.R. 1840.1684, this site is a 1.5 ha. sherd scatter on the summit of a hill. One kilometer to nearest water. Five percent Iron I, also Iron II. Iron I pottery includes cooking pots triangular-rimmed with molded lower edge, cooking pots with ridge just below the lip, collared-rimmed pithoi, and punctured jar handles (Herrmann 1964: 67; Finkelstein 1986: 132; Finkelstein, Lederman, and Bunimovitz 1997: 546).

ESH-SHEIKH MUSHARAF — see MAJDAL, KH.

SHEIKH NASRALLAH, KH. ESH-
                          M.R. 18085.17935

0.5–0.7 ha. site, covering two adjacent knolls together called ez-Zahrah on Jebel el-Kebir. Spring just east across the Najame road from Salim, southwest of Salim. Finds: from the east slope, near many cisterns, just northwest of the Weli: some Iron I (Jaroš and Deckert 1977: 33; Finkelstein 1986: 133 found one sherd, Wachter 1968: 67 found two; Campbell 1991: 31 found one collared-rim pithos, one krater, and two cooking pots), also Iron II.

SHEIKH SABAR, TELL ESH-
                          M.R. 1620.2061

2.5 ha. site on hill 45 m above terrain. Rendzina soil. Five kilometers to nearest spring. Ten percent Iron I, also Iron II (Zertal 1988: 99).

SHEIKH SAFIRIYYAN, KH. ESH
(Kh. Safiriyya)   M.R. 1815.2007

0.7-2.0 ha. site on slope seven meters above valley. Eroded soil and alluvium. 6 km to nearest water at spring of Ein Giniyya. 10%–14% Iron I sherds, also LB and Iron II. Iron I includes collared-rimmed pithoi (including long-collared with thick folded rim) and punctured jar handles (Zertal 1988: 115; 1996: 117–19).

SHEIKH SALIH, KH. ESH- — see SALIH, KH. ES-

SHEIKH SIFRY, TELL — see HILU, KH. TELL EL-

SHIH, KHALLET ESH-   M.R. 17155.14130

0.45 ha. site on slope. Eighteen percent Iron I, including collared-rimmed pithoi, also Iron II (Finkelstein and Magen 1993: 163–64).

SHILLO, NAHAL   M.R. 145765.16526

49×35 m site on slope west of Migdal Aphek. Scanty Iron I finds, also Iron II (Kochavi and Beit-Arieh 1994: 45*, 65).

SHREIM, KH. — see SHUREIM, KH. ESH-

SHUK, ESH- — see SHUKAH, TEL

SHUKAH, TEL (esh-Shuk)   M.R. 1933.2115

Iron I pottery includes a large baking tray and Philistine cooking pots (Zori 1962: 185).

SHUKRA, KHALLET ESH- M.R. 1847.1836

0.31 ha. site located in a small depression fifty meters above the Wadi Farah valley. Terra Rosa soil. 1.2 km to nearest water at Ein Farr spring. 10%–20% Iron I sherds, the rest Iron II. Iron I ceramics include hemispherical bowls with simple, rounded rims and cooking pots with plain rims (Finkelstein 1986: 166; Zertal 1996: 403–4).

SHUNA   M.R. 17600.16600

0.25 ha. site on hill. 800 m to nearest water. No LB or Iron II (Finkelstein, Lederman, and Bunimovitz 1997).

SHUNA, KH. ESH-
(Kh. el-Meidan)   M.R. 15890.15190

3.5 ha. site on east slope of hill. 1.2 km to nearest water. 0.8%–2.5% Iron I sherds, seemingly entirely found in rock-cut pits, presumably dating to Iron I. Also Iron II. Iron I ceramics include collared-rimmed pithoi (Finkelstein 1988a: 173, 181; Finkelstein, Lederman, and Bunimovitz 1997: 63).

SHUNET EL-MASNA'A — see KAZIYYA ER-RATRUT

SHUREIM, KH. ESH-   **M.R. 16985.18745**

0.1 ha. site fifteen meters up valley side. Rendzina soil. Thirty percent of sherds Iron I, also Iron II (Zertal 1992: 415–16).

SHUWEIHA, KH. (Kh. Bir esh-Shuweiha)
M.R. 18555.17855

0.6 ha. site on a spur of Jebel el-Kebir in the farthest northeast corner of the plain of Sahal et-Tahtani. 2.4 km to nearest water. Eighty percent of sherds Iron I, also LB and Iron II—most Iron I from peak and south slopes (Bull and Campbell 1968: 26; Campbell 1984: 69; 1991: 33–34; Finkelstein 1986: 133; Otto 1997: 11). Three cisterns date to Iron I (Kuschke 1958: 15). More Iron I pottery was found on the track from the site to the village of Beit Dajan (Bull and Campbell 1968: 26; Campbell 1991: 33).

SIFRY, TELL — see HILU, KH. TELL EL-

SIMADI, TELL ES- — see SAMADI, WAQF ES-

SINIYYA, KH. — see ED-DEIR, KH.

ES-SIRTASSA   **M.R. 1669.1905**

1.5 ha. site on 100 m-high hilltop. Rendzina soil. 1.5 km to nearest spring. 25% Iron I, also LB and Iron II (Zertal 1988: 147; 1992: 296).

ES-SIYAR   **M.R. 186025.16570**

Caves totaling 0.4 ha. in area. 1.2 km to water. 6.3% Iron I sherds, no LB or Iron II (Finkelstein, Lederman, and Bunimovitz 1997: 547).

ES-SKHRA   **M.R. 1875.1912**

1 ha. site on level terrain in valley. Terra Rosa soil. Twenty percent Iron I sherds, no LB or Iron II. Iron I sherds include pithoi, both hole-mouth and high-necked with simple rim (Zertal 1996: 205–6).

SOFAR, TELL (Tell Sufan; Tel Tzfari)
M.R. 1733.1818

1 ha. site guarding the west end of the Shechem pass (Nandrasky 1964: 90). Nearest water sources are springs of Ein el-Jisr and Ein es-Subyan. Six occupation levels. LB sherds found, although LB was not one of the six levels (Campbell 1967: 9). Level 6 is Iron I (Sofar 1973: 13; Campbell 1983: 269; 1991: 80), with remains both on the summit of the tell and on the north and west terraces (Bull and Campbell 1968: 36). Also Iron II (Bull and Campbell 1968: 36; Jaroš and Deckert 1977: 33).

SUFAN, TELL — see SOFAR, TELL

SUFI EL-KHUREIBAT — see KHREBAT, KH. EL- (A)

SULTAN, TELL ES- (Tel Jericho)
M.R.1925.1420

0.4 ha site in oasis on Jordan Valley plain. Spring of Ein es-Sultan on northeast edge of site. Iron II occupation. Kenyon stated that no Iron I was present, but some have argued that there was an 11th-century reoccupation (Holland 1992: 736; 1997: 223). In the "Well-hill" area of the Sellin-Watzinger excavations, Area I6 west of Ein es-Sultan, an area of Iron II houses, there was habitation in Iron I (Weippert and Weippert 1976: 131, 137), as well as in F.376, F.677, and L.278. Also Iron I occupation in Area G/H.5/6 (Sellin/Watzinger and Kenyon excavations) on top of the MBII-LB "Bit-Hilani" house (Weippert and Weippert 1976: 144).

Finds: southern-style goblets (#E.10.a–b; Weippert and Weippert 1976: 119); amphoriskoi

(#B1 and #E.1.a) with body-handles, brown burnish, and painted brown and red stripes on neck and body, as at southern sites such as Lachish and Tell el-Fara South (Weippert and Weippert 1976: 122); krater (#E2; Weippert and Weippert 1976: 119) small with neck-to-rim handle and ornamental frieze in the handle area, as Tel Qasile and Megiddo and Beth Shean; pilgrim flasks (#E.4.a–b; Weippert and Weippert 1976: 128) with small body, two handles, red and black painted concentric circles with clear glaze, as at Tell el-Farah South, Gezer, Beth Shemesh, and Sahab; pyxide #Garstang 23: 6 (Weippert and Weippert 1976: 129) with partition slanting from neck to base, short neck, lug handles, painted bands on body and shoulder as at Megiddo, Hazor, Afula, and Tell Abu Hawwam.

Tombs: Garstang's Cremation Pit Tomb 11 from the 1932 excavations is Iron I (Garstang 1933: 36). It is a unique form, round, deep, in the northeast part of the necropolis. Finds: 10 objects (#PAM 1064-1073, housed in the Rockefeller Museum), including XIX Dynasty steatite scarab #722 (32.1580; Rowe 1936: 173) with a beared male figure with cone helmet and two horns in front and a tassel on back, wearing a leopard skin, with a sack on a stick over his shoulder (or a yoke with two objects on it), standing on a bull—this figure is an Egyptian ideogram, Sign No. A33 (Gardiner's *Egyptian Grammar*, p. 438); a Thutmose III scarab; bronze bracelet; iron bracelet; pottery.

SUMRA, KH. ES- — see ESUR, TEL; FUQAHA, KH.

## SUR, KH. (A)				M.R. 17225.17865

0.525 ha. site on slope above valley. Spring at the site. Fifty percent Iron I pottery, mostly from the western edge of the site, along with LB and Iron II (Bull and Campbell 1968: 37; Campbell 1991: 70; Jaroš and Deckert 1977: 33; Finkelstein 1983a: 141).

## SUR, KH. (B)				M.R. 17375.16445

0.8 ha. site on ridge at south end of Wadi Ali valley. 1.45 km to nearest water source. Fifty percent Iron I sherds, also Iron II. Iron I pottery includes cooking pots with erect or slanted rims, outcurving, lipped-rim cooking pots, cooking pots with sharp, triangular slanted rims, collared-rimmed pithoi, and punctured jar handles (Finkelstein 1988a: 155, 179; Finkelstein, Lederman, and Bunimovitz 1997: 400).

## SURREY HILL				M.R. 17375.14690

0.15 ha. site on ridge. One kilometer to nearest water. 36.8% Iron I, no LB or Iron II (Finkelstein, Lederman, and Bunimovitz 1997: 307).

## SUWEIDA, KH. ES-				M.R. 1997.1887

4 ha. site on slope thirty meters above surrounding terrain. Mediterranean Brown Forest soil. Five kilometers to water at Ein Hilu spring. Five percent Iron I sherds, also Iron II. Iron I includes cooking pots having sharp triangular slanted rim with ridge on bottom edge of rim and cooking pots with ridge just below the lip (Zertal 1996: 530–35).

TAIASIR — see TAYASIR

## TAIYIBEH, ET- EAST			M.R. 17845.15130

T. L. Thompson (1979) confused the records for this site with those of the et-Taiyibeh on the Nahal Issachar in Galilee. The one here in question is the hilltop site occupied by a modern Arab village. Nearest water is 1.2 km away. Twenty percent Iron I sherds, mostly from the west slope. Also Iron II. Iron I is represented by cooking pots with erect or slanted rims cooking pots, collared-rimmed and hole-mouth storejars, and a krater (Ben-Yosef 1983: 18; Finkelstein 1983a: 144; 1988a: 160, 180; Finkelstein, Lederman, and Bunimovitz 1997: 368–69).

TAIYIBEH WEST (Taiba, et-Taiyiba)
M.R. 1514.185

Iron I tomb. Contents included hand-burnished red-slipped bowls, Cypriote Black-on-red ware, and closed-wick lamps (Yannai 1995: 279).

TALL   **M.R. 1720.2062**

0.8 ha. site 22 m above the Dothan Valley. Ten percent Iron I, also Iron II (Zertal 1984: 91–92; 1992: 96).

TANA EL-FOQA, KH.   **M.R. 18515.1759**

0.5-0.7 ha. site on south slope (although others have estimated the full size as about four hectares; Williams and Campbell 1965: 6). Two kilometers to nearest spring. Seven percent Iron I sherds, also Iron II. Iron I pottery includes cooking pots having sharp, triangular rims that are flattened and unaccentuated, collared-rimmed pithoi, and punctured jar handles (Ilan 1973: 297; Finkelstein 1986: 134; 1988a: 179; Campbell 1991: 37).

TANA ET-TAHTA, KH.   **M.R. 18740.17332**

0.8 ha. site on hillock. 550 m to nearest spring. Minimal Iron I sherds, along with Iron II and possible LB. Iron I includes collared-rimmed and hole-mouth pithoi (Elliger 1970: 95; Campbell 1984: 73 n.13; 1991: 37–39; Finkelstein 1986: 131; 1988a: 179; Marcus 1991-92: 2.108; Finkelstein, Lederman, and Bunimovitz 1997: 583).

TANNIN, KH.   **M.R. 18225.20235**

0.5 ha. site on edge of plain, twenty meters above the terrain. Terra Rosa soil. 35 m to nearest spring. Forty percent Iron I sherds, also LB and Iron II. From Iron I or LB comes a small clay figurine 4.1×2.8 cm. From Iron I comes an inscribed sherd 58×71×7–10 mm, inscribed with *ŠMN*[?] ("oil"?), or, if read left-to-right, *nimiš* = "wasp" (A. Mazar 1982b: 142; Lemaire 1985: 14; Zertal 1992: 167, 509, 528).

TARAFEIN, KH. (Ras et-Turfineh)
M.R. 17015.1556

1.5-2.0 ha. site on south side of hilltop. 200 m to nearest water. Thirty percent Iron I sherds, also Iron II. Iron I sherds include collared-rimmed and hole-mouth pithoi (Finkelstein 1986: 152; 1988a: 181; Finkelstein, Lederman, and Bunimovitz 1997: 331).

ET-TARUD — see ATARUD, KH.

TAYASIR (Taiasir)   **M.R. 1875.19415**

1 ha. site on hillside. Terra Rosa soil. Six kilometers to nearest water at Ein el-Mitah. Two percent Iron I sherds, no LB or Iron II. Iron I sherds include non-carinated cooking pots (Finkelstein 1986: 131; Zertal 1996: 193–94).

ET-TELL   **M.R. 175.147**

10 ha. site (Vincent 1936: 234) with no LB occupation. 500 m to spring, down deep ravine to the north, the volume of which is 5 gallons/hour (Callaway 1965a: 412). Many Iron I cisterns (ʾAi 1971a: 22) surround the site. Complete publication of the site has not been forthcoming; the following analysis is a result of the author's own research.

Founded 1225, with the "Cobblestone Street Stratum" (Callaway 1976: 30; 1984: 53), variously called Intermediate Stratum IX (Callaway 1980: 245), Level IA, "Wall E Iron Age Phase" (Callaway 1965b: 40), or Phase II (Callaway, draft of final report: "The Iron I Village at Ai (et-Tell)"). This stratum is unwalled (Callaway 1976: 30; 1984: 53).

In Site B (central tell), 1.2 ha. are built up (Herzog 1992: 235). There are pier-constructed and pillared houses (see below), complex cisterns, and terraces (Callaway 1976: 29–30). There are two compounds with a 80 cm-wide, 0.2 m high E-W wall running 20 m between them and no doorway (Callaway 1969b: 57). These compounds contain four large 3/4-room houses (#5, 6, 10, 11) totaling 9.6×7.5 m (Stager 1985: 19; Braemer

1982: 169), equaling 54% of the excavated area, with a shared an exterior work space.

On the south side of the fence, the central house is House B.XV (found in Squares B.XV, XVII, XXII, and XXIV), also called the "Pillared Building," under Byzantine Wall A (Callaway 1968a: 316; 1969b: 6). This may have been a two-story building, since a threshold of cobblestones in B.XVII leads to the upper part of one room, which opens thru a small door to the lower level on the opposite side (Callaway 1968b: 4). The house has four hewn-stone pillars done with hammer and bronze chisel, piers, and stone walls (Callaway 1965a: 412). The roof had to be 1.8 m up off the packed-earth floor (Callaway 1965b: 26; 1969b: 57). This main building has a second roofed structure of six rooms adjoining it on the east with corbel-arched passageways 0.8 m high (for animals; Callaway 1969b: 59; 1970a: 13–15, 18; ʾAi 1969b: 15). There is also a long, narrow enclosure adjoining that second structure, with a manger for caprovids (Callaway 1969b: 59; 1970a: 13–15, 18; ʾAi 1969b: 15) and two bell-shaped cisterns. The "North Bench House" is another house to the north of the main one, also piered, with cisterns and benches (Callaway 1970a: 13, 16). It is in Squares B.XVII, XVIII, XXI, and XXIII. Here a forged bronze chisel was found (Callaway 1969b: 57).

There is also the "Southern Bench House" B.V–VI, IX–XI. It has an arch in its eastern Wall S which may also lead to a side room enclosed by Wall W (Callaway, draft of "The Iron I Village at ʾAi (et-Tell)").

Also from this strata is the public area of the "Cobblestone Street," demarcated by Walls A and AN found in B.I, V, IX, and XIII at the edge of the lower terrace (Callaway 1965b: 22).

In Site C (west side of tell), there is occupation in Area C.II, Field 100.8–10, Layer 2; Area C.III, Field 200.5-6, Layer 2; Area C.IV, Field 302.1, Layer 2; Area C.VI, Field 500.2–3, Layer 2; Area C.VII, Field 600.4–5, Layer 2; Area C.VIII, Field 700.2, Layer 2; Area C.IX, Field 800.2-3, Layer 2; Area C.XI, Field 1000.2, Layer 2. There are no houses.

Site G (south-east central area of tell) has terrace Wall A (Callaway 1980: 245); Area G.II,

Field 100.3a, Layer 5; Area G.IV, Field 300.3a–4, Layer 5; Area G.VI, Fields 500.4 and 501.1, Layer 5; Area G.VIII, Field 700.4, Layer 5; Area G.IX, Field 800.5, Layer 5. No houses (Callaway 1967: 4).

Finds: collared-rimmed pithoi with long collar and thick folded rim (Callaway 1968a: 316; Cooley 1997a: 33); handmade hole-mouth pithoi (Callaway 1980: figs. 147–150); outcurving, lipped-rim cooking pots and cooking pots with sharp, triangular slanted rims (Callaway 1968a: 316; Stager 1968: 8); bowls, many red-slipped and burnished, both wheeled and handmade, some with painted lines; rims vertical, ledge, or incurving (Callaway 1980: figs. 147–50); jugs with rims outcurving, all handmade (Callaway 1980: figs. 147–50).

In 1150, the site was destroyed (Callaway 1976: 30; contra earlier statements that it was not destroyed, as in Callaway 1964: 7).

In 1125 began the Silo Granary Stratum (Callaway 1976), also called Level IB, "Wall A Iron Age Phase" (even though Wall A is Byzantine; Callaway 1965b: 40), Phase X (Callaway 1980: 245), or Phase III (Callaway, draft of "The Iron I Village at Ai (et-Tell)"). The site is still unwalled (Callaway 1965a: 412; 1966: 4). Now it has a bigger population, new crude buildings, less public areas, and subdivisions of the old buildings (Fritz 1995: 56; Callaway 1976: 29–30). For example, a *tabun* and silos above ground were constructed through the cobblestone roads in the public area (Callaway 1976: 29–30). Cisterns were built with the houses, some in every house (Callaway 1969a: 58). Also many were built in an open area 2 km E of site. One house has three cisterns—all bell-shaped, making a sort of a system with settling basin and filter-trap (Callaway 1976: 30; 1984: 55). The total water storage provides a minimum of one gallon a day for up to eighty people between rainy seasons ("Glenn 1970–71" Report in Nicol Museum).

In this phase, a high wall was built in a semicircle, using the EB wall in the northwest, west, and southwest, and houses built along the rest of the perimeter, in order to set off two house-compounds in the east (Zevit 1983: 29; Callaway 1976: 22–23).

In Site B, North Bench House B.XV is not rebuilt, and lay in ruins (Callaway 1968a: 316; Stager 1968: 8). But the South Bench House B.V–VI,IX–X continues (Callaway 1965b: 26–27), with stone floors now replacing the beaten earth ones. In Site C, however, there were crude 2 to 3 room dwellings (Shiloh 1978: 45): House 152 (+150), which is 13.5×5.1 m and is of a type with a rectangular space bordered with walled-off rooms on one short side (Braemer 1982: 344); House 189 (+190, 183, 184, 208), which is 13.5×6 m and of no clear plan; and House 207 (+206), of the same type as House 152. The EB terrace wall here, Wall AE, is reinforced with rubble Wall AF (Layer 1c) in order to go all across Site C (Callaway 1980: 245).

Occupation is also registered for Site C, in Area C.I, Fields 1.4 and 1.9, Layer 1c; Area C.II, Field 100.11–14, Layer 1c; Area C.III, Field 200.3–4, Layer 1c; Area C.VII, Field 600.3, Layer 1b; Area C.IX, Field 800.1a, Layer 1b; Area C.X, Field 900.1a, Layer 1b, and terrace Walls B, C, and D (Callaway 1969b: 16).

In the Site D Acropolis (north central edge of tell), there are very irregular casemate-like houses (D.I, D.II, D.V) with a N-S orientation in two parallel bands, densely occupying one E–W terrace each (Callaway 1965b: 32; 1984: 22). Site D also has silos, cisterns, and underground storage (Vincent 1936: 255). People moved into large Room A of the EB Palace (Marquet-Krause 1935: 339), put a divider across the middle, and used it as two houses. They also built houses on the terraces east of the temple (Callaway 1965b: 38; 1984: 54) and subdivided EB Palace Hallway B into rooms (Marquet-Krause 1935: 339). These were clearly squatters because they put their fires directly on floors (Callaway 1965b: 38–39).

At end of a street in Site D, there is tiny Room #65 (8.5×2.5 m), with a bench at foot of its wall all the way around, well-preserved on the south and west sides. Here was found a 4-story, 80 cm tall biconical fenestrated incense burner with two loop handles and lions paws as a base (Marquet-Krause 1935: 340; Vincent 1936: 255). Analogous pieces are from Megiddo (P6055 and others), two from Tell Qasile, and three from Beth Shean (Allen 1980: 38, 60). Inside the burner were a carnelian

and glass beaded necklace and a clay animal figure #1081 (Gilmour 1995: 172), which is 5 cm long and depicts either a greyhound dog or a jackal similar to one found by Sellin at Taanach—it is not a mouse (Allen 1980: 11-13). Also in the room were an everted-rim funnel chalice (#1054= a bowl for a cult stand, having a chalice profile with a tang; Gilmour 1997b: 9), a bovine figurine (Gilmour 1995: 172–73; Thomsen 1936/37: 95), and a bowl (#1055) with flat base and a row of breasts around the carination.

Site G has agricultural terraces such as Terrace A (Callaway 1969b: 16). There was also occupation in Site G, Area G.II, Field 100.3, Layer 4; Area G.IV, Field 300.3, Layer 4; Area G.VI, Field 500.3a, Layer 4; Area G.VIII, Field 700.3, Layer 4; Area G.IX, Fields 800.4 and 802.1, Layer 4.

Finds: no Philistine wares (Bunimovitz and Finkelstein 1993: 160). Many sling-stones (Cooley 1997a: 33); collared-rim pithoi (H. Weippert 1988: 399), including types with short, thick everted rims, ones with long collars and thick folded rims, and some with long collars and short necks and narrow rims (Callaway 1968a: 317; Stager 1968: 8; Cooley 1997a: 33), also some with molded rims with ridge at the bottom of the rim that has merged with the rim itself rather than separate on the neck (Callaway 1980: fig. 150: 15-30), simple-rimmed with high neck, and curved-rimmed (Brandfon 1983); cooking pots variously outcurving lipped-rim, flattened triangular-rimmed, triangular-rimmed with lower edge pointing below horizontal, some having sharp triangular slanted rim with ridge on bottom edge of rim, some with ridge just below the lip, some outflaring-necked non-carinated, as well as cooking pots with plain rims (Callaway 1968a: 316; 1980: figs. 147–50); jugs wheeled, with rims vertical or outcurving or incurving; some spouted, some with rim handles (Callaway 1980: fig. 150: 15–30); bowls with vertical or out-curving rims; all wheeled, none slipped (Callaway 1980: figs. 147–50), including (Brandfon 1983), large bell-shaped bowls, large bowls with thickened, folded, and inverted rims, and hemispherical bowls with simple, rounded rims; ledge-rimmed kraters (Brandfon 1983);

saddle querns, mortars, stone pestles; small round ovens (Callaway 1976: 29); flint sickles (Callaway 1969b: 59); 2 iron bracelets (Marquet-Krause 1935: 340); carnelian necklace (in a shallow deposit in earth and ash; Vincent 1936); caprovid bones (Callaway 1969b: 59); bronze ring; worked antler tip from a gazelle or row deer (not fallow deer, whose antlers do not have tips). From the Site B houses: 16 sling stones ("1964 Objects Registry" p. 28). From the Pillared Bldg (B.XV): iron point 6.5 cm long (Reg #430; "1964 Registered Objects" p. 43). From the North Bench House: bronze chisel (Callaway 1970a: 18). From B.IV: hollow bull-shaped piece of a spout (#100; Allen 1980: 11, 54). Flints from Site G: a retouched sickle, a blade, and a ridge blade used to make the core into a blade core for running blades (Callaway 1980: 270). From Sites D and G: iron tweezers, iron lance head, iron dagger, 2 iron knives, iron nail, another unidentifiable iron piece (Waldbaum 1978: 25). From Site D: in Room 10 lugged-blade axe, symmetrically sharpened, even on the rear portion of its blade as well as the narrow part opposite the crest (Meron 1985: 69)—one of the three types of Iron I axes (Meron 1985: 163); this type is found at 12th-century Tel Masos, 11th-century Megiddo and Tell Abu Hawwam, and is an Anatolian type which seems to arrive with the Sea Peoples (Meron 1985: 84, iv). From another place in Site D: iron spearbutt, iron tool (Meron 1985: 25).

From one of the two Iron I strata, the following finds: Phoenician globular jugs with round base and lip (Briese 1985: 12), some with slender handle and angular back (Briese 1985: 14), some red painted (Briese 1985: 20), some with funnel-shaped neck (Briese 1985: 16), some with "running" lip and "snapped-off" mouth (Briese 1985: 16); from Site B, B.XIX, Locus 1801.4, a figurine of a goose 7.5 cm long, similar to ones at Beth Shean ("Denyer 1976" Report in Nicol Museum).

Level II is the destruction layer of Level I, especially visible in Site D (Callaway 1965b: 38; 1969b: 7), also called Phase XI—some early reports held for no destruction, just a light third occupation phase almost totally eroded (Callaway 1964: 7). No Iron II.

TELL, KH. ET-   **M.R. 15860.16810**

2–3 ha. site on hilltop and ridge. 3.85 km to nearest water. 6.9% Iron I sherds, also Iron II. Iron I includes cooking pots with sharp, triangular slanted rims and collared-rimmed pithoi (Finkelstein 1988a: 164, 180; Finkelstein, Lederman, and Bunimovitz 1997: 113).

TELL, KH. ET-   **M.R. 16385.16905**

3 ha. site on hilltop. 3.4 km to nearest water. 8.2% Iron I sherds, no LB or Iron II. Iron I finds include cooking pots, some with sharp, triangular slanted rims, and collared-rimmed pithoi (Finkelstein 1988a: 163, 180; Finkelstein, Lederman, and Bunimovitz 1997: 252).

TELL, KH. ET-   **M.R. 17490.15870**

1.5 ha. site on hilltop. 600 m to nearest water. 4.8%–9% Iron I sherds, also Iron II. Iron I includes cooking pots with erect or slanted rims and collared-rimmed pithoi (Finkelstein 1983a: 143; 1988a: 180; Finkelstein, Lederman, and Bunimovitz 1997: 357).

TEOMIM, TEL   **M.R. 1987.2054**

Two tells, one 120×40 m and the other 80×30 m. Iron I sherds all from beside cistern, including flasks, including some of Black-on-Red ware, lamps with flat bases, storejars, and Philistine sherds (Zori 1962: 175).

TERUMOT, TEL (Kh. el-Khomrah)
M.R. 1965.2052

15×20 m tell. LB and Iron I remains. Iron I pottery includes bowls, many ring-rimmed, many with flat bases (Zori 1962: 175).

THUGHRA, ETH-   **M.R. 17585.13475**

0.52 ha. site in declivity in Wadi Jurat Kamakh. Twenty percent Iron I, also LB and Iron II (Finkelstein and Magen 1993: 368).

TIBNAH, KH. — see TIBNE, KH.

TIBNE, KH. (Kh. Tibnah) M.R. 16035.15725

1.5–3.5 ha. site on north slope of hilltop. 100 m to nearest spring. 6%–7.9% Iron I pottery, also Iron II. Iron I includes cooking pots with sharp, triangular slanted rims and collared-rimmed pithoi (Finkelstein 1986: 151; 1988a: 181; Finkelstein, Lederman, and Bunimovitz 1997: 182).

TIRAT ZVI — see KEREN ZEITIM

TITTORAH, HORVAT (Burj el-Hubis; Qalat Tantura)   M.R. 1521.14555

Although Finkelstein (1988a: 122) found no Iron I, more recent work by Egon Lass in conjunction with the Modiʻin Project has found Iron I and II (S. Gibson and Lass 1997).

TRUNET EL-ʻAUJA, TELL — see ʻAUJA EL-FOQA, KH. EL-

TRUNI, TELL ET — see ʻAUJA EL-FOQA, KH. EL-

TZFARI, TEL — see SOFAR, TELL

ET-TUGHRAH   M.R. 1873.1921

0.15 ha. site 140 meters above the surrounding terrain. Rendzina soil. Six kilometers to nearest water, at Ein el-Farah spring. 60%-80% Iron I sherds, also Iron II. Iron I pottery includes hemispherical bowls with simple, rounded rims and cooking pots with outcurving, lipped-rim or sharp triangular slanted rim with ridge on bottom edge of rim (Finkelstein 1986: 140; Zertal 1996: 290–91).

ET-TUWEILAT   M.R. 1648.1855

Entirely Iron I site of 0.1 ha., twenty meters above valley floor. Terra Rosa soil. 800 m to nearest water (Zertal 1992: 360).

TZUR NATAN — see BIR EL-HADAB

UKASHA   M.R. 18255.16565

0.5 ha. site on hill. 2.4 km to nearest water. 44.7% Iron I sherds, no LB or Iron II (Finkelstein, Lederman, and Bunimovitz 1997: 532).

UMM EL-ʻALAQ, KH.   M.R. 1456.2174

Iron I and II site (Hirschfeld 1991: 12).

UMM EL-BUTM, KH.   M.R. 1785.2035

1 ha. site forty meters above valley. Mediterranean Brown Forest soil. Three kilometers to nearest spring. Ten percent Iron I, no LB or Iron II (Zertal 1988: 110; 1992: 160).

UMM EDH-DHIYAB, KH. — see ZEʻEVIM, TEL

UMM EL-HAFFEH, KH. — see MUHAFFAR, TELL EL-

UMM EL-HOSR, KH. — see YUSUF, KH.

UMM ER-RAMMIN, KH. — see RAMMUN

UMM SAFA — see KAZIYYA ER-RATRUT

UMM ES-SAMAYEH, TELL — see MISKI, TELL

UMM ESH-SHARAYIT, KH.
**   M.R. 16966.14370**

4 ha. site on slope. Four percent Iron I sherds, also Iron II (Finkelstein and Magen 1993: 31*, 158–59). 1995 excavations by the Palestinian Department of Antiquities led by Hamdan Taha, Jihad Yassine, and Jamal Bargouth have not yet been published.

UNEIZIYYA, KH. EL- — see **ABU MU'AMMAR, KH.**

EL-UNUQ   **M.R. 1852.1840**

1.49 ha. site fifty meters above the Wadi Farah, on both sides of the wadi. Terra rosa soil. Ninety percent of pottery found is Iron I, twenty percent being Einun ware. The remainder is Iron II. Iron I, in addition to Einun ware, includes large bowls with thickened, folded, and inverted rims, hemispherical bowls with flat, rectangular rims, collared-rimmed pithoi with short, thick everted rims, pithoi with simple rims and high necks,, punctured jar handles, long-necked piriform jugs, and lug-handled pyxides (Finkelstein 1986: 162; Zertal 1991: 42–43; 1996: 394–97).

URMA, KH. EL-   **M.R. 18805.17265**

1.2ha-1.5 ha. site on summit of Jebel el-Urmeh. 850 m to nearest well (Jaroš and Deckert 1977: 24). Five percent of sherds Iron I (Finkelstein 1986: 136), also LB and Iron II. In Iron I the site was fortified using old MB and LB walls: retaining walls (Campbell 1991: 50), buttress walls (Campbell 1991: 50), and defensive walls (Campbell 1991: 51). Iron I also had a massive water storage system of several huge cisterns, one 1800 kL (Campbell 1991: 52–53; Bull and Campbell 1968). These may have been built in MB, but they were definitely in use in Iron I. Iron I finds are from on top, east slopes, bedrock quarry south of the acropolis, west slopes, and northeast slopes (Campbell 1991: 51): 4 outcurving, lipped-rim cooking pots, 8 collared-rim and 3 neckless pithoi (Finkelstein 1988a: 179).

WASIL, KH. (Kh. Wuseil)   **M.R. 1593.1953**

0.24 ha. site one hundred meters above the surrounding terrain. Rendzina soil. Four kilometers to water at well of Bir es-Sama. Five percent Iron I, no LB or Iron II (Zertal 1988: 126).

WUSEIL, KH. — see **WASIL, KH.**

YALO, TEL — see **YALU**

YALU (Tel Yalo)   **M.R. 1524.1386**

Hilltop site of two hectares, with spring to the east. Occupation from LB, Iron I, and Iron II (Albright 1924a: 10; Finkelstein 1996: 239). Iron I pottery includes large bowls with thickened, folded, and inverted rims and hemispherical bowls (Peterson 1977: 350). Iron I pottery has not been reconfirmed for the site of Tell el-Koka/Tell el-Qauq'a, 300 m to the east (cf. Kochavi 1972: 236).

YANUN   **M.R. 183.172**
***and* YANUN, KH.**   **M.R. 18425.17385**

The site of Khirbet Yanun is 0.4 ha. (Finkelstein 1988a: 144), on the level of the terrain. Alluvial soil. 100 m to spring, 21 m to a well. Iron I was found at both Khirbet and modern Yanun (Wallis 1961: 44; Otto 1978; Finkelstein 1988a: 142; Jaroš and Deckert 1977: 33). Also Iron II. There is an Iron Ia citadel at Khirbet Yanun which was abandoned before the end of the 12th century (Otto 1978). Finds include cooking pots with sharp, triangular slanted rims, cooking pots with outcurving, lipped-rims, collared-rim pithoi, neckless pithoi, punctured jar handles, one "man's face" punctured jar handle (Finkelstein 1988a: 179).

YAQLUM, KH. EL — see **KH. MARAH EL-'INAB**

YARZA, KH. (A) — see **YERZAH, TELL**

YASID   **M.R. 1765.1892**

1.5 ha. site on a fifty-meter high hill in a mountainous area. Terra Rosa soil. Seven kilometers to nearest spring. Thirty percent of sherds Iron I, also Iron II (Zertal 1992: 469).

YERZAH, TELL
(Kh. Yarza [A])   **M.R. 1913.1904**

1.1 ha. tell twenty meters above the Wadi Malih.

Terra Rosa soil. Three kilometers to nearest water at Ein el-Mita spring. Twenty percent of sherds Iron I, also Iron II. Iron I pottery includes hemispherical bowls with beveled rims whose upper surface slopes outward diagonally, outflaring-necked non-carinated cooking pots, and punctured jar handles (Finkelstein 1986: 149; Zertal 1996: 300–301).

YIZRE'EL, TEL — see JEZREEL, TEL

YOSEF HAYASHNAH, TEL — see SHEIKH HASAN, TELL ESH-

YUSUF, KH. (Kh. Umm el-Hosr)
M.R. 1948.1879

6 ha. site ten meters above valley floor. Rendzina soil. Nearest water 6.5 km away at Ein Hilu springs. Five percent Iron I sherds, also LB. Iron I includes triangular-rimmed cooking pots with an upper lip that has been folded inward (Zertal 1996: 317–19).

ZA'ATARA, KH.   M.R. 1796.20355

0.8 ha. site five meters above valley. Mediterranean Brown Forest soil. Four kilometers to nearest spring. Three percent Iron I, also Iron II (Zertal 1992: 162).

ZEBABIDEH   M.R. 1807.1992

3 ha. site ten meters above valley. Eroded soil. Six kilometers to nearest spring at Ein Giniyya. Ten percent of sherds Iron I, also Iron II (A. Mazar 1982b: 142; Zertal 1988: 118; 1996: 124–25).

ZEBUBEH   M.R. 169.217

LB and Iron I site 300×300 m, located northwest of the village of Zebubeh (Zori 1977: 51).

ZE'EVIM, TEL (edh-Medhiab; Kh. Umm edh-Dhiyab)   M.R. 1545.2063

Iron I "fortress" (so Ne'eman 1990: 34*, 41–42) on lofty hill. Also Iron II.

ZERIN — see JEZREEL, TEL

UNNAMED   M.R. 1457.1653

Iron I and II site of minimal size (Finkelstein 1978: 20).

UNNAMED   M.R. 15465.22150

Iron I and II site 40×50 m in size (Olami 1981: 91–92).

UNNAMED   M.R. 15675.15990

0.5 ha. site on ridge. 200 m to nearest water. 4%–7.7% Iron I sherds, also Iron II. Iron I includes outcurving, lipped-rim cooking pots and collared-rimmed pithoi (Finkelstein 1986: 151; Finkelstein, Lederman, and Bunimovitz 1997: 60).

UNNAMED   M.R. 15795.15350

0.25 ha. site on hill. 1.4 km to nearest water. Seventeen percent of sherds Iron I, no LB or Iron II. Iron I includes collared-rimmed pithoi (Finkelstein 1986: 152–53; Finkelstein, Lederman, and Bunimovitz 1997: 61).

UNNAMED   M.R. 15805.15900

0.1 ha. hill 400 m from nearest water. 4.2% Iron I, no LB or Iron II (Finkelstein, Lederman, and Bunimovitz 1997: 71).

UNNAMED   M.R. 1587.2206

0.45 ha. site with Iron I and II occupation (Olami 1981: 99–100).

UNNAMED   M.R. 16005.17160

0.15 ha. site on ridge. 500 m to water. Eighty percent Iron I, also Iron II (Finkelstein, Lederman, and Bunimovitz 1997: 276).

UNNAMED   **M.R. 16415.17010**

1 ha. site on hill. 2.8 km to nearest water. 11.1%–18% Iron I sherds, no LB or early Iron II (Finkelstein 1986: 146; Finkelstein, Lederman, and Bunimovitz 1997).

UNNAMED   **M.R. 16675.15830**

0.15 ha. site on ridge. 500 m to water. 27.3% Iron I, also Iron II (Finkelstein, Lederman, and Bunimovitz 1997).

UNNAMED   **M.R. 16760.15740**

0.4 ha. site on hill. One kilometer to water. 14.3% Iron I, also Iron II (Finkelstein, Lederman, and Bunimovitz 1997: 224).

UNNAMED   **M.R. 16825.14490**

1.05 ha. site on hilltop in the city of Ramallah, on the southwest side of the street to Beitunia. 700 m to nearest water. Twenty percent Iron I sherds, including collared-rimmed pithoi, also LB and Iron II (Sapin 1968–69: 7–8, 23; Finkelstein and Magen 1993: 156).

UNNAMED   **M.R. 16830.14370**

1 ha. site in declivity in Wadi Bir ed-Deir. Water nearby in the wadi, at the well of Bir ed-Deir, and at the spring of Ein Umm Elisha. 38% Iron I, also LB and Iron II. Iron I finds include collared-rimmed pithoi and rounded-rimmed jars (Sapin 1968–69: 7–8, 23; Finkelstein and Magen 1993: 155).

UNNAMED   **M.R. 16960.15405**

0.55 ha. site on ridge. 300 m to nearest water. Half of sherds Iron I, no LB or Iron II. Iron I includes collared-rimmed pithoi (Finkelstein 1986: 152; Finkelstein, Lederman, and Bunimovitz 1997: 232).

UNNAMED   **M.R. 17115.16910**

0.8 ha. site on slope. 1.3 km to water. 1.6% Iron I, no LB or Iron II (Finkelstein, Lederman, and Bunimovitz 1997: 392).

UNNAMED   **M.R. 17190.16560**

0.15 ha. site on ridge. 600 m to nearest water. 37.5% Iron I, no LB or Iron II. Iron I includes collared-rimmed pithoi (Finkelstein 1986: 140; Finkelstein, Lederman, and Bunimovitz 1997: 387).

UNNAMED   **M.R. 17203.13723**

Iron I and II remains in the Wadi Zimri. Iron I finds include, from Locus 52, neckless pithos (Maitlis 1989: 14, 50, fig. 3.9).

UNNAMED   **M.R. 17315.16530**

0.4 ha. site on level plain. 1.4 km to nearest water. 6.9% Iron I, also Iron II (Finkelstein, Lederman, and Bunimovitz 1997: 401).

UNNAMED   **M.R. 17350.14665**

0.5 ha. site in the Wadi Abu el-Leimun. Sixteen percent Iron I, also Iron II (Finkelstein and Magen 1993: 34*).

UNNAMED   **M.R. 17375.14690**

0.15 ha. site on slope in Wadi esh-Shami. One kilometer to nearest water. 57% of sherds Iron I, possibly Iron II also. Iron I sherds include outcurving, lipped-rim cooking pots, cooking pots with ridge just below the lip, and collared-rimmed pithoi (Finkelstein 1986: 146; Finkelstein and Magen 1993: 22*, 81–82).

UNNAMED   **M.R. 1759.1332**

Although Finkelstein and Magen (1993: site #466) found no Iron I, Shimon Gibson has found Iron I sherds on the east slope at the Roman tombs, along with Iron II (Gibson 1995: 428).

UNNAMED   **M.R. 17630.16200**

1.2 ha. site on slope. 1.3 km to nearest water. Two percent Iron I, no LB or Iron II (Finkelstein, Lederman, and Bunimovitz 1997: 421).

UNNAMED   **M.R. 17690.13530**

600 m² site on bank of Wadi er-Rawabi. Twelve percent Iron I sherds, also LB and Iron II (Finkelstein and Magen 1993: 379).

UNNAMED   **M.R. 17690.16280**

0.15 ha. site on slope. 400 m to nearest water. Iron I surface pottery is between 26.7% and 60% (widely different survey results). Also Iron II. Iron I includes cooking pots with ridge just below the lip, and collared-rimmed and hole-mouth pithoi (Finkelstein 1986: 142; Finkelstein, Lederman, and Bunimovitz 1997: 422).

UNNAMED   **M.R. 17830.14395**

In a declivity in the Wadi Suneisil between Ras el-Muhala and Jebel Tu'mur are fifty MB shaft and cave tombs and cisterns. Thirty percent of the pottery collect from this MB site was Iron I, with no LB or Iron II (Finkelstein and Magen 1993: 39*, 202).

UNNAMED   **M.R. 17980.15970**

0.1 ha. site on ridge. 2.6 km to nearest water. Twenty percent Iron I sherds, no LB or Iron II (Finkelstein, Lederman, and Bunimovitz 1997: 377).

UNNAMED   **M.R. 17980.16220**

0.05–0.1 ha. site on slope. 1.8 km to nearest water. Surveys have found between 15% and 21.4% Iron I sherds, including collared-rimmed pithoi. Also Iron II (Finkelstein 1986: 142; Finkelstein, Lederman, and Bunimovitz 1997: 438).

UNNAMED   **M.R. 18090.14850**

0.2 ha. entirely Iron I site on ridge. 3.8 km to nearest water (Finkelstein, Lederman, and Bunimovitz 1997: 486).

UNNAMED   **M.R. 18115.16665**

1.5 ha. site. 1.6 km to nearest water. 8.1% Iron I finds, including cooking pots having sharp triangular slanted rim with ridge on bottom edge of rim, and cooking pots with ridge just below the lip, collared-rimmed pithoi, and punctured jar handles (Finkelstein 1986: 140; Finkelstein, Lederman, and Bunimovitz 1997: 522).

UNNAMED   **M.R. 18120.16150**

0.3 ha. site on hill. One kilometer to water. 89.5% Iron I, no LB or Iron II (Finkelstein, Lederman, and Bunimovitz 1997: 520).

UNNAMED   **M.R. 18190.15540**

0.3 ha. site on ridge. 300 m to nearest water. Sixteen percent Iron I, no LB or Iron II (Finkelstein, Lederman, and Bunimovitz 1997: 502).

UNNAMED   **M.R. 18300.15000**

0.5 ha. site on slope. 2.4 km to water. 4.7% Iron I, also Iron II (Finkelstein, Lederman, and Bunimovitz 1997: 509).

UNNAMED   **M.R. 18475.17420**

Single building (lodge?) of one phase, built in Iron I and continuing into the 10th century. One cistern accompanies it. Iron I pottery collared-rimmed and hole-mouth pithoi, triangular-rimmed cooking pots with molded lower edge, and "man's face" puncturing (Finkelstein 1986: 130; Finkelstein, Lederman, and Bunimovitz 1997: 576).

UNNAMED   **M.R. 18540.16060**

0.2 ha. site on slope. 400 m to water. 4.2% Iron I, no LB or Iron II (Finkelstein, Lederman, and Bunimovitz 1997: 543).

UNNAMED   **M.R. 18695.16750**

0.1 ha. site on slope. 2.1 km to water. 23.1% Iron I, no LB or Iron II (Finkelstein, Lederman, and Bunimovitz 1997: 552).

UNNAMED   **M.R. 18710.16880**

0.2 ha. site on slope. 2.8 km to water. Ten percent Iron I, no LB or Iron II (Finkelstein, Lederman, and Bunimovitz 1997: 554).

REFERENCES

Abel, F.-M.
1928   Notes sur les environs de Bir-Zeit. *JPOS* 8: 49–55.
1937   Un Mention Biblique de Birzeit. *RB* 46: 217–24.

Abercrombie, R.
1979   *Palestinian Burial Practices from 1200 to 600 B.C.E..* Ph.D. diss., The University of Michigan, Ann Arbor.

Aharoni, Y.
1957   Archaeological Survey in the North. *Bulletin of the Department of Antiquities of the State of Israel* 5/6: 45–49.
1969   Rubute and Ginti-Kirmil. *VT* 19: 137–45.
1971   Khirbet Raddana and Its Inscription. *IEJ* 21: 130–35.

Aharoni, Y., Dothan, T., and Frumstein, H.
1950   Researches of the Circle for Historical Geography. *Yediot* 16(3–4): 45–51. In Hebrew.

Ahituv, S.
1979   *The Egyptian Topographical Lists Relating to the History of Palestine in the Biblical Period.* Ph.D. diss., The Hebrew University, Jerusalem. In Hebrew.
1984   *Canaanite Toponyms in Ancient Egyptian Documents.* Jerusalem: Magnes Press.

Ahlström, G.
1990   The Bull Figurine from Dhahrat et-Tawileh. *BASOR* 280: 77–82.

ʾAi
1969a   ʾAi — 1968. *HA* 28/29: 38–39. In Hebrew.
1969b   ʾAi — 1969. *HA* 31/32: 15–16. In Hebrew.
1971a   ʾAi — 1970. *HA* 37: 22. In Hebrew.
1971b   Ha-ʾAi — 1971. *HA* 40: 21–22. In Hebrew.

Ain Samiya
1970   Ain Samiya. *HA* 36: 11–12. In Hebrew.
1971   Ain Samiya. *HA* 37: 23. In Hebrew.
1976   Tell Marjama (Ain Samiya). *HA* 57/58: 23–24. In Hebrew.
1978   Kh. Marjeme (Ain Samiya). *HA* 65/66: 28–29. In Hebrew.

Albright, W. F.
1923   The Ephraim of the Old and New Testaments. *JPOS* 3: 36–40.
1924a   Researches of the School in Western Judaea. *BASOR* 15: 2–11.
1924b   *Excavations and Results at Tell el-Ful.* AASOR 4. New Haven: Yale University Press.
1924c   The Excavations at Gibeah of Saul. *Qobets* 1: 53–60.
1929   New Israelite and Pre-Israelite Sites. *BASOR* 35: 1–14.
1933   A New Campaign of Excavations at Gibeah of Saul. *BASOR* 52: 6–12.
1934   The Kyle Memorial Excavation at Bethel. *BASOR* 56: 2–15.
1935   Observations on the Bethel Report. *BASOR* 57: 27–30.
1936   Additional Note [to Blair, 1936 and Bergman, 1936]. *BASOR* 62: 25–26.
1946   The Late Bronze Town at Modern Djett. *BASOR* 104: 25–26.

Albright, W. F., and Kelso, J.
1968   *The Excavations at Bethel.* AASOR 39. Cambridge, MA: American Schools of Oriental Research.

Allen, M. W.
1980   A Synthetic Reconstruction of the Religion of Iron Age Ai and Raddanah. J. A. Callaway Archives. Nicol Museum, Southern Baptist Theological Seminary, Louisville.

Alt, A.
1925   *Die Landnahme der Israeliten in Palästina.* Leipzig: Drukerei D. Wergemeinschaft.
1929   The God of the Fathers. Repr. 1968 in *Essays on Old Testament History and Religion.* Garden City: Doubleday and Co., Inc.

Amiran, R.
1970   *Ancient Pottery of the Holy Land.* New Brunswick, NJ: Rutgers University Press.

Amit, D., and Zilbarbod, I.
1996   Survey of Mazor. *HA* 106: 99–100. In Hebrew.

Amitai, J., ed.
1985   *Biblical Archaeology Today.* Jerusalem: Israel Exploration Society.

Amizur, H.
1993   "Between Ramah and Bethel in the Hills of Ephraim." Vol. 3, pp. 181–87 in Erlich, 1987–93. In Hebrew.

Astour, M. C.
1995   Overland Trade Routes in Ancient Western Asia. *Civilizations of the Ancient Near East* 3: 1401–1420.

Aviram, J., ed.
1973   *Eretz Shomron: The 30th Archaeological Convention, September 1972.* Jerusalem:

Israel Exploration Society. In Hebrew.

Bach, R.
1958   Zur Siedlungsgeschichte des Talkessels von Samaria. *ZDPV* 74: 41–54.

Badè, W. F.
1927   Excavation of Tell en-Nasbeh. *BASOR* 26: 1–7.
1928   *Excavations at Tell en-Nasbeh.* Palestine Institute Publications 1. Berkeley: Palestine Institute.
1929   Tell en-Nasbeh in 1929. *Bulletin of the Pacific School of Religion* 8(3): 3–12. = The Tell en-Nasbeh Excavations of 1929. Pp. 483–94 in *Smithsonian Report for 1930.* Washington, DC: Smithsonian Institute. = The Tell en-Nasbeh Excavations of 1929. *PEFQSt* 1930: 8–19.
1936   New Discoveries at Tell en-Nasbeh. Pp. 30–36 in *Werden und Wesen des Altes Testaments*, ed. P. Volz, F. Stummer, and J. Hembel. BZAW 66. Berlin: Alfred Töpelmann.

Beck, B.
n.d.   The Surface Exploration Techniques Employed at Khirbet Kefire. J. A. Callaway Archives. Nicol Museum, Southern Baptist Theological Seminary, Louisville.

Ben-Nun, Y.
1985   The Building on Mt. Ebal and Its Identification as an Altar. Pp. 137–62 in Erlich, 1985. In Hebrew.

Ben-Tor, A.
1980   The Regional Study. *BAR* 6.1: 30–44.

Ben-Tor, A.; M. Avisar; R. Bonfil; I. Zerzetsky; and Y. Portugali.
1987   A Regional Study of Tel Yoqne'am and Its Vicinity. *Qadmoniot* 20: 2–17.

Ben-Yosef, S.
1983   *Nahal Mikhmas, Nahal Yitev.* 2d ed. Jerusalem: Society for the Protection of Nature. In Hebrew.

Bennett, B. M., Jr.
1972   The Search for Israelite Gilgal. *PEQ* 104: 111–22.

Beth Dagon
1966   Beth Dagon. *HA* 17: 10.

Biran (Bergman), A.
1936a   Soundings at the Supposed Site of Old Testament Anathoth. *BASOR* 62: 22–25.
1936b   Anathoth? *BASOR* 63: 22–23.
1964   *Yalqut HaParsumim.* Jerusalem: Department of Antiquities. In Hebrew.
1983   'Anata. *HA* 83: 21–22.

Biran (Bergman), A., and Brandstetter, R.
1941   Explorations in the Valley of Beth-Shan. *Yediot* 8: 85–90. In Hebrew.

Biran, A.; Mazar, B.; Aharoni, Y.; Dothan, M.; and Yeivin, S.
1968   *The Archaeological Survey of Judea, Samaria, and the Golan.* = HA 26. In Hebrew.

Birch, W. F.
1911   Gibeah of Saul and Zela. *PEFQSt* 101–9.

Blair, E. P.
1936   Soundings at Anata. *BASOR* 62: 18–21.

Blizzard, R. B., Jr.
1973/74 Intensive Systematic Surface Collection at Livingston's Proposed Site for Biblical Ai. *Westminster Theological Journal* 36: 221–30.

Böhl, F. M. T.
1960?   The Excavations of Shechem. In Horn, 1960?. Translation of *Die Ausgrabung von Sichem.* Ziest: G. J. A. Ruys' Uitgevers-Mij., 1927.

Boraas, R. S.
1986   Iron IA Ceramics at Tell Balatah. Pp. 249–64 in *The Archaeology of Jordan and Other Studies*, ed. L. T. Geraty and L. T. Herr. Berrien Springs: Andrews University Press.

Borée, W.
1930   *Die alten Orstnamen Palästinas.* Leipzig: Eduard Pfeiffer Press.

Borowski, O.
1987   *Agriculture in Iron Age Israel.* Winona Lake: Eisenbrauns.

Braemer, C.
1982   *L'Architecture domestique du Levant a l'Age du Fer.* Protohistoire du Levant 8. Paris: Recherches sur les Civilisations.

Brandfon, F. R.
1983   *The Beginning of the Iron Age in Palestine.* Ph.D diss., The University of Pennsylvania, Philadelphia.

Brandl, B.
1986–87 Two Scarabs and a Trapezoidal Seal from Mt. Ebal. *TA* 13–14: 166–72.
1993a   Clay, bone, metal and stone objects. Pp. 223–62 in Finkelstein, Bunimovitz, and Lederman, 1993.
1993b   Scarabs and Other Glyptic Finds. Pp. 203–22 in Finkelstein, Bunimovitz, and Lederman, 1993.

Briese, C.
1985   Früheisenzeitliche Bemalte Phönizische Kannen von Fundplätzen der Levanteküste. *Hamburger Beiträge zur Archäologie* 12: 7–118.

Brodsky, H.
1992   Bethel. *Anchor Bible Dictionary* 1: 710–12. Garden City: Doubleday & Co., Inc.

Brug, J. F.
1985   *A Literary and Archaeological Study of the Philistines*. BARInt 265. Oxford: British Archaeological Reports.

Buhl, M. -L., and Holm-Nielsen, S.
1969   *Shiloh*. Publications of the National Museum Archeological-Historical Series 1.12. Copenhagen: The National Museum of Denmark.

Bull, R. J.
1960   A Re-examination of the Shechem Temple. *BA* 23: 110–19.

1998   On the Composition and Orientation of Two Temples on the Acropolis of Tell Balatah (Shechem). Paper presented at annual meeting of the American Schools of Oriental Research, Orlando.

Bull, R. J., and Campbell, E. F., Jr.
1968   The Sixth Campaign at Balatah (Shechem). *BASOR* 190: 2–41.

Bunimovitz, S.
1993   Area C. Pp. 15–34 in Finkelstein, Bunimovitz, and Lederman, 1993.

Bunimovitz, S., and Finkelstein, I.
1993   Pottery. Pp. 81–196 in Finkelstein, Bunimovitz, and Lederman, 1993.

Burga
1972   Tel Burga. *RB* 79: 576–77.

Burgeta
1966   Tel Burgeta. *HA* 18/19: 11–12. In Hebrew.

Byers, G.
1994   An Iron I Tomb from Khirbet Nisya. Paper presented at annual meeting of the American Schools of Oriental Research annual, Chicago.

1995   An Iron I Tomb from Khirbet Nisya. Paper presented at annual meeting of the American Schools of Oriental Research, Philadelphia.

Cahill, J. M., Lipton (Lipovich), G., and Tarler, D.
1988   Tell el-Hammah. *IEJ* 38: 191–94.

Cahill, J. M., Tarler, D., and Lipton (Lipovich), G.
1989a   Tell el-Hammah. *ESI* 9: 134–35.

1989b   Tell el-Hammeh in the 10th Century BCE. *Qadmoniot* 22: 33–38.

Callaway, J. A.
1964   Excavations at Ai (et-Tell). *ASOR Newsletter* 1964–65(1): 3–8.

1965a   Ai. *RB* 72: 409–15.

1965b   The 1964 ʾAi Excavations. *BASOR* 178: 13–40.

1966   The 1966 ʾAi Excavations. *ASOR Newsletter* 1966–67(2): 2–4.

1968a   Evidence on the Conquest of ʾAi. *JBL* 87: 312–20.

1968b   The 1968 ʾAi Excavations. *ASOR Newsletter* 1968–89(5): 1–6.

1969a   The Significance of the Iron Age Village at ʾAi. Vol. 1, pp. 56–61 in *Proceedings of the Fifth World Congress of Jewish Studies*, ed. P. Peli. Jerusalem: R. H. HaCohen Press.

1969b   The 1966 ʾAi Excavations. *BASOR* 196: 2–16.

1969c   The 1969 ʾAi Excavations. *ASOR Newsletter* 1969–70(2): 1–5

1970a   The 1968–1969 ʾAi Excavations. BASOR 198: 7–31.

1970b   Khirbet Raddanah. *IEJ* 20: 230–32.

1970c   The 1968 ʾAi Excavations. *PEQ* 102: 42–44.

1973   The Date of the Raddanah Inscription. Paper presented at annual meeting of the Society for Biblical Literature.

1974   Khirbet Raddana. *RB* 81: 91–94.

1976   Excavating ʾAi: 1964–1972. *BA* 39: 18–30.

1980   *The Early Bronze Citadel and Lower City at Ai (et-Tell)*. Joint Archaeological Expedition to Ai (et-Tell) 2. Cambridge, MA: ASOR.

1984   Village Subsistence. Pp. 51–66 in *The Answers Lie Below*, ed. H. O. Thompson. Lanham, MD: University Press of America.

1985a   A New Perspective on the Hill Country Settlement of Canaan in Iron Age I. Pp. 31–49 in *Palestine in the Bronze and Iron Ages*, ed. J. N. Tubb. University of London Institute of Archaeology Occasional Publications 11. London: University of London Press.

1985b   Response. Pp. 72–78 in Amitai, 1985.

1988   The Settlement in Canaan. Pp. 53–84 in *Ancient Israel*, ed. H. Shanks. Washington: Biblical Archaeology Society.

Callaway, J. A., ed.

n.d. Village Life at Ai (et-Tell) and Raddanah in Iron Age I. = Davis, 1982; Mariottini, 1981; Harmon, 1983; and Denyer, 1973. J. A. Callaway Archives. Nicol Museum, Southern Baptist Theological Seminary, Louisville, KY.

Callaway, J. A., and Cooley, R. E.

1971 A Salvage Excavation at Raddana, In Bireh. *BASOR* 201: 9–19.

Campbell, E. F.

1960 Excavations at Shechem, 1960. *BA* 23: 102–9.

1967 The 1966 Shechem Expedition. *ASOR Newsletter* 1966–67(2): 5–10.

1969 Tell Balatah (Shechem) and Tell er–Ras. *ASOR Newsletter* 1968–69(10): 1–8.

1983 Judges 9 and Biblical Archaeology. Pp. 263–71 in *The Word of the Lord Shall Go Forth*, ed. C. L. Meyers and M. O'Connor. Winona Lake: Eisenbrauns.

1984 The Boundary Between Ephraim and Manasseh. Pp. 67–76 in *The Answers Lie Below*, ed. H. O. Thompson. Lanham, MD: University Press of America.

1991 *Shechem II: Portrait of a Hill Country Valley*. ASOR Archaeological Reports 2. Atlanta: Scholars Press.

1993 Developments in the Excavation and Reexcavation of Shechem/Tell Balatah. Pp. 598–605 in *Biblical Archaeology Today 1990*, ed. A. Biran and J. Aviram. Jerusalem: Israel Exploration Society.

Campbell, E. F., and Wright, G. E.

1965 Sichem. *RB* 72: 415–22.

Chambon, A.

1984 *Tell el-Farah I*. Paris: Editions Recherche sur les Civilisations.

Cockerham, C.

1995 *Burial Practices at Tell Dothan*. M.A. Thesis, Gordon-Conwell Theological Seminary, Wenham, MA.

Contenson, H. de.

1964 The 1953 Survey in the Yarmuk and Jordan Valleys. *ADAJ* 8: 30–46.

Coogan, M.

1987 Of Cults and Cultures. *PEQ* 119: 1–8.

Cooke, F. T.

1925 The Site of Kirjath-Jearim. *AASOR* 5: 105–20.

Cooley, R. E.

1975 Four Seasons of Excavations at Khirbet Raddana. *Near East Archaeological Society Bulletin* n.s. 5: 5–20.

1980 Brief Report on Project, Dothan II: A Late Bronze Age Tomb at Tell Dothan. Memorandum to Albert E. Glock.

1983 Tell Dothan. In *The Living and Active Word of God*, ed. M. Inch and R. Youngblood. Winona Lake: Eisenbrauns.

1997a Ai. Pp. 32–33 in *Oxford Encyclopaedia of the Ancient Near East* volume 1, ed. Eric M. Meyers. Oxford: Oxford University.

1997b Raddanah, Khirbet. Pp. 401–2 in *Oxford Encyclopaedia of the Ancient Near East* 4, ed. Eric M. Meyers. Oxford: Oxford University.

1998 Archaeological History at Tel Dothan. Lecture presented at Jerusalem University College, Jerusalem.

Cooley, R. E., and Pratico, G. D.

1994 Gathered to His People. Pp. 70–92 in *Scripture and Other Artifacts*, ed. M. D. Coogan, et al. Louisville: Westminster/John Knox.

1995 Tell Dothan: The Western Cemetery. Pp. 147–50 in *Preliminary Excavation Reports*, ed. W. G. Dever. AASOR 52. Baltimore: ASOR Press.

Cox, R. L.

1974 The Pool of Gibeon. *Bible and Spade* 3: 40–44.

Cross, F. M., and Freedman, D. N.

1971 An Inscribed Jar Handle from Raddanah. *BASOR* 201: 19–22.

Crowfoot, G. M., Kenyon, K., and Sukenik, E.

1942 *Samaria–Sebastia I*. London: Palestine Exploration Fund.

Crowfoot, J. W., Crowfoot, G. M., and Kenyon, K.

1957 *Samaria-Sebastia III*. London: Palestine Exploration Fund.

Currid, J. D.

1989 A Note on the Function of Building 5900 at Shechem — Again. *ZDPV* 105: 42–46.

Dagan, Y.

1996 Trans-Israel Highway: Southern Route. *ESI* 15: 122.

Dajani, A.

1953 An Iron Age Tomb at Al-Jim [sic]. *ADAJ* 2: 66–74.

1956 An Iron Age Tomb at Al-Jib. *ADAJ* 3: figs.19–22.

Daliyat

1978 Tel Daliyat. *HA* 67/68: 29–30. In Hebrew.

Dar, S.
1977   *Ancient Settlements in Emek Hefer.* Maaberot: Kibbutz Maaberot. In Hebrew.
1986   *Landscape and Pattern.* 2 vols. BARInt 308. Oxford: British Archaeological Reports.
1992   Samaria (Place): Archaeological Survey of the Region. Trans. M. Erez. *Anchor Bible Dictionary* 5: 926–31. Garden City: Doubleday & Co., Inc.

Dar, S.; Hanun, E.; Tapar, Y.; Levy, B.; and Ruth, Y., eds.
1971   *Land of Benjamin.* Tel Aviv: Publishing House of the Department of "Knowledge of the Land" in the Kibbutz Movement. In Hebrew.

Dare, B.
1969   A Survey of the Deir Dibwan Region. Waterloo Lutheran University, Waterloo, Ont. Typescript.

Davis, J. B.
1982   Availability and Use of Water Resources in Hill Country Villages in Iron Age I. Paper presented at Society of Biblical Literature Southeastern Regional meeting.
1984   *Hill Country Village Subsistence Strategy in the Period of the Judges.* Ph.D. diss., Southern Baptist Theological Seminary, Louisville, KY.

De Groot, A., and Lehmann, G.
1996   Izbet Sartah. *HA* 106: 170. In Hebrew.

Denyer, D.
1973   A Conical Seal from Khirbet Raddanah. J. A. Callaway Archives. Nicol Museum, Southern Baptist Theological Seminary, Louisville.

Dever, W. G.
1972   Middle Bronze Age I Cemeteries at Mirzbaneh and ʾAin-Samiya. *IEJ* 22: 93–110.
1973   Excavations at Shechem at Mt. Gerazim. Pp. 8–9 in Aviram, 1973.
1991   Archaeology and Israelite Origins. *BASOR* 279: 89–96
1992   How to Tell a Canaanite from an Israelite. Pp. 26–61 in *The Rise of Ancient Israel,* ed. H. Shanks. Washington: Biblical Archaeology Society.
1997a   Ain es-Samiyeh. *Oxford Encyclopaedia of the Ancient Near East* 1: 35–36.
1997b   Bethel. *Oxford Encyclopaedia of the Ancient Near East* 1: 300–301.

Dinur, I.
1985   ʿAnata. *HA* 86: 21–22, 38–39. In Hebrew.
1987a   Survey Northeast of Jerusalem. *HA* 90: 43–46. In Hebrew.
1987b   Hizma. *HA* 89: 37. In Hebrew.

Donner, H.
1995   *Geschichte Volkes Israel und seiner Nachbarn in Grundzügen.* Vol. 1. Ergänzungsreihe/Grundrisse zum ATD 4/1. Gottingen: Vandenhoeck & Ruprecht.

Dorsey, D. A.
1987   Shechem and the Road Network of Central Samaria. *BASOR* 268: 57–70.
1989   *The Roads and Highways of Ancient Israel.* ASOR Library of Biblical and Near Eastern Archaeology. Baltimore: The Johns Hopkins University Press.

Dotan, A.
1981   A New Light on the Izbet Sartah Ostracon. *TA* 8: 160–72.

Dothan II
1980   *A Guide for the Dothan II Publication Project.* Albright Institute of Archaeological Research Archives, Jerusalem. Mimeo.

Dothan, M.
1955   The Excavations at ʿAfula. *Atiqot* 1: 19–70.

Dothan, T.
1982   *The Philistines and Their Material Culture.* New Haven: Yale University Press.
1989   The Arrival of the Sea Peoples. Pp. 1–14 in *Recent Excavations in Israel,* ed. S. Gitin and W. G. Dever. AASOR 49. Winona Lake, IN: American Schools of Oriental Research.
1990   Ekron of the Philistines Part I: Where They Came From, How They Settled Down and the Places They Worshiped In. *BAR* 16(1): 26–36.

Dothan, T., and Gitin, S.
1993   Miqne, Tel (Ekron). *The New Encyclopaedia of Archaeological Excavations in the Holy Land* 3: 1051–59.

Edelman, D. V.
1988   Saul's Journey through Mt. Ephraim and Samuel's Ramah. *ZDPV* 104: 44–58.
1996   Saul ben Kish in History and Tradition. Pp. 142–60 in Fritz and Davies, 1996.

Edelstein, G.
1968   Tel Amal. *RB* 75: 395–96.

Eitam, D.
1981   Badiʿa Map. *HA* 77: 56. In Hebrew.

Elizur, Y.
1985   Identifications of the "Land of Nof" and "The Ramah," City of Samuel. Pp. 101–15 in Erlich, 1985. In Hebrew.
1993   A New Proposal for the Identification of an Israelite City at Ein Samia. Vol. 3, pp. 17–28 in *Judea and Samaria Research Studies*, ed. Z. H. Erlich and Y. Eshel. Kedumim-Ariel: The College of Judea and Samaria Research Institute. In Hebrew.

Elliger, K.
1930   Die Grenze zwischen Ephraim und Manasse. *ZDPV* 53: 18–309.
1937   Tappuah. *Palästinajahrbuch* 33: 7–22.
1938   Neues über die Grenze zwischen Ephraim und Manasse. *JPOS* 18: 7–16.
1970   Michmethat. Pp. 91–100 in *Archäologie und Altes Testament*, ed. A. Kuschke and E. Kutsch. Tubingen: J. C. B. Mohr.

Elon, Z., and Demsky, A.
1987   Gibit: Ancient Settlement in the Desert Fringe. Vol. 1, pp.114–30 in Erlich, 1987–93. In Hebrew.

Emek Hefer
1980   Emek Hefer — 1979. *HA* 73: 19–20. In Hebrew.

Eran, A.
1994   Weights from Excavations 1981–1984 at Shiloh. *ZDPV* 110: 151–57.

Erlich, Z., ed.
1985   *"Before Ephraim and Benjamin and Manasseh"*. Ophrah: Land of Benjamin High Schools. In Hebrew.
1987–93 *Samaria and Benjamin*. 3 vols. Jerusalem: Society for the Preservation of Nature in Israel. In Hebrew.

Eshel, H.
1982   The Possible Location of Ophra, Town of Gideon. *Cathedra* 22: 3–8. In Hebrew.
1990   Nob, City of Priests. Vol. 1, pp. 17–22 in Erlich, 1987–93. In Hebrew.
1994   Archaeological Research in the Judean Desert between 1967 and 1992. Vol. 4, pp.103–20 in *Judea and Samaria Research Studies*, ed. Z. H. Erlich and Y. Eshel. Kedumim–Ariel: The College of Judea and Samaria Research Institute. In Hebrew.

Et-Taiyiba
1991   Et–Taiyiba Map, Survey. *ESI* 10: 18–19.

Feig, N.
1983   Tel Amal. *IEJ* 33: 264.

Feldstein, A.
1993   Migron and the Battle of Michmash. Vol. 3, pp. 83–90 in Erlich, 1987–93. In Hebrew.

Finkelstein, I.
1978   *Rural Settlement in the Foothills and in the Yarqon Basin in the Israelite–Hellenistic Periods*. M.A. thesis, Tel Aviv University, Tel Aviv. In Hebrew.
1981   Israelite and Hellenistic Farms in the Foothills and in the Yarkon Basin. *EI* 15: 331–48. In Hebrew.
1983a   *The 'Izbet Sartah Excavations and the Israelite Settlement in the Hill Country*. Ph.D. diss., Tel Aviv University, Tel Aviv. In Hebrew.
1983b   Tel Shiloh. *ESI* 2: 95–100.
1985a   *Izbet Sartah*. BARInt 299. Oxford: British Archaeological Reports.
1985b   ed–Dawara, Khirbet. *ESI* 4: 20.
1986   *The Archaeology of the Period of the Settlement and Judges*. Tel–Aviv: HaKibbutz HaMeuchad Publishing House. In Hebrew.
1987   Khirbet Ed–Dawara. *ESI* 6: 48
1988a   *The Archaeology of the Israelite Settlement*. Jerusalem: Israel Exploration Society.
1988b   Khirbet ed–Dawwar [sic], 1985–86. *IEJ* 38: 79–80.
1988–89 The Land of Ephraim Survey 1980–87, Preliminary Report. *TA* 15–16: 117–83.
1990a   Excavations at Kh. Ed–Dawwara. *TA* 17: 163–209.
1990b   The Emergence of Early Israel. = Review of Lemche, 1985 and R. B. Coote and K. Whitelam, *The Emergence of Israel in Historical Perspective*, 1987, Sheffield: Almond Press. *JAOS* 110: 677–86.
1992a   Ephraim (Archaeology). *Anchor Bible Dictionary* 2: 551–55. New York: Doubleday.
1992b   Izbet Sartah. *Anchor Bible Dictionary* 3: 588–59. New York: Doubleda.
1992c   Seilun, Khirbet. *Anchor Bible Dictionary* 5: 1069–72. New York: Doubleday & Co.
1992d   Pastoralism in the Highlands of Canaan in the Third and Second Millennia B.C.E. Pp. 133–42 in *Pastoralism in the Levant*, ed. O. Bar–Yosef and A. Khazanov. Madison: University of Wisconsin Press.
1993a   The Sociopolitical Organization of the Central Hill Country in the Second Millennium B.C.E. Pp. 110–31 in *Biblical Archaeology Today 1990 Supplement*, ed. A. Biran

and J. Aviram. Jerusalem: Israel Exploration Society.

1993b   Excavation Results in Areas E, G, J, K, L
and M. Pp. 65–80 in Finkelstein,
Bunimovitz, and Lederman, 1993.

1993c   The History and Archaeology of Shiloh
from the Middle Bronze Age II to the Iron
Age II. Pp. 371–93 in Finkelstein,
Bunimovitz, and Lederman, 1993.

1996   The Philistine Countryside. *IEJ* 46: 225–
42.

Finkelstein, I., Bunimovitz, S., and Lederman, Z. eds.

1993   *Shiloh: The Archaeology of a Biblical Site.*
Tel Aviv: Institute of Archaeology.

Finkelstein, I.; Bunimovitz, S.; Lederman, Z.; Hellwig,
S.; and Sadeh, M.

1985   Excavations at Shiloh. *TA* 12: 123–80.

Finkelstein, I., Lederman, Z., and Bunimovitz, S.

1997   *Highlands of Many Cultures.* 2 vols. Tel
Aviv University Institute of Archaeology
Monographs 15. Tel Aviv: Tel Aviv Uni-
versity Press.

Finkelstein, I., and Magen, Y.

1993   *Archaeological Survey of the Hill Country
of Benjamin.* Jerusalem: Israel Antiquities
Authority.

Finkelstein, I., and Na'aman, N., eds.

1994   *From Nomadism to Monarchy.* Washington: Biblical Archaeology Society.

Flanagan, J.

1988   *David's Social Drama.* JSOTSup 129.
Sheffield: JSOT Press.

Fowler, M. D.

1981   Cultic Continuity at Tirzah? *PEQ* 113: 27–
31.

1983   A Closer Look at the "Temple of El Berith"
at Shechem. *PEQ* 115: 49–53.

Free, J.

1954   Dothan. *ADAJ* 3: 79–80.

1955   The Third Season at Dothan. *BASOR* 139:
3–9.

1956a   The Excavations of Dothan. *BA* 19: 43–48.

1956b   The Fourth Season at Dothan. *BASOR* 143:
11–17.

1957   Radiocarbon Date of Iron Age Level at
Dothan. *BASOR* 147: 36–37.

1958   The Fifth Season at Dothan. *BASOR* 152:
10–18.

1959   The Sixth Season at Dothan. *BASOR* 156:
22–29.

1960   The Seventh Season at Dothan. *BASOR*
160: 6–15.

1962   The Seventh Season of Excavation at
Dothan. *ADAJ* 6/7: 117–20.

Frick, F.

1985   *The Formation of the State in Ancient Israel. The Social World of Biblical Antiquity 4.* Sheffield: Almond/JSOT Press.

Fritz, V.

1995   *The City in Ancient Israel.* Biblical Seminar 29. Sheffield: Sheffield Academic
Press.

1996   *Die Enstehung Israels im 12. und 11. Jh. v.
Chr..* Biblische Enzyklopädie 2. Stuttgart:
Kohlhammer.

Fritz, V., and Davies, P. R., eds.

1996   *The Origins of the Ancient Israelite States.*
JSOTSup 228. Sheffield: Sheffield Aca-
demic Press.

Gal, Z.

1979   An Early Iron Age Site Near Tel Menorah
in the Beth-shan Valley. *TA* 6: 138–45.

1980   *Ramat Issachar.* Tel Aviv: HaKibbutz
HaMeuchad Publishing House Ltd. In Hebrew.

1991a   *Map of Gazit.* Archaeological Survey of
Israel 46. Jerusalem: Israel Antiquities Authority.

1991b   The Period of the Israelite Settlement in the
Lower Galilee and the Jezreel Valley. Vol.
1, pp. 101–15 in *Let Your Colleagues
Praise You,* ed. R. J. Ratner, L. M. Barth,
M. L. Gevirtz, and B. Zuckerman. =
Maarav 7. Rolling Hills Estates, CA: West-
ern Academic Press.

1992   *Lower Galilee During the Iron Age.* ASOR
Dissertation Series 8. Winona Lake:
Eisenbrauns.

1994   Iron I in Lower Galilee and the Margins of
the Jezreel Valley. Pp. 35–46 in Finkelstein
and Na'aman, 1994.

Galling, K.

1965   Kritische Bemerkungen zur Ausgrabung
von el–Jib. *Bibliotheca Orientalis* 22: 242–
45.

Garbini, G.

1978   Sull'Alfabetario di Izbet Sarta. *Oriens
Antiquus* 17: 287–95.

Garsiel, M., and Finkelstein, I.

1977   The Settlement of the House of Joseph in
the West Part of its Inheritance. *Bar–Ilan*
14/15: 58–69. In Hebrew.

1978   The Westward Expansion of the House of

Joseph in Light of the 'Izbet Sartah Excavations. *TA* 5: 192–98.

Garstang, J.
1933   Jericho. *Liverpool Annals of Archaeology and Anthropology* 20: 3–42.

Geographical Index
n.d.   *Geographical Index of the Historical Sites in Judaea and Samaria and in the Gaza Strip.* In Hebrew and English.

Gibson, S.
1995   *Landscape Archaeology and Ancient Agricultural Field Systems in Palestine.* Ph.D. diss., University College, London.
1996   Tell el–Ful and the Results of the Northeast Jerusalem Survey. Pp. 9*–23* in *New Studies on Jerusalem*, ed. A. Faust. Ramat Gan: Bar Ilan University Press.

Gibson, S., and Lass, E.
1997   The Lost City of the Maccabees: The Modiin Project. Report presented at the Albright Institute for Archaeological Research, Jerusalem.

Gilmour, G. H.
1995   *The Archaeology of Cult in the Southern Levant in the Early Iron Age.* Ph.D. diss., Oxford University, Oxford.
1997a   The Nature and Function of Astragalus Bones from Archaeological Contexts in the Levant and Eastern Mediterranean. *Oxford Journal of Archaeology* 15: 167–73.
1997b   *Early Israelite Religion During the Period of the Judges.* Kaplan Centre for Jewish Studies and Research, University of Cape Town, Occasional Papers 1. Cape Town: University of Cape Town Press.

Gitin, S., and Dothan, T.
1987   The Rise and Fall of Ekron of the Philistines. *BA* 50: 197–222.

Glass, J., Goren, Y., Bunimovitz, S., and Finkelstein, I.
1993   Petrographic Analysis of Middle Bronze Age III, Late Bronze Age and Iron Age I Ceramic Assemblages. Pp. 271–77 in Finkelstein, Bunimovitz, and Lederman, 1993.

Glock, A. E.
1993   Taanach. *New Encyclopaedia of Archaeological Excavations of the Holy Land* 4: 1428–33.

Glueck, N.
1943   Three Israelite Towns in the Jordan Valley. *BASOR* 90: 2–23.
1951   *Explorations in Eastern Palestine.* Vol. 4.

AASOR 28. New Haven: American Schools of Oriental Research.

Gophna, R., and Beit–Arieh, I.
1997   *Map of Lod.* Archaeological Survey of Israel 80. Jerusalem: Israel Antiquities Authority.

Gophna, R., and Kochavi, M.
1966   An Archaeological Survey of the Plain of Sharon. *IEJ* 16: 143–44.

Graham, J. A.

1981   New Light on the Fortress; and Iron I at Tell el–Ful. Pp. 23–38 in N. Lapp, 1981.

Greenhut, Z.
1996   The Periphery of Jerusalem in the Bronze & Iron Ages. Pp. 3–8 in *New Studies on Jerusalem*, ed. A. Faust. Ramat Gan: Bar Ilan University Press. In Hebrew.

Grintz, J. M.
1961   Ai Which is Beside Beth-Aven. *Biblica* 42: 201–16.

Gunneweg, J.; F. Asaro; H. V. Michel; and I. Perlman.
1994   Interregional Contacts between Tell en-Nasbeh and littoral Philistine centers in Canaan during Early Iron Age I. *Archaeometry* 36: 227–40.

Guthe, H.
1915   Beiträge zur Orstkunde Palästinas 13: Naara, Neara. *ZDPV* 38: 41–49.

Guy, P. L. O.
1924   An Early Iron Age Cemetery Near Haifa. *Palestine Museum Bulletin* 1: 47–55.

Hagemeyer, F.
1908   *Gibea, die Stadt Sauls.* Halle: Ehrhardt Karras.

Halbe, J.
1975   Gibeon und Israel. *VT* 25: 613–41.

Hallote, R.
1997   Gibeon. *Oxford Encyclopaedia of the Ancient Near East* 2: 403–404.

Hamilton, R. W.
1944   Schedule of Historical Monuments and Sites. *Palestine Gazette* 1375: Supplement 2.

Haran, M.
1961   Shiloh and Jerusalem. *Tarbiz* 31: 317–25. In Hebrew.

Harel, M.
1984   *Journeys and Campaigns in Ancient Times.* Jerusalem: Israel Ministry of Defense. In Hebrew.

Harmon, G. E.
1983   *Floor Area and Population Determination.* Ph.D. diss., Southern Baptist Theological Seminary, Louisville, KY.

Harrelson, W.
1978   Shechem in Extra–biblical References. *BAReader* 2: 258–64.

Hellwing, S., Sadeh, M., and Kishon, V.
1993   Faunal Remains. Pp. 309–50 in Finkelstein, Bunimovitz, and Lederman, 1993.

Herrmann, S.
1964   Operationen Pharao Schoschenks I. im östlichen Ephraim. *ZDPV* 80: 55–69.
1985   Basic Factors of Israelite Settlement in Canaan. Pp. 47–53 in Amitai, 1985.

Herzog, Z.
1992   Iron Age Fortifications. Pp. 231–74 in Kempinski and Reich, 1992.

Hesse, B.
1990   Pig Lovers and Pig Haters. *Journal of Ethnobiology* 10: 195–225.

Hirschfeld, Y.
1991   Ramat HaNadiv — 1989/1990. *ESI* 10: 9–12.

Hodder, I., and Orton, C.
1976   *Spatial Analysis.* Cambridge: Cambridge University Press.

Holland, T. A.
1992   Jericho (Place). *Anchor Bible Dictionary* 3: 723–37. Garden City: Doubleday & Co., Inc.
1997   Jericho. *Oxford Encyclopaedia of the Ancient Near East* 3: 220–24.

Hopkins, D. C.
1983   The Dynamics of Agriculture in Monarchic Israel. *SBLSP* 1983: 177–202.

Horn, S. H.
1962   Scarabs from Shechem. *JNES* 21: 1–14.
1964   Shechem: History and Excavations of a Palestinian City. *Jaarbericht van het Vooraziatisch–Egyptisch Genootschap Ex Orient Lux* 18: 284–306.
1966   Scarabs and Scarab Impressions from Shechem — II. *JNES* 25: 48–56.
1968   Objects from Shechem. *Jaarbericht van het Vooraziatisch–Egyptisch Genootschap Ex Orient Lux* 20: 17–90.
1973   Scarabs and Scarab Impressions from Shechem — III. *JNES* 32: 281–89.

Horn, S. H., ed. and trans.
1960?   Preliminary Reports of the Excavations of Shechem. Albright Institute of Archaeo-logical Research Archives, Jerusalem. Mimeo.

Horn, S. H., and Moulds, L. G.
1969   Pottery from Shechem. *Andrews University Seminary Studies* 7: 17–46.

Horwitz, L. K.
1986–87   Faunal Remains from the Early Iron Age Site on Mount Ebal. *TA* 13–14: 173–89.
1993   Identification of Bone Raw Material Used in Artefact Manufacture. Pp. 263–64 in Finkelstein, Bunimovitz, and Lederman, 1993.

Hunt, M. L.
1985   *The Iron Age Pottery of the Yoqneam Regional Project.* Ph.D. diss., University of California, Berkeley.

Ibrahim, M.; Sauer, J. A.; and Yassine, K.
1976   The East Jordan Valley Survey 1975. *BASOR* 222: 41–66.

Ilan, Z.
1973   *Jordan Valley and Desert of Samaria.* Tel Aviv: Am Oved–Tarbut ve–Khinukh. In Hebrew.
1985   Tabur ha–Aretz. *Israel Land and Nature* 10: 146–50. = Eng. Trans. of *Beth Mikra* 89/90 (1982): 122–26.

Israel Department of Antiquities and Museums.
1976   *Geographic List of the Records Files 1918–1948.* Jerusalem: Ministry of Education and Culture. In Hebrew and English.

Jamieson–Drake, D. W.
1991   *Scribes and Schools in Monarchic Judah.* JSOTSup 109. Sheffield: Almond Press.

Jaroš, K.
1976   *Sichem.* OBO 11. Freiburg: Universitäts-verlag.

Jaroš, K., and Deckert, B.
1977   *Studien zur Sichem–Ära.* OBO 11a. Freiburg: Universitätsverlag.

Jenni, E.
1958   Historisch–topographische Untersuchungen zur Grenze zwischen Ephraim und Manasse. *ZDPV* 74: 35–40.

Jirku, A.
1952   Einige Altertümer aus Dschett. *Bibliotheca Orientalis* 9: 175–76.

Joffe, A. H.
1997   Farah, Tell el– (North). *Oxford Encyclopaedia of the Ancient Near East* 2: 303–304.

Kallai (Kleinmann), Z.
1954   Beeroth. *EI* 3: 111–15. In Hebrew.

1956   Notes on the Topography of Benjamin. *IEJ* 6: 180–87.

1958   The Town Lists of Judah, Simeon, Benjamin, and Dan. *VT* 8: 134–60.

1971   Baal Shalisha and Ephraim. Pp. 191–206 in *Bible and Jewish History*, ed. B. Uffenheimer. Tel Aviv: Tel Aviv University Press. In Hebrew.

1986a   The Settlement Traditions of Ephraim. *ZDPV* 102: 68–74.

1986b   *Historical Geography of the Bible*. Leiden: E. J. Brill.

Kappus, S.

1968   Oberflächenuntersuchungen im mittleren wadi far'a. *ZDPV* 82: 74–82.

Karmon, Y.

1956   Geographical Conditions in the Sharon Plain and their Impact on its Settlement. *Yediot* 23: 111–12. In Hebrew.

Kaufman, A. S.

1988   Fixing the Site of the Tabernacle at Shiloh. *BAR* 14(6): 46–52.

Kelso, J. L.

1934   The Kyle Memorial Excavations at Bethel. *Bibliotheca Sacra* 104: 415–20.

1955   The Second Campaign at Bethel. *BASOR* 137: 5–10.

1956   Excavations at Bethel. *BA* 19: 36–43.

1958   The Third Campaign at Bethel. *BASOR* 151: 3–8.

1961a   The Fourth Campaign at Bethel. *BASOR* 164: 5–19.

1961b   Sensational Finds Made at Bethel. *Pittsburgh Seminary Panorama* 1(4): 2.

1962   Béthel. *Bible et Terre Sainte* 47: 8–15.

Kempinski, A.

1986.   Joshua's Altar — An Iron Age I Watchtower. *BAR* 12/1: 42, 44–49.

Kempinski, A., and Reich, R., eds.

1992   *The Architecture of Ancient Israel from the Prehistoric to the Persian Period*. Jerusalem: Israel Exploration Society.

Kafr 'Aana

1962   The Excavations at Kafr 'Aana. *HA* 3: 14–15. In Hebrew.

Killebrew, A.

1998   Ceramic Typology and Technology of Late Bronze II and Iron I Assemblages from Tel–Miqne Ekron. Pp. 379–405 in *Mediterranean Peoples in Transition*, ed. S. Gitin, A. Mazar, and E. Stern. Jerusalem: Israel Exploration Society.

Kislev, M.

1993   Food Remains. Pp. 354–61 in Finkelstein, Bunimovitz, and Lederman, 1993.

Kjaer, H.

1930   The Excavation of Shilo. *JPOS* 10: 1–88.

1931   Shiloh. *PEFQS* 1931: 1–18, 71–88.

Knierim, R.

1969   Oberflächenuntersuchungen im Wadi el–Far'a II. *ZDPV* 85: 51–62.

Kochavi, M.

1977   An Ostracon from the Period of the Judges from 'Izbet Tsartah. *TA* 4: 1–13.

1985   The Israelite Settlement in Canaan in the Light of Archaeological Survey. Pp. 54–60 in Amitai, 1985.

1989   The Identification of Zeredah, Home of Jeroboam son of Nebat, King of Israel. *EI* 20: 198–201. In Hebrew.

Kochavi, M., ed.

1972   *Judea, Samaria, and the Golan: Archaeological Survey 1967–68*. Jerusalem: Carta. In Hebrew.

Kochavi, M., and Beit–Arieh, I.

1994   *Map of Rosh Ha–'Ayin*. Archaeological Survey of Israel 78. Jerusalem: Israel Antiquities Authority.

Kochavi, M., and Demsky, A.

1978   An Israelite Village From the Days of the Judges. *BAR* 4(3): 19–21.

Kurinsky, S.

1991   *The Glassmakers*. New York: Hippocrene Books.

Kuschke, A.

1958   Lehrkurs 1957. *ZDPV* 74: 7–34.

1962   New Contributions to the Historical Topography of Jordan. *ADAJ* 6/7: 90–95.

Landes, G. M.

1975   Report on an Archaeological "Rescue Operation" at Suwwanet eth–Thaniya in the Jordan Valley North of Jericho. *BASORSup* 21: 1–22.

Lapp, N. L.

1997   Ful, Tell el–. *Oxford Encyclopaedia of the Ancient Near East* 2: 346–47.

Lapp, N. L., ed.

1981   *The Third Campaign at Tell el–Ful*. AASOR 45. Cambridge, MA: American Schools of Oriental Research.

Lapp, P. W.

1965   Tell el–Ful. *BA* 28: 2–10.

1975   The Salvage Excavation at Tell el–Ful. Pp. 83–90 in *The Tale of the Tell*, ed. N. L.

Lapp. Pittsburgh Theological Monographs 5. Pittsburgh: Pittsburgh Theological Seminary.

Lederman, Z., and Finkelstein, I.
1993   Area D. Pp. 35–48 in Finkelstein, Bunimovitz, and Lederman, 1993.

Le Du, C.
1996   *Á la decouverte de Naplouse, Sichem, & Sébastiyeh*. La Bibliothèque Palestinienne 1. Nablus: Centre Culturel Français de Naplouse.

Lemaire, A.
1985   Notes d'Epigraphie Nord–Ouest Semitique. *Semitica* 35: 13–17.

Lemche, N. P.
1985   *Early Israel*. VTSup 37. Leiden: E. J. Brill.

Levy, G. R., and Richmond, E. T.
1927   *Selected Types of Iron Age and Hellenistic Pottery = Bulletin of the Palestine Museum* 4.

Levy, S.
1962   Tel 'Amal. *IEJ* 12: 147.

Levy, S., and Edelstein, G.
1972   Cinq Années de Fouilles á Tel 'Amal. *RB* 79: 325–67.

Liphschitz, N.
1986–87 Paleobotanical Remains from Mount Ebal. *TA* 13–14: 190–91.

Livingston, D.
1971–72 Traditional Site of Bethel Questioned. *Westminster Theological Journal* 34: 39–50.
1990   The 1987 and 1990 Excavations at Khirbet Nisya, Israel. *Near East Archaeological Society Bulletin* n.s. 35: 2–19.
1994   Further Considerations on the Location of Bethel and el–Bireh. *PEQ* 126: 154–59.

Lod
1975   Map of Lod. *HA* 54/55: 45–46. In Hebrew.

Loffreda, S.
1968   Typological Sequence of Iron Age Rock–Cut Tombs in Palestine. *Liber Annuus* 18: 244–87.

Macalister, R. A. S.
1909   Archaeological Discoveries at Nablus. *PEFQSt* p.74.

Maitlis, Y.
1989   *Agricultural Settlements in the Environs of Jerusalem during the Iron Age*. MA thesis, Hebrew University. Jerusalem.

Marcus, M.
1986   *The Northern Desert of Judah*. Jerusalem:

Nature Reserve Authority. In Hebrew.
1991/92 *The Hill–Country of Bethel*. 2 Vols. Jerusalem: Nature Reserve Authority. In Hebrew.
1993   *The Hill Country of Jerusalem*. Jerusalem: Nature Reserve Authority. In Hebrew.

Mariottini, C. F.
1981   The Village Pastoral—Agrarian Economy in the Period of the Judges. Paper presented at Society for Biblical Literature Southeastern Regional meeting.

Marquet-Krause, J.
1933/34 Palestine Department of Antiquities File. Israel Antiquities Authority Archives, Jerusalem. In Hebrew.
1935   La Deuxième Campagne de Fouilles á Ay. *Syria* 16: 325–45.
1949   *Les Fouilles de 'Ay*. Institut Français d'Archeologie de Beyrouth Bibliotheque Archéologique et Historique 45. Paris: Librairie Orientaliste Paul Geunthner.

Masterman, E. W. G.
1913   Tell el–Ful and Khurbet [sic] 'Adaseh. *PEFQSt* pp. 132–37.

Mazar, A.
1976   Khirbet Marjame. *IEJ* 26: 138–39.
1977   An Israelite Fortress–City near ʾAin Samiya. *Qadmoniot* 10: 111–13.
1982a   The Bull Site. *BASOR* 247: 27–42.
1982b   Three Israelite Sites in the Hills of Judah and Ephraim. *BA* 45: 167–78.
1982c   A Cultic Site from the Period of the Judges in the Northern Samarian Hills. *EI* 16: 135–35. In Hebrew.
1983   Bronze Bull Found in Israelite "High Place" From the Time of the Judges. *BAR* 9/5: 35–40.
1990   *Archaeology of the Land of the Bible*. Anchor Bible Reference Library. Garden City: Doubleday.
1992   The Fortifications of the Israelite City at Khirbet Marjama in the Hills of Ephraim. *EI* 23: 174–93. In Hebrew.
1994a   The Northern Shephelah during the Iron Age. Pp. 247–67 in *Scripture and Other Artifacts*, ed. M. D. Coogan, J. C. Exum, and L. E. Stager. Louisville: Westminster/John Knox.
1994b   Jerusalem and its Vicinity in Iron Age I. Trans. N. Panitz–Cohen. Pp. 70–91 in Finkelstein and Na'aman, 1994.
1994c   The 11th Century in the Land of Israel. Pp. 39–57 in *Cyprus in the 11th Century BC*,

ed. V. Karageorghis. Nicosia: University of Cyprus Press.

1997   Bull Site. *Oxford Encyclopaedia of the Ancient Near East* 1: 383–84.

Mazar, A., and Rosen, S.
1982   A Cultic Site From the Period of the Judges in the Northern Samaria Hills. *EI* 16: 135–45. In Hebrew.

Mazar, B.
1954   Gath and Gittaim. *IEJ* 4: 227–35.
1973   The 'Place of Shechem'. Pp. 1–7 in Aviram, 1973.
1975   *Cities and Districts in Eretz–Israel*. Jerusalem: Bialik Institute. In Hebrew.

McClellan, T. L.
1975   *Quantitative Studies in the Iron Age Pottery of Palestine*. 2 vols. Ph.D. diss., The University of Pennsylvania, Philadelphia.
1985   Town Planning at Tell en-Nasbeh. *ZDPV* 100: 53–69.
1987   Review of Chambon, 1984. *BASOR* 267: 84–86.

McCown, C. C.
1947   Tell en-Nasbeh. *PEFQSt* 1947: 145–50.

McCown, C. C., and Wampler, J. C.
1947   *Tell en-Nasbeh*. 2 vols. Berkeley: The Palestine Institute of the Pacific School of Religion.

Medebielle, P.
1976   *Birzeit*. Jerusalem: Latin Patriarchate Press.
1993   *Ephrem–Taybeh*. Jerusalem: Latin Patriarchate Press.

Mellaart, J.
1962   Preliminary Report of the Archaeological Survey in the Yarmouk and Jordan Valley. *ADAJ* 6–7: 126–57.

Menorah
1975   A Site Near Tel Menorah. *HA* 56: 21. In Hebrew.

Meron, E.
1985   *Axes and Adzes in Israel and its Surroundings*. MA Thesis, Tel Aviv. In Hebrew.

Miller, J. M.
1975   Gebah/Gibeah of Benjamin. *VT* 25: 145–66.

Miller, R. D., II.
1997   The Archaeology of Society in Early Iron Age Palestine. *Hausseminar* presented at the Jerusalem Institute of the Görres-Gesellschaft, Jerusalem.
1998a   Abimelech and Anthropological Archaeology. Paper presented at annual meeting of

the Society of Biblical Literature, Orlando.
1998b   Iron I Shiloh as Complex Chiefdom. Paper presented at annual meeting of the American Schools of Oriental Research, Orlando.
1998c   A Social History of Israel in the Iron I Period. Lecture presented at the British School of Archaeology in Jerusalem, Jerusalem.
1999   Daily Life in the Days of Samuel. *Holy Land* 19(3): 3–6.
2000a   Ephraim. In *Eerdmans Dictionary of the Bible*, ed. D. N. Freedman, A. C. Myers, and A. B. Beck. Grand Rapids: Wm. B. Eerdmans Publishing Co.
2000b   The Israelites are Philistine: The Trope of Ethnicity in the Archaeological Record. Paper presented at annual meeting of the American Schools of Oriental Research, Nashville.
in press a *Chieftains of the Highland Clans: A Social History of Israel in the 12th and 11th Centuries B.C.*. In preparation.
in press b Modeling the Farm in Early Iron Age Israel. In *Daily Life in the Ancient Near East*, ed. R. E. Averbeck, M. W. Chavalas, and D. B. Weisberg. Bethesda, MD: CDL Press.

Mittmann, S.
1970   *Beiträge zur Seidlungs und Territorialgeschichte des nördlichen Ostjordanlandes*. Abhandlungen des Deutschen Palästinavereins. Wiesbaden: Otto Harrassowitz.

Molin, G.
1954–56 Dothan. *Archiv für Orientforschungen* 17: 218.

Möller, H.
1915   Die Lage von Gibea Benjamin. *ZDPV* 38: 49–53.

Monson, J. M.
1983   *The Land Between*. Rockford, IL: Bible Backgrounds, Inc.

Moorey, P. R. S.
1971   A Bronze Statuette of a Bull. *Levant* 3: 90–91.

Moulds, L. G.
1967   *The Whole and Restored Pottery of the 1913, 1914 Shechem Campaigns*. M. Th. Thesis, Andrews University. Berrien Springs, MI.

Muhaffar
1971   Tell Muhaffar. *HA* 38: 4. In Hebrew.

Muilenberg, J.
1955   The Site of Ancient Gilgal. *BASOR* 140: 11–27.

Müller, H. W.
1987   *Der Waffenfund vom Balata–Sichem und Die Sichelswerter*. Munich: Bavarian Academy of Science Press.

Naʻaman, N.
1985   Bethel and Beth-Aven. *Zion* 50: 15–25. In Hebrew.
1986a   *Borders and Districts in Biblical Historiography*. Jerusalem Biblical Studies 4. Jerusalem: Simor Ltd.
1986b   Migdal–Shechem and the "House of El–Berith." *Zion* 51: 259–80. In Hebrew.

Nandrasky, K.
1964   Part III of Remarks and Observations on the Historical Topography of Jordan, ed. H. Donner. *ADAJ* 8–9: 89–90.

Naveh, J.
1978   Some Considerations on the Ostracon from Izbet Sartah. *IEJ* 28: 31–35.

Neef, H. -D.
1995   *Ephraim*. BZAW 238. Berlin: de Gruyter.

Ne'eman, Y.
1990   *Map of Maʻanit*. Archaeological Survey of Israel 54. Jerusalem: Israel Antiquities Authority.

Negbi, O.
1991   Were There Sea People in the Central Jordan Valley at the Transition from the Bronze Age to the Iron Age? *TA* 18: 205–43.

News from the Survey
1963   News from the Survey. *HA* 5: 20–22. In Hebrew.

Nielsen, E.
1954   *Shechem*. Copenhagen: G. E. C. Gad.

Noth, M.
1957   Lehrkursus 1956. *ZDPV* 73: 1–58.
1966   Lehrkursus 1965. *ZDPV* 82: 255–73.
1967   Lehrkursus 1966. *ZDPV* 83: 109–22.

Oeming, M.
1989   Der Tell Jesreel. *Jahrbuch des Deutsches Evangelisches Institut für Altertumswissenschaft des Heiliges Landes* 1: 56–78.

Ofer, A.
1993   *The Highland of Judah During the Biblical Period*. Ph.D. diss., Tel Aviv University. In Hebrew.

Olami, Y.
1981   *Survey of the Daliya Map*. Archaeological Survey of Israel 31. Jerusalem: Archaeological Survey of Israel.

Otto, E.
1978   Survey–archaeologische Ergebnisse zur Geschichte der früheisenzeitlichen Siedlung Janoah. *ZDPV* 94: 108–18.
1997   *Kontinuum und Proprium*. Orientalia Biblica et Christiana 8. Weisbaden: Harrassowitz.

Paley, S. M., and Porath, Y.
1980   The Regional Project in ʻEmeq Hefer 1980. *IEJ* 30: 217–19.
1982   The Emek Hefer Regional Project, 1981. *IEJ* 32: 66–67.

Paley, S. M., Porath, Y., and Steiglitz, R.
1985   Tel Hefer — 1984. *ESI* 3: 44–45.

Petersen, A.
1997   Jaljuliya. *Levant* 29: 95–114.

Peterson, J. L.
1977   *A Topographical Surface Survey of the Levitical Cities of Joshua 21 and 1 Chronicles 6*. Ph.D. diss., Seabury–Western Theological Seminary.

Porat, N.
1993   Macroscopic Description of Stone Objects. P. 265 in Finkelstein, Bunimovitz, and Lederman, 1993.

Porat, P., Feder, O., and Agadi, S.
1988/89 Tel Yizreʻel — 1987–1988. *ESI* 7/8: 189–91.

Porath, Y.
n.d.   Survey of Samaria II. Israel Antiquities Authority Archives, Jerusalem. In Hebrew.
1986   The Land of Hefer. Pp. 75–80 in *Samaria Studies*, ed. S. Dar and Z. Safrai. Tel Aviv: HaKibbutz HaMeuchad Publishing House. In Hebrew.

Porath, Y., Dar, S., and Applebaum, S.
1985   *The History and Archaeology of Emek–Hefer*. Kibbutz Meuchad: HaKibbutz HaMeuchad Publishing House Ltd. In Hebrew.

Porath, Y., Ne'eman, Y., and Boshnino, A.
1989   Jatt. *HA* 93: 59–60. In Hebrew.

Porath, Y., and Paley, S.
1982a   Emeq Hefer Regional Project, 1981. *IEJ* 32: 66–67.

Porath, Y., Paley, S., and Stieglitz, R.
1982   Emeq Hefer Regional Project, 1982. *IEJ* 32: 259–61.
1984   Emeq Hefer Regional Project, 1984. *IEJ* 34: 276–77.

Portugali, J.
1982   A Field Method for Regional Archaeology. *TA* 9: 170–88.

Pritchard, J. B.
1956   The Water System at Gibeon. *BA* 19: 66–75.
1957   The Discovery of Biblical Gibeon. *University of Pennsylvania Museum Bulletin* 21.1: 3–26.
1958   A Second Season at Gibeon. *University of Pennsylvania Museum Bulletin* 22.2: 12–24.
1959   Gabaon. *Bible et Terre Sainte* 18: 8–14.
1960a   Gibeon's History in Light of Excavation. Pp. 1–12 in *Congress Volume Oxford*. VTSup 7. Leiden: E. J. Brill.
1960b   Industry and Trade at Biblical Gibeon. *BA* 23: 23–29.
1961   *The Water System of Gibeon*. University of Pennsylvania Museum Monographs. Philadelphia: University of Pennsylvania Press.
1962a   *Gibeon*. Princeton: Princeton University Press.
1962b   Excavations at el–Jib, 1960. *ADAJ* 6/7: 121–22.
1963   Gabaon. *Bible et Terre Sainte* 56: 7–15.
1964a   *Winery, Defense, and Soundings and Gibeon*. Philadelphia: University of Pennsylvania Press.
1964b   El–Jib Excavations, 1962. *ADAJ* 8/9: 86–87.
1976   Gibeon. In *Archaeological Discoveries in the Holy Land*, ed. J. B. Pritchard. New York: Thomas Y. Crowell Co.

Qala'
1981   Qala'. *HA* 77: 16–17. In Hebrew.

Raban, A.
1982   *Survey of the Nahalal Map*. Archaeological Survey of Israel 28. Jerusalem: Archaeological Survey of Israel.
1998   A Reassessment of the Iron Age I Collared–Rim Pithoi. Paper presented at annual meeting of the American Schools of Oriental Research, Orlando.

Rainey, A. F.
1984   *A Handbook of Historical Geography*. Jerusalem: American Institute of Holy Land Studies.

Redford, D. B.
1992   *Egypt, Canaan, and Israel in Ancient Times*. Princeton: Princeton University Press.

Reed, W. L.
1967   Gibeon. Pp. 231–43 in Thomas, 1967.

Reisner, G. A., Fisher, C. S., and Lyon, D. G.
1924   *Harvard Excavations at Samaria*. Cambridge, MA: Harvard University Press.

Reviv, H.
1989   *The Elders in Ancient Israel*. Trans. L. Plitmann. Jerusalem: Magnes Press.

Ribar, J. W.
1973   *Death Cult Practices in Ancient Palestine*. Ph.D. diss., The University of Michigan, Ann Arbor.

Richmond, E. T.
1929   *Provisional Schedule of Historical Sites and Monuments*. Jerusalem: Department of Antiquities of Palestine.

Rösel, H.
1975/76 Studie zur Topographie der Kriege in den Buchern Josua und Richter. *ZDPV* 91: 159–90; 92: 11–26.

Rosen, A. M.
1986   *Cities of Clay: The Geoarchaeology of Tells*. Prehistoric Archaeology and Ecology 1. Chicago: University of Chicago Press.

Rosen, S.
1993   Economy and Subsistence. Pp. 362–70 in Finkelstein, Bunimovitz, and Lederman, 1993.

Ross, J. F.
1971   Shechem 1971: Final Report, Field IV. Albright Institute of Archaeological Research Archives, Jerusalem.

Ross, J. F., and Toombs, L.
1961   Three Campaigns at Biblical Shechem. *Archaeology* 14: 171–79.
1962   Les découvertes effectuées au cours des dernières campaignes de fouilles á Sichem. *Bible et Terra Sainte* 44: 6–15.
1976   Six Campaigns at Biblical Shechem. Pp. 119–28 in *Archaeological Discoveries in the Holy Land*, ed J. B. Pritchard. New York: Thomas Y. Crowell Co.

Routledge, B.
1996   Structural Constraints on Family Size in Iron Age Palestine. Paper presented at annual meeting of the American Schools of Oriental Research, New Orleans.

Rowe, A.
1936   *Catalogue of the Egyptian Scarabs, Scaraboids, Seals and Amulets in the Palestine Archaeological Museum*. Cairo: French Institute of Oriental Archaeology.

Rubin, Z.
1989   Historical Geography of Eretz–Israel. Pp.
        23–36 in *The Land That Became Israel*, ed.
        R. Kark. New Haven: Yale University
        Press.
Salem, H. J.
1993   *Introduction and Bibliography to Surveys
        and Excavations*. Palestinian Institute of
        Archaeology Handbooks 1. Birzeit: Pales-
        tinian Institute of Archaeology.
Sapin, J.
1968/69 *Le Plateau Central de Benjamin*. Memoire,
        Ecole Biblique et Archéologique Française.
        Jerusalem.
Sayej, G., and Neyruz, J.
1993   Étude archéologique du site de Bir–Zeit.
        Birzeit University, Birzeit. Typescript.
Schaeffer, C. F. A.
1939   *The Cuneiform Texts of Ras Shamra–
        Ugarit*. London: The British Academy.
Schenke, H. –M.
1968   Jakobsbrunner – Josephsgrab – Sychar.
        ZDPV 84: 159–84.
Schley, D. G.
1988   *Shiloh*. JSOTSup 63. Sheffield: Sheffield
        Academic Press.
Schmidt, B. B.
1994   *Israel's Beneficent Dead*. Forschungen zum
        Alten Testament 11. Tubingen: J. C. B.
        Mohr (Paul Siebeck).
Schmitt, G.
1980   Bet-Awen. Pp. 33–76 in *Drei Studien zur
        Archäologie und Topographie Altisraels*,
        ed. R. Cohen and G. Schmitt. BTAVO
        B.44. Wiesbaden: Ludwig Reichert.
Schunck, K. –D.
1962   Bemerkungen zur Orstliste von Benjamin.
        ZDPV 78: 143–58. = pp. 33–48 in Schunck,
        1989.
1963   *Benjamin*. BZAW 86. Berlin: Verlag
        Alfred Töpelmann.
1989   *Altest Testament un Heiliges Land*. Vol. 1.
        Beiträge zur Erforschung des Alten Testa-
        ments und des Antiken Jüdentums 17.
        Frankfurt: Peter Lang.
Seger, J. D.
1970   Balatah: 1969. *ASOR Newsletter* 1970–
        71(1): 1–2.
1972   Shechem Field XIII, 1969. *BASOR* 205:
        20–35.
1997   Shechem. *Oxford Encyclopaedia of the
        Ancient Near East* 5: 19–23.

Sellin, E.
1914   *Vorläufiger Bericht über die diesjährige
        Frühsjahrskampagne der Ausgraben in
        Balata–Sichem*. Vienna: Kaiserliche
        Akademie der Wissenschaft.
1917   *Gilgal*. Leipzig: A. Deichertsche
        Verlagsbuchhandlung Werner Scholl.
1922   *Wie würde Sichem eine Israelitische Stadt?*
        Leipzig: A.   Deichertsche
        Verlagsbuchhandlung.
1960?   Preliminary Report Concerning the Results
        of the Excavations at Balatah–Shechem. In
        Horn, 1960?. = E.T. of *Anzeiger der
        Kaiserlichen Akademie der Wissenschaften
        in Wein* 51 (1914): 35–40.
Sellin, E., and Steckeweh, H.
1941   Kurzer vorläufiger Bericht über die
        Ausgrabung von *balata* (Sichem) im
        Herbst 1934. *ZDPV* 64: 1–20.
Shaath, S., ed.
1985–88 *ALESCO: Studies in the History and Ar-
        chaeology of Palestine*. 3 Vols. Aleppo:
        Aleppo University Press.
Shanks, H.
1988   Two Early Israelite Cult Sites Now Ques-
        tioned. *BAR* 14(1): 48–52.
Shantur, B., and Labadi, Y.
1971   Tomb 204 at Ain Samiya. *IEJ* 21: 73–77.
Shavit, A.
1992   *The Ayalon Valley and Its Vicinity During
        the Bronze and Iron Ages*. M.A. thesis, Tel
        Aviv. In Hebrew.
1993   Tel Malot. *ESI* 12: 49–50.
Shechem
1968a   Shechem and Tell er-Ras — 1968. *HA* 27:
        21–23. In Hebrew.
1968b   Survey of the Region of Shechem. *HA* 25:
        28–30. In Hebrew.
1972   Shechem 1972. *HA* 43: 9. In Hebrew.
1973   Shechem (Tell Balatah) — 1972. *HA* 45:
        17–18. In Hebrew.
Shiloh
1965   Shiloh. *Buried History* 2(4): 20–24.
1983   Tel Shiloh — 1982/1983. *ESI* 2: 95–100.
Shiloh, Y.
1973   The Camp in Shiloh. Pp. 10–18 in Aviram,
        1973.
1978   Elements in the Development of Town
        Planning in the Israelite City. *IEJ* 28: 36–
        51.
1987   The Casemate Wall, the Four Room House,

and Early Planning in the Israelite City. *BASOR* 268: 2–16.

Shimon, O.
1995   Survey of the Qlia Map. *HA* 104: 80–81. In Hebrew.

Shmueli, A.; Grossman, D.; and Ze'evy, R., eds.
1977   *Judea and Samaria.* Jerusalem: Canaan Publishing House. In Hebrew.

Simons, J.
1937   *Handbook for the Study of Egyptian Topographical Lists Relating to Western Asia.* Leiden: E. J. Brill.
1959   *The Geographical and Topographical Texts of the Old Testament.* Nederlands Instituut voor het Nabije Oosten, Studia Francisci Scholten Memoriae Dicata AB/2. Leiden: E. J. Brill.

Sinclair, L. A.
1960   *An Archaeological Study of Gibeah (Tell el–Ful).* AASOR 34. New Haven: American Schools of Oriental Research.

Sofar
1973   Tell Sofar. *HA* 47: 12–13. In Hebrew.

Soggin, J. A.
1967   Bemerkungen zur alttestamentlichen Topographie Sichems. *ZDPV* 83: 183–98.

Spanier, Y.
1991   The Geographic and Archaeological Aspects of East Samaria. In vol. 1 of *Judea and Samaria Research Studies,* ed. Z. H. Erlich and Y. Eshel. Kedumim–Ariel: The College of Judea and Samaria Research Institute. In Hebrew.
1994   Map of el–Mughayir, Survey. *ESI* 14: 78–79.

Stager, L. E.
1968   The Archaeology of Palestine in the 11th Century. J. A. Callaway Archives. Nicol Museum, Southern Baptist Theological Seminary, Louisville, KY. Mimeo.
1974   Hill Country and Plains Life. Lecture presented at the University of Michigan, Ann Arbor.
1980   Anatomy of the Highland Village. Pp. I.1–I.18 in 'Ai/et-Tell: A Case Study in Biblical History, ed. J. A. Callaway. J. A. Callaway Archives. Nicol Museum, Southern Baptist Theological Seminary, Louisville, KY.
1981a   Farming in the Judean Desert during the Iron Age. *BASOR* 221: 145–58.
1981b   Highland Village Life in Palestine Some

Three Thousand Years Ago. *News and Notes, Oriental Institute* 69: 1–3.
1985   The Archaeology of the Family in Ancient Israel. *BASOR* 260: 1–35.
1990   Shemer's Estate. *BASOR* 277/278: 93–107.
1998   The Temple of El–Berith at Shechem. Paper presented at annual meeting of the Society of Biblical Literature, Orlando.

Steinfeld, P.
1983   Nahal Alexander Regional Survey. Pp. 357–60 in *Archaeological Survey in the Mediterranean,* ed. D. R. Keller and D. W. Rupp. BARInt S155. Oxford: British Archaeological Reports.

Stern, E., and Beit–Arieh, I.
1979   Excavations at Tel Kedesh. *TA* 6: 1–25.

Sternberg, G.
1915   Bethel. *ZDPV* 38: 1–40.

Stone, G. R.
1991   Digging up Jezreel. *Buried History* 27: 42–56.

Stroebe, H. J.
1964   Lehrkursus 1962. *ZDPV* 80: 1–45.
1966   Lehrkursus 1964. *ZDPV* 82: 1–45.

Sukenik, E. L.
1948   *Archaeological Investigations at 'Affula.* Jerusalem: Rubin Mass.
1951   Topography and Archaeology of Moza. Repr., pp. 280–82 in Dar, et al., 1971.

Tappy, R.
1992   *The Archaeology of Israelite Samaria.* Vol. 1. Harvard Semitic Studies 44. Atlanta: Scholars Press.

Thomas, D. W.
1967   *Archaeology and Old Testament Study.* Oxford: Clarendon Press.

Thompson, T. L.
1979   *The Settlement of Palestine in the Bronze Age.* BTAVO 34. Wiesbaden: Reichert.

Thomsen, P.
1936/37 Ai (et-Tell). *Archiv für Orientforschung* 11: 94–95.

Toombs, L. E.
1963   Sichem. *RB* 70: 425–33.
1972   The Stratigraphy of Tell Balatah (Shechem). *ADAJ* 17: 99–111.
1976   The Stratification of Tell Balatah (Shechem). *BASOR* 223: 57–59.
1979   Shechem. Pp. 69–83 in *Symposia Celebrating the 75th Anniversary of ASOR,* ed. F. M. Cross. Cambridge, MA: American Schools of Oriental Research.

1992   Shechem. *Anchor Bible Dictionary* 5: 1174–86.

Toombs, L.; Campbell, E. F.; and Ross, J. F.
1971   The Eighth Campaign at Balatah (Shechem). *BASOR* 204: 2–17.

Toombs, L., and Kee, H. C.
1957   The Second Season of Excavation at Biblical Shechem. *BA* 20: 82–105.

Toombs, L., and Wright, G. E.
1961   The Third Campaign at Balatah (Shechem). *BASOR* 161: 11–54.
1962   Sichem. *RB* 69: 257–66.
1963.   The Fourth Campaign at Balatah (Shechem). *BASOR* 169: 1–60.

Tufnel, O.
1948   Review of McCown and Wampler, 1947. *PEQ* 80: 145–50.

Ussishkin, D., and Woodhead, J.
1992   Excavations at Tel Jezreel 1990–1991. *TA* 19: 3–56.
1994   Excavations at Tel Jezreel 1992–1993. *Levant* 26: 1–48.
1997   Excavations at Tel Jezreel 1994–1996. *Tel Aviv* 24: 6–72.

Vaux, R. de.
1951a   La troisième campagne de fouilles á Tell el–Farah, près Naplouse. *RB* 58: 393–430, 566–90.
1951b   La quatrième campagne de fouilles á Tell el–Farah. *Comptes Rendus de l'Académie des Inscriptions et Belles-Lettres* pp.347–50.
1952   La quatrième campagne de fouilles á Tell el–Farah, près Naplouse. *RB* 59: 551–83.
1955a   Les fouilles de Tell el Farah, près Naplouse, Cinquième Campagne. *RB* 62: 541–89.
1955b   La cinquième campagne de fouilles á Tell el–Farah. *Comptes Rendus de l'Académie des Inscriptions et Belles-Lettres* pp. 36–43.
1956   The Excavations of Tell el–Farah and the Site of Ancient Tirza. *PEQ* 88: 125–40.
1957   Les fouilles de Tell el Farah, près Naplouse, Sixième Campagne. *RB* 64: 552–80.
1967.   Tirzah. In Thomas, 1967.
1971   La Thèse de l'Amphictyoni Israëlite. *HTR* 64: 415–36.
1973   *La Period des Juges.* Vol. 2 of *Histoire ancienne d'Israël.* Etudes Bibliques 13. Paris: Libraire Lecoffre.

Vaux, R. de, and Steve, A. M.
1947   La premiere campagne de fouilles á Tell el–Farah, près Naplouse. *RB* 54: 394–433, 573–89.

Vestri, L.
1962   Betel. *Bibbia e Oriente* 4: 53–56.

Vincent, L. –H.
1936   Les Fouilles d'et-Tell = 'Ai. *RB* 231–66.

Vogel, E. K.
1971   Bibliography of Holy Land Sites. *HUCA* 42: 1–96.

Vogel, E. K., and Holtzclaw, B.
1981   Bibliography of Holy Land Sites, Part II. *HUCA* 52: 1–92.

Vriezen, K. J. H.
1975   Hirbet Kefire — Ein Oberflächenuntersuchungen. *ZDPV* 91: 133–56.
1977   Khirbet Kefire. *RB* 84: 412–16.

Wachter, L.
1968   Zur Lage von Michmethath; Salem bei Sichem. *ZDPV* 84: 55–72.

Waldbaum, J. C.
1978   *From Bronze to Iron.* Studies in Mediterranean Archaeology 54. Göteborg: Šströms.

Wallis, G.
1961   Thaanath–Silo. *ZDPV* 77: 38–45.

Watkins, L.
1997a   Izbet Sartah. *Oxford Encyclopaedia of the Ancient Near East* 3: 198–99.
1997b   Shiloh. *Oxford Encyclopaedia of the Ancient Near East* 5: 28–29.
1997c   Southern Samaria, Survey of. *Oxford Encyclopaedia of the Ancient Near East* 5: 66–68.

Weinfeld, M.
1993   Traces of Hittite Cult in Shiloh, Bethel, and Jerusalem. Pp. 455–72 in *Religionsgeschichtliche Beziehungen zwischen Kleinasien, Nordsyrien und dem Alten Testament,* ed. B. Janowski, K. Koch, and G. Wilhelm. OBO 129. Fribourg: University Press.

Weippert, H.
1988   *Palästina in Vorhellenistischer Zeit.* Handbuch der Archäologie Vorderasien 2.1. Munich: C. H. Beck'sche Verlagsbuchhandlung.

Weippert, H., and Weippert, M.
1976   Jericho in der Eisenzeit. *ZDPV* 92: 105–48.

Welten, P.
1965   Bezeq. *ZDPV* 81: 138–65.

Welter, G.
1932a   *Ausgrabungen in Sichem*. Sonderabdruck aus dem Jahrbuch des Deutschen Archäologischen Instituts 3/4. Berlin: Walter de Gruyter and Company.
1932b   Stand der Ausgrabungen in Sichem. *Archäologisher Anzeiger* 3/4: 290–314.
Wengrow, D.
1996   Egyptian Taskmasters and Heavy Burdens: Highland Exploitation and the Collared–Rim Pithos of the Bronze/Iron Age Levant. *Oxford Journal of Archaeology* 15: 307–26.
Wenning, R., and Zenger, E.
1986   Ein bauerliches Baal–Heiligtum im samarischen Gebirge aus der Zeit der Anfänge Israels. *ZDPV* 102: 75–86.
Wilhelm, G.
1970   Tell Balata. *Archiv für Orientforschungen* 23: 183–85.
Williams, P. H., Jr., and Campbell, E. F., Jr.
1965   *ASOR Newsletter* 6: 1–6.
Wolf, C. U.
1966   The Location of Gilgal. *Biblical Research* 11: 42–52.
Wolff, S.
1994a   Senior Fellow Report. *ASOR Newsletter* 44: 3.
1994b   Archaeology in Israel. *American Journal of Archaeology* 98: 481–519.
1995   Ein Haggit. *HA* 104: 53–54. In Hebrew.
Wood, B. G.
1983   Shiloh — Israel's First Holy City. *Bible and Spade* 12: 34–41.
Wright, G. E.
1947   Tell en-Nasbeh. *BA* 10: 69–77.
1948   Review of McCown and Wampler, 1947. *American Journal of Archaeology* 52: 470–72.
1957   The Second Campaign at Tell Balatah. *BASOR* 148: 11–28.
1959   Israelite Samaria and Iron Age Chronology. *BASOR* 155: 13–29.
1965   *Shechem*. New York: McGraw–Hill.
1967   Shechem. Pp. 355–70 in Thomas, 1967.
1973   Co–ordinating the Survey of Shechem Over 60 Years. *ZDPV* 89: 188–96.
Wright, G. R. H.
1967   Some Cypriote and Aegean Pottery Recovered from the Shechem Excavations 1964. *Opuscula Atheniensia* 7: 47–80.
1968   Temples at Shechem. *ZAW* 80: 1–35.
1970   The "Granary" at Shechem and the Underlying Storage Pits. *ZAW* 82: 275–78.
1971   Shechem and League Shrines. *VT* 21: 572–603.
1985   *Ancient Building in South Syria and Palestine*. 2 vols. Handbuch der Orientalistik 7. Leiden: Brill.
1987   Temple and Gate in Palestine. Vol. 2, Pp. 173–83 in Shaath, 1985–88.
1992a   The Place Name Balatah and the Excavation at Shechem. Pp. 1–9 in *Obiter Dicta*. London: Aquiline Press; Leiden: Netherlands Institute for Near East; and Nicosia: Spectrum. = *ZDPV* 83 (1967): 199–202.
1992b   The Mythology of Pre-Israelite Shechem. Pp. 10–21 in *Obiter Dicta*. London: Aquiline Press; Leiden: Netherlands Institute for Near East; and Nicosia: Spectrum. =*VT* 20 (1970): 75–82.
1993–94   Section Drawing at Shechem. *Archiv für Orientforschung* 40/41: 320–37.
1994   Mensuration and Monuments at Shechem. Pp. 321–28 in *Beitrage zur Altorientalischen Archäologie und Altertumskunde*, ed. P. Calmeyer, K. Hecker, L. Jakob–Rost, and C. B. F. Walker. Wiesbaden: Harrassowitz Press.
1997   Building Materials and Techniques: Bronze and Iron Ages. *Oxford Encyclopaedia of the Ancient Near East* 1: 363–67.
Yalqut
1965   *Yalqut HaPersumim* 1164. In Hebrew.
1967a   *Yalqut HaPersumim* 1327. In Hebrew.
1967b   *Yalqut HaPersumim* 1390. In Hebrew.
1976   *Yalqut HaPersumim* 2279. In Hebrew.
Yannai, E.
1995   A Group of Early Iron Age Lamps from the Northern Sharon Valley. *TA* 22: 279–81.
Yeivin, S.
1970   The Settlement of the Benjaminites in the West of their Inheritance. Pp. 369–85 in *Sefer Yosef Braslavi*, ed. I. Ben-Shem, H. M. Gevaryahu, and V. Z. Lurya. Writings of the Association for Biblical Research in Israel 21. Jerusalem: Kiriat Sefer. In Hebrew.
1971   The Benjamin Settlement in the Western Part of Their Territory. *IEJ* 21: 141–54.
Yogev, O.
1988/89   Tel Yizre'el — October 1987–January 1988. *ESI* 7/8: 191–95.

Yoqne'am

n.d.   The Yoqne'am Regional Project Typology
          for Iron Age Pottery. Albright Institute of
          Archaeological Research Archives, Jerusa-
          lem. Mimeo.

Zertal, A.

1983a   Har Menashe, Survey — 1982. *ESI* 2: 43–
          44.

1983b   Mount Ebal. *ESI* 2: 72.

1984   *Arruboth, Hefer, and the Third Solomonic
          District*. Tel Aviv: Kibbutz Meuchad.

1985   Has Joshua's Altar Been Found on Mt.
          Ebal? *BAR* 11(1): 26–43.

1986   How Can Kempinski Be So Wrong! *BAR*
          12(1): 43, 49–53.

1986–87   An Early Iron Age Cultic Site on Mount
          Ebal. *TA* 13–14: 105–66.

1988   *The Israelite Settlement in the Hill Coun-
          try of Manasseh*. Haifa: Haifa University.
          In Hebrew.

1992   *The Manasseh Hill Country Survey*. Haifa:
          Israel Exploration Society and Israel De-
          fense Department. In Hebrew.

1994   "To the Land of the Perizzites and the Gi-
          ants": On the Israelite Settlement in the Hill
          Country of Manasseh. Pp. 47–69 in
          Finkelstein and Na'aman, 1994.

1996   *The Manasseh Hill Country Survey*. Vol.
          2. (The Eastern Valleys and the Fringes of
          the Desert). Haifa: Haifa University Press.
          In Hebrew.

1997   Northern Samaria, Survey of. *Oxford
          Encyclopaedia of the Ancient Near East* 4:
          164–66.

Zevit, Z.

1983   Archaeological and Literary Stratigraphy
          in Joshua 7–8. *BASOR* 251: 23–35.

1985   The Problem of 'Ai. *BAR* 11(2): 58–69

Zimhoni, O.

1992   The Iron Age Pottery from Tel Jezreel. *TA*
          19: 57–70.

1997a   Clues from the Enclosure–fills: Pre-Omride
          Settlement at Tel Jezreel. *TA* 24: 83–109.

1997b   *Studies in the Iron Age Pottery of Israel*.
          Tel Aviv: Tel Aviv University Press.

Ziso, B., Suleimani, G., and Weiss, D.

1997   Shaar HaGay Survey. *HA* 107: 100–102.
          In Hebrew.

Zobel, H.-J.

1966   Abel Mehola. *ZDPV* 82: 83–108.

Zohar, M.

1980   Tell Marjameh. *IEJ* 30: 219–20.

Zohary, M.

1966–86   *Flora Palaestina*. 4 vols. Jerusalem: Israel
          Academy of Sciences and Humanities.

Zori, N. (=Tsori, N).

1954   Archaeological Survey of the Beth-Shan
          Valley. *Yediot* 18: 78–90. In Hebrew.

1962   An Archaeological Survey of the Beth
          Shean Valley. Pp. 135–98 in *The Beth
          Shean Valley, The 17th Archaeological
          Convention*. Jerusalem: Israel Exploration
          Society. In Hebrew.

1971   *Tel-Josef area in Antiquity*. Tel–Aviv:
          Neographica Press. In Hebrew.

1975   Middle Bronze I and Early Iron I Tombs
          near Tel Rehov in the Beth Shean Valley.
          EI 12: 9–17. In Hebrew.

1977   *The Land of Issachar Archaeological Sur-
          vey*. Archaeological Survey of Israel.
          Jerusalem: Israel Exploration Society. In
          Hebrew.

Zorn, J.

1993   *Tell en-Nasbeh*. 4 vols. Ph.D. diss., Pacific
          School of Religion, Berkeley.

1997   Nasbeh, Tell en-. *Oxford Encyclopaedia of
          the Ancient Near East* 4: 101–3.